CROSSCURRENTS

Katie Glaskin is an Associate Professor in Anthropology at the University of Western Australia. She has worked as an anthropologist on native title claims since 1994, and has published widely in the area of native title. While most of her anthropological work has been in the Kimberley region of Western Australia, she has also lived and worked in India, Nepal, Israel and Japan. Katie's other major research interests include personhood, dreams, sleep and creativity. In much of this work she takes a neuroanthropological approach, drawing on neuroscience as well as anthropology. In 2015, she won the Royal Anthropological Institute of Great Britain and Ireland's prestigious Curl essay prize. Katie studied painting as an undergraduate and continues to practice as a painter.

CROSSCURRENTS

*LAW AND SOCIETY IN A NATIVE TITLE
CLAIM TO LAND AND SEA*

KATIE GLASKIN

U W
A P
UWA PUBLISHING

First published in 2017 by
UWA Publishing
Crawley, Western Australia 6009
www.uwap.uwa.edu.au

UWAP is an imprint of UWA Publishing
a division of The University of Western Australia

THE UNIVERSITY OF
WESTERN
AUSTRALIA

National Library of Australia
Cataloguing-in-Publication entry:
Glaskin, Katie, author.
Crosscurrents : law and society in a native title claim to land and sea / Katie Glaskin.
ISBN: 9781742589442 (paperback)
Includes bibliographical references and index.
Australia. Federal Court. Sampi on behalf of the Bardi and Jawi People v Western Australia.
Native title (Australia)
Native title (Australia)—Western Australia—Kimberley.
Native title (Australia)—Government policy—Australia.
Native title—Law and legislation—Western Australia—Kimberley.
Aboriginal Australians—Land tenure—Law and legislation—Western Australia—Kimberley.
Aboriginal Australians—Legal status, laws, etc.—Western Australia—Kimberley.
Aboriginal Australians—Western Australia—Kimberley.
Bardi (Australian people)
Jawi (Australian people)

Cover image by Christopher Pease, *Down the rabbit hole II*, 2013, oil on canvas,
61.5 × 90.5 cm (h, w), The University of Western Australia Art Collection,
University Senate Grant and Gift of the Friends of the Lawrence Wilson Art Gallery,
2014 © Christopher Pease.
Typeset in 12 point Bembo by Lasertype
Printed by Lightning Source

uwapublishing

Readers of this book should be warned that many of the people whose names appear, both Aboriginal and non-Aboriginal, have now passed away.

For Jamaji, Uju, Janjan and Wotjularr

Contents

List of Maps and Figures

Preface and Acknowledgements

This book is about a native title claim to an area of land and sea in north-west Western Australia. The claim ('Sampi') was first determined by the Federal Court in 2005 (*Sampi v State of Western Australia* [2005] FCA 777) before proceeding to appeal in 2007. The appeal was determined in 2010 (*Sampi v State of Western Australia* [2010] FCAFC 26). Some of the issues that came to impact on the case along the path to its final resolution in 2010 included those that would have impacted any native title case in Australia during the same period; others were specific to the case.

I began writing this book knowing many of the people who have had direct involvement in the Sampi case may disagree with some or more of the analysis and interpretations of issues I offer here. To write about a case of this length and complexity with its many differently situated actors means there will inevitably be disagreement about certain aspects of the case. It would be strange if there were not. I have tried not to overload the reader with the complexity of native title nor the social and political lives of people as they are required to interact with it, though I hope the reader will emerge with a sufficient sense of these things without the detail becoming too overwhelming.

Like most other groups pursuing native title around Australia, Bardi and Jawi claimants had to rely on a Native Title Representative Body to pursue the claim on their behalf. Native Title Representative bodies are statutorily charged with representing the interests of local indigenous constituents in native title. These organisations are notoriously underfunded and overstretched, and many have considerable staff turnover. The Kimberley Land Council (KLC) represented Bardi and Jawi in the Sampi case. During the period of their claim, from when they first issued instructions to pursue a claim in 1993 until the conclusion of the appeal in 2010, Sampi claimants frequently encountered new personnel who were dealing with their case. By my count, at least six instructing solicitors and five barristers represented Bardi and Jawi claimants' legal interests at different times, though there may have been more. I worked for the land council during 1994 and 1995, when I began research for the Sampi claim with Geoffrey Bagshaw, who was contracted to the organisation as the senior anthropologist on the claim. Between 1996 and 2007 the land council also engaged me for periods of time to work on various aspects of the case.

My postgraduate research also enabled me to spend time with Bardi and Jawi claimants. My fieldwork in 1997 and 1998 focused on the effects of participating in native title processes, research inspired by my early experiences of working with them in relation to native title. Historical and oral historical material presented in chapters Two, Three and Four is largely derived from research undertaken for my doctoral thesis (Glaskin 2002); I am grateful to the Australian National University and to the Kimberley Land Council for their support in conducting this research. Francesca Merlan, Tim Rowse and Ian Keen were my supervisors and I remain indebted to them for their feedback and encouragement throughout that process. I have previously published some of the material in Chapter Four (Glaskin 2007b) derived from this research.

This book also draws on my postdoctoral research, made possible through the award of the Berndt Foundation's inaugural postdoctoral fellowship at the University of Western Australia. This allowed me to pursue my interest in how the courts were dealing with aspects of native title. This research (2002–05) coincided with the period during which a number of significant native title determinations were handed down: *Yorta Yorta v Victoria* [2002] HCA 58, *Western Australia v Ward* [2002] HCA 28, *Neowarra v Western Australia* [2003] FCA 1402, *Daniel v Western Australia* [2003] FCA 666 and *Gumana v Northern Territory of*

Australia [2005] FCA 50 among them. During this period I was able to attend the Perth Registry of the Federal Court of Australia to hear the expert evidence in native title hearings *Harrington-Smith v Western Australia (no.9)* [2007] FCA 31, *Neowarra v Western Australia* [2003] FCA 1402, and *Bennell v Western Australia* [2006] FCA 1243. A University of Western Australia Teaching Relief Grant (awarded in 2012) granted me some time (in 2013) to begin drafting chapters for this book.

From the outset, the reader should be aware of what I have and have not sought to do. I have not sought to detail the contributions of all land council personnel during this period; for example, field and project officers were engaged with the claimants and the claim to differing degrees over a period of years. Nor have I examined the contributions made by all the instructing solicitors and barristers in the case. I do not discuss the material presented by linguists, archaeologists and historians, although the interested reader can find discussion of these in the 2005 judgment. Nor have I attempted to analyse the contributions anthropologists (Geoffrey Bagshaw and myself) made to the outcome of this case, although I do discuss some elements of the disagreements between the claimants' anthropologists and those acting for the respondent parties as relevant to the unfolding case. Justice French's review of Bagshaw's anthropological evidence (paragraphs 801–883) found 'the bulk of the anthropological evidence appears to have been based upon information provided by Aboriginal persons to the anthropologists', and that it was 'supported by reference to other writers' (*Sampi v State of Western Australia* [2005] FCA 777 at paragraph 801). Indeed, where the 2005 judgment in the case details aspects of Aboriginal land and sea tenure, it relies extensively on material found in Bagshaw's anthropological reports. It is the transcript of the applicant evidence, however, on which the findings about the case are mainly based.

I have not discussed the many meetings held at Djarindjin or One Arm Point in order for KLC lawyers to receive instructions from their clients and to update them about the progress of the claim. Through the many years of legal process, it would be no surprise if claimants primarily thought about their native title experience in terms of the constant meetings to give instruction to solicitors, and the experience of court itself. Talk about 'fighting' for native title encapsulates these experiences and the constant efforts required in relation to them. Beyond this, the experiences that continue to have the most salience in regard to native title are a mixture of the conflicts that native title is considered to have generated, tempered only slightly by the humorous events that sometimes unfolded which were somehow connected with native title, and events that made a good story to be retold. The intensity of being involved in a protracted legal case has faded, but the politics about country that were also part of people's experience, both before native title and during the years of focusing on rights and interests and entitlements and genealogical connections, remains. Some people have interests in adjoining native title claims that keeps them involved in native title processes and associated politics. My primary focus here though is on law as process, and in this, I am interested not only in legal reasoning but in how judicial precedent and case strategies interact with a claim's history and recorded ethnography.

The reader will notice that my examination of the evidence in the case as against the evidence in transcript is confined to the islands that were excluded from the 2005 determination on the basis that these were considered to have been Jawi islands at the time of colonisation, but which the claimants had argued were Bardi. There are two reasons for this: first, it simply would not have been feasible to examine all the evidence in this way. Second, viewing all the islands as Jawi was fundamentally linked to the 2005 determination that limited native title recognition to the mainland and the intertidal zone, thus excluding any native title rights in the sea. This focus on specific islands means the evidence I look at is mainly connected to certain individuals, especially Bardi man Jimmy Ejai and Jawi man Khaki Stumpagee, both of whom are now sadly deceased. It has not been feasible to discuss this evidence without naming them, and I hope doing so will not be distressing for any of their relatives who read this book. I also hope I have conveyed something of the enormous contribution to this native title case both men made over a number of years.

Others whose evidence I have not dwelt upon in the same way also made important contributions to the outcome of this case. Many of these people have now passed away and the reader should note that sensitivity should be exercised with regard to their names. They include, but are not limited to, the following (in alphabetical order): Phillip Albert, Bernadette Angus, Hamlet Angus, Laurel Angus, Mercia Angus, Vincent Angus, Freddie Bin Sali, Rosie Bin Sali, Charles Coomerang, Marie Coomerang, Dennis Davey, Frank Davey, Irene Davey, Joe Davey, Maryanne Doyle, Eugenia George, Kevin George, Madeleine Gregory, Aggie Ishmael, Victor James, Bella Lauder, Anna Phillips, Elizabeth Puertollano, Kevin Puertollano, Joe Rock, Lena Stumpagee, Leslie Stumpagee, Joe Sammat, Terry Sammat, Paul Sampi, Aubrey Tigan and David Wiggan. I have not dwelt on their evidence because it mainly concerned areas on the mainland that were subject to a positive determination of native title at first instance. Many others contributed to the claim in numerous ways although they did not give evidence. While it is not possible to name everyone, they include the following (in alphabetical order): Patsy Ah Choo, Laurel Angus, Maureen Angus, Violet Carter, Biddy Chaquebor, Brendan Chaquebor, Locki Coomerang, Lucy Coomerang, Audrey Davey, Henry Davey, Maggie Davey, Margaret Davey, Bessie Ejai, Peter Gregory, Eric Hunter, Maureen Hunter, Nellie Hunter, Adrian Isaac, Nancy Isaac, Elaine James, Julie Lauder, Brian Lee, Turkoi Mowarlajarlai, Sandy Paddy, Roma Puertollano, Bonnie Sampi, Patrick Sampi, Jacob Sesar, Peter Sibosado, Barry Stumpagee, Ingrid Thomas, Rosa Tigan, Douglas Wiggan, Jody Wiggan, Katie Wiggan, Margaret Wiggan, Roy Wiggan, Valerie Wiggan and Monty Wilfred.

Throughout this book, I have used English names when quoting documents already available on the public record (such as Federal Court transcripts) that identify individuals in this way. When referring to comments made by Bardi or Jawi people during fieldwork, I use personal ('bush') names rather than English names. Many Bardi and Jawi have more than one bush name, and some bush names are more private than others. I use the bush names other Bardi and Jawi freely use in relation to these individuals (rather than those that are more private) so that, whether now or sometime in the future, Bardi and Jawi can recognise these names in this book if they choose to read it, but their identities will not be readily identifiable to others.

With the exception of personal ('bush') names, language names, place names and outstation names, Aboriginal words appearing in this book are italicised. Unless stated otherwise, Aboriginal terms appearing in this book are in Bardi. The orthography I have used follows the reports submitted to the Federal Court in this case (Bagshaw 1999, 2001a, 2001b, Bagshaw & Glaskin 2000, Glaskin & Bagshaw 1999). This orthography was based on Robinson (1973) and Metcalfe (1975). The first Bardi dictionary (Aklif 1999) used a slightly different orthography (for example, a double 'o' for a long 'u' sound, such that, for example, the name Galalung would be written Galaloong), and this is the orthography used by linguists working in the area since (e.g., Bowern 2012). At the time of submitting initial reports to the Federal Court, though, the Bardi dictionary had not yet been published; it was published later that year. With the exception of mistranscriptions (see Chapter Eight), the orthography used in the anthropological reports is reflected in the transcript in the Federal Court. As I refer to the case's transcript on numerous occasions throughout this book, I have followed the orthography used in the case.

There are dialectical differences within the Bardi language, and this is not uncommon in the languages of Australia: for example, Hosokawa (1994, p. 497) distinguishes linguistic

PREFACE AND ACKNOWLEDGEMENTS

varieties within the Yawuru language; Thieberger (1993, p. 156) identifies three dialects of Karajarri. Robinson (1973, p. 107) says the linguistic style attributed to Bardi who occupied the Pender Bay region was said to be 'precisely articulated' or 'slow', and was described as 'slow Bardi'. Nyul Nyul referred to them as Barda or Bardu, and speakers of 'slow Bardi', who interacted closely with Nyul Nyul, would at times refer to themselves using these terms (Robinson 1973, p. 107). This linguistic distinction is rarely referred to today, although I heard small hints of it during the 1990s from some elderly people who are now deceased. The distinction more commonly made is between Bard and Bardi, and this also has historical dimensions through people's associations with Lombadina and Sunday Island missions. 'Light Bardi' speakers speak quickly and tend to drop final vowels from their words and, as Robinson (1973, p. 108) says, 'may refer to themselves as Bard rather than Bardi'. Today, the people who refer to themselves as Bard are usually those who are or have been associated with Lombadina mission. 'Heavy Bardi' speakers come from the northern and eastern regions of Bardi country and include those who lived at the mission on Sunday Island. Robinson (1973, p. 108) describes them as having 'slower' speech and occasionally incorporating Jawi words; they refer to themselves as Bardi. Today, most of that population lives in One Arm Point. These dialectical distinctions also appear in the ethnographic literature. Unless discussing specific distinctions between Bard and Bardi people's perspectives, my references to Bardi throughout this book should be taken to refer to both.

The transcript of the hearing (Federal Court of Australia, Western Australia District Registry, Before Beaumont J. File No.: WAG49/98, Re: Paul Sampi and Others, Applicants, and The State of Western Australia and Others, Respondents) was produced by Transcript Australia. With the exception of the gender-restricted portions of the transcript, I had access to this as one of the participants in the case. A copy of the transcript usually remains on the court file at the appropriate Federal

Court Registry (in this case, Perth) where it may be possible to access it. The transcript of the appeal (Transcript of Proceedings, Federal Court of Australia, Western Australian District Registry, before Branson J, North J, Mansfield J, in Paul Sampi and Others and State of Western Australia and Others, No. WAD 188 of 2006) was produced by Auscript Australia. I attended the final submissions for the original case and made extensive notes of the arguments made; when I first drafted Chapter Seven, which draws on these arguments, I wrote it from these notes. In the interest of being as accurate as possible, I subsequently referenced the transcript rather than relying on these notes, but the fact that I could attend the final submissions in the Federal Court and make these notes underscores the public nature of Federal Court proceedings. I was not able to attend the final submissions in the Full Court appeal as I was then living in Tokyo, and rely wholly on transcript in relation to my discussion of that part of the case.

Toni Bauman, Paul Burke, Timothy Dauth, Tony Redmond, Michael Robinson, Moya Smith, Nick Smith, Celine Travési, David Trigger and James F. Weiner have all offered encouragement when I have mentioned the idea of this book to them at various times over the years. I am most grateful to Ingrid Ward, who drew the maps that appear in this book for me; Paul Davill, Peter Veth and Ben Ripper, who assisted me to clarify specific issues in their respective areas of expertise; Bruno Jordanoff for sharing his Kimberley collection with me; Nicholas Reid and Patrick Nunn for sharing their work on Aboriginal oral traditions and sea-level rise; the South Australian Museum for permission to publish an extract from Tindale's (1974, p. 146) map, and the State Library of Western Australia for permission to publish William J. Jackson's (1917) photographs included in this book. For their support and presence throughout the process of writing, I especially thank David Walker and Koto and Umi; for their encouragement in important moments, Rita Armstrong, Victoria Burbank, Dianne Carmody, Jim Campbell, Laurent Dousset, Catie Gressier, Kaye Johnson, Nicholas Harney, Mitchell Low,

Julie McCormack, Julie Potts, Graham Walker, Jill Woodman, Angela Zeck and my parents. I am indebted to Geoffrey Bagshaw, the senior anthropologist in the Sampi case, who generously read and commented on the draft of this book. As a recent graduate of anthropology, I learned enormous amounts through working with Geoff ('Juljinabur'). Over the course of working on this case, we shared some extraordinary experiences, both good and difficult. While I have not focused on these in this book, the reader will get a sense of some of the issues that became part of our experience in this case. All errors, of course, necessarily remain my own.

My greatest debt is to the many Bardi and Jawi people who shared their hospitality and spent many hours talking with me about things that must have seemed self-evident to them, who told me their stories, their jokes and their dreams, who showed me their country and taught me to see it in a different way. Many of the people I once knew have now passed away; I miss them still.

Native title they say it was for the Aborigine people, they know that was our traditional land and we know we owned that land. But in the *gardiya's* [European Australians'] way, we have to be really strong, fill in the papers and some documents to be recognised that we own that. But in Aborigine way, Law, we know that we own them (Galiwar, One Arm Point, 1 December 1996).

Chapter One

Law's Metaphysics

Records of the bare bones of judgments...do not by any means reflect either the judicial process or the substantive law. The record of a case involves the pleas of the parties, the evidence of the witnesses, and cross-examination, as well as the judges' decisions (Gluckman 1955, p. 35).

An Ethnography of Law

It is one thing to know what the law says: it is another to try to understand what it means and how it comes to be applied. In native title, which deals with indigenous relationships with country through the lens of a Western property rights regime, this complexity is seriously magnified. The resolution of a legal case can take years, and native title claims are no exception. When a determination is made, it becomes the defining feature of a claim. It comes to stand for all the actions and social relations that have each had their own effects that have, in some way, culminated in the litigation. In this way, a judgment can itself become a kind of history that produces 'facts' through which the past may be read and the future defined. This, I contend, is problematic because, although determinations reflect the cases that go to trial, they necessarily conceal most of their processual aspects, including those that have played a significant role in an eventual outcome.

This book centres on the claim to native title made to an area of land and sea in the north-west Kimberley region of Western Australia. I was one of the two anthropologists who worked on behalf of the applicants, the Bardi and Jawi people, who had brought the case. The case, *Sampi v State of Western Australia* [2005] FCA 777 ('Sampi'), was initially determined in 2005. As the judgment was delivered in the Perth District Registry of the Federal Court of Australia, it became apparent that the claim had only partly succeeded. Native title rights to Bardi country on the mainland had been recognised; native title rights to Bardi islands, Jawi islands and to sea country had not. The main reason for this was the finding that Jawi society had become incorporated into Bardi society.

As I listened to the judge explain his findings, a senior Jawi man's words replayed through my mind. *I'm not a Bardi, I'm a Jawi.* In 1997, when he had said this, we were sitting at an outstation in his country at a place called Guwarngun, located in the south of Sunday Island off the coast of the Dampier Peninsula, more than 2,000 kilometres away from the Perth Federal Court Registry. I was on the island doing fieldwork with my colleague Geoffrey Bagshaw and the old man and his wife and other members of his family. The events that had elicited his response were about tourism not about native title, but they came back to me at that moment because they were such a strong assertion of a distinct Jawi identity. *Have they got a song for this place,* he had asked rhetorically to anyone at his small outstation within earshot.

The Sampi determination of 2005 was the initial catalyst for me to write this book; both as a participant, and with an interest in native title processes more generally, I was concerned about how the concept of 'society' had been applied in the case. Jawi islands and sea country had been excluded from the native title determination, based on the view that Jawi society had been incorporated into Bardi society. These two things – the exclusion of Jawi country and the edict about Jawi society – were both a legacy of this one word, 'society', which had only been introduced

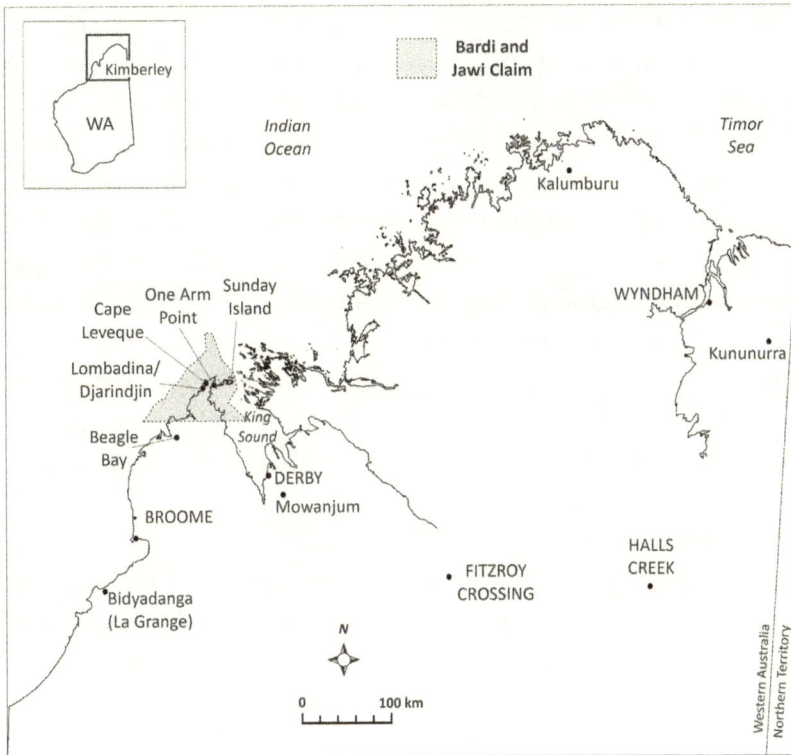

Figure 1: Location of Bardi and Jawi claim, Kimberley region, north-west Australia.

into native title jurisprudence in 2002 through a precedent set in the High Court of Australia's decision in the Yorta Yorta native title case (*Members of the Yorta Yorta Aboriginal Community v Victoria* [2002] HCA 58). Speaking about his identity as a Jawi person, the old man had said *I'm not a Bardi, I'm a Jawi. They see it wrong, that's why everything buckle up.* At this point, I was inclined to agree with him.

This book is an exploration of how the claim and its outcome were shaped by different events; some that occurred when the first non-Aboriginal people were settling in the area, others during the claim process itself. Its focus is on the relationships between different actors and events that led to the claim being made and how they interacted to shape subsequent actions and events that preceded and accompanied the legal action. I approach the case not as a discrete thing, but as a series of interconnected and related events. When the 2005 determination was handed down, some explanation for what had occurred seemed warranted. Clearly, a number of others have thought so too (e.g., Brennan 2007; Burke 2010; Burns 2011; Strelein 2005; Redmond 2011). Legal and anthropological commentary focused on the way the concept of 'society' was applied in the case. A term introduced into native title law only in 2002, its deployment and effects in the Sampi case illustrate the impacts that evolving judicial precedent may have on a case in graphic detail: the legal crosscurrents in which this case was caught.

In this case, how the term 'society' was applied also became fundamentally connected with how the question of the claim to native title offshore would be decided. The Bardi and Jawi claim was made to an area of land and sea that included a number of islands, reefs and other marine features. The 2005 determination recognised native title on the mainland and in the intertidal zone, but contained no recognition of native title to the sea or the islands. The exclusion of Jawi country on the basis that Jawi were now part of a Bardi society was taken to mean that there was no recognition of native title offshore although, by my reckoning, this correlation did not follow. This was only justifiable if one took the view that Bardi had no customary interests offshore, something that appeared unsustainable (e.g., Akerman 1975; Green 1988; Rouja 1998; Smith 1984–85). How did this happen?

Law's Metaphysics

In litigated claims, the facts upon which a judge will ultimately make their decision depend on a complex interaction between applicant and expert evidence, procedural issues (such as how applicant evidence is elicited, and how cases are run and argued), and interpretations of the ethnographic and historical record.

This means that what is taken to be a fact is necessarily already a judgment of some kind. As Burke (2011, p. 18–19) says, while 'the work of the judge at trial level has long been conceived of as the application of law to facts', facts themselves may be reconstructions of the past, 'guesses on which basic legal rights depend'. Given that such facts have a subjective quality to them, how we understand the application of law also needs to be qualified. In contrast to the legal formalist view that law is 'found or discovered, not made by judges', legal realists argue that law alone does not decide cases (Donovan 2008, p. 91). Because no two cases are identical, rules drawn 'from a preceding case can never be purely and simply applied to a new case' (Bourdieu 1987, p. 826). Such rules, then, are inherently ambiguous, and cannot be applied in any 'mechanical' kind of way; cases can always be interpreted in various ways, and 'the resulting indeterminacy of abstract legal concepts' means they can be manipulated via precedent (MacLean 2012, p. 26). Consideration of how the concept of 'society' found expression in the Sampi case illustrates these points well.

One of my purposes in writing this book is to understand how judgments are made. This is not something I take to be separate to the many processes shaping the case that is ultimately decided. Another is to explore issues Aboriginal people face in having their rights in country recognised under the auspices of the Western legal system. These two matters are, of course, closely connected. For the most part, native title claims are examined from the vantage point of the determination and what this reveals about the judge's reasoning and their application of law to the facts. Scholarly attention to specific native title claims then has focused on how judges have applied and interpreted native title law, the role of anthropology and its intersection with law, and on the relationship between the ethnographic archive and the determination.[1] What usually remains invisible, except to those who are participants in a case, is the historical context of claims and claimant groups, front and backstage aspects of the hearing, the impact of evolving case law, and legal strategies and pleas that also contribute to the outcome of a case.

In their studies of litigation in the United States, O'Barr and Conley (1988) have pointed out that different actors hold different ideologies about the law. Disputants who bring their cases to be resolved usually understand the law to be about justice, whereas, they argue, for legal personnel the law is primarily about settling disputes (1988, p. 345). Bardi and Jawi, with whom I worked in relation to this claim, saw the case as being about justice, about the recognition of their pre-existing land and sea entitlements. Part of the context of this case, then, is that for most of those who were engaged in it the recognition of their customary land and sea entitlements was more than a legal issue; it had moral significance as well. O'Barr and Conley's (1988, p. 345) view that legal personnel might primarily see the law as about settling disputes (in contrast to applicants who largely see it as about justice) is not to deny the justice orientation of many who enter into the legal profession, nor the many who do so for the express purpose of 'making a difference'. Rather, it is to highlight the functional aspects of the law. Their studies revealed there is often a 'dissonance' between what claimants expect from a case in terms of their understandings of a just result, and its eventual outcomes. This is especially relevant, of course, to an adversarial system of law, as practised in the United States, Australia and Britain, as distinct from an inquisitorial system, practiced in some European countries, in which the judge would appear to have greater capacity to inquire independently into the truth of a matter, rather than being constrained by the pleadings and evidence put before them. Thus, in considering the outcome of the Sampi case in its initial (2005) determination, it is important to consider the constraints on the trial judge in these terms. Judges are also limited by the relevant legislation (in this case native title) and by case law. But judges interpret both legislation and precedent even as they weigh up the evidence before them in the light of the case put and the pleadings made. Given that the aim in the adversarial context is to win the case, these pleadings and the evidence are themselves also shaped to greater or lesser extent by legal precedent.

This book describes and explores native title as a social process. Part of that process and the cultural basis that underpins it is the legal dispossession of Aboriginal people and the evidentiary requirements subsequently made of them through law to reclaim country their ancestors held. While legal processes may create a sense of a level playing field, they can also mask a range of inequalities inherent in the process itself, including that indigenous peoples can only make their claims 'in the language of the jurisprudence and property-rights regime of those responsible for their plight in the first place' (Dirlik 2001, p. 181). I therefore consider not only the context of the case but also 'the juridical field': the 'judges, lawyers and, at lower levels, witnesses, performing their roles in a court case', as formally 'recorded in court documents, transcripts and reasons for decision' (Burke 2011, p. 15). While it is not possible to access much of the 'less accessible informal dimension' Burke (2011, p. 15) identifies – 'the judge's private thought processes, corridor discussions with court staff, other judges and counsel appearing for the parties,' among other things – some parts of the formal dimension of the juridical field, such as transcripts and legal submissions, do provide insight into the approach of various actors, and are part of the overall context in which judicial weight is accorded to some aspects of a case or associated arguments in preference to others. Accordingly, the transcripts for the final submissions in the 2005 case and for the appeal to the Full Federal Court brought in 2007 are an important part of the material I examine in this book.

Native Title, Continuity and Society

In Australia, the Commonwealth passed the *Native Title Act 1993* in response to the High Court's decision in Mabo (*Mabo v Queensland (No. 2)* [1992] HCA 23). In Mabo, the Court found the Murray Islanders of the Torres Strait had common law rights to the island of Mer 'as against the whole world', conferring exclusive possession.[2] This decision set a precedent that applied beyond the island of Mer in the Torres Strait, and established the existence of Indigenous Australians' native title within the common law of Australia. The High Court's finding that Indigenous Australians' *sui generis* (unique) form of title had not necessarily been extinguished as a consequence of colonisation had a profound social impact in Australia more broadly. There were those who believed the existence of native title threatened to 'fracture the skeleton' of the common law of Australia; others greeted the recognition of Indigenous Australians' prior ownership of land as being long overdue.[3] The Australian Federal Government responded quickly to Mabo, and, having consulted and negotiated with various groups that would be most affected, passed the *Native Title Act 1993* (Cth) within eighteen months of the decision. The Act provides the legal framework for Aboriginal Australians and Torres Strait Islanders to make claims to their ancestral lands. It came into effect on the 1st January 1994.

Native title in Australia shares its English common law origins with Indian title law in the US and Aboriginal rights law in Canada (Connolly 2006, p. 39). The Mabo decision thus drew on Canadian and US legal cases, despite the 'several juristic foundations – proclamation, policy, treaty or occupation – on which native title has been rested in Canada and the United States'.[4] Judicial decisions about native title in both Canada and Malaysia have similarly drawn on Australian native title jurisprudence.[5] In Australia, native title is established through the 'traditional laws and customs that give rise to rights and interests in land and waters'.[6] Other Commonwealth countries dealing with issues of aboriginal land title have similarly based their legal recognition of indigenous land rights on notions of 'tradition'. As Connolly (2006, p. 28) has observed of the Canadian context:

> The concept of tradition is semantically indeterminate enough
> to permit judges – and others – a significant degree of choice

in how they interpret and utilise it in their practices. One interpretative strategy a number of judges have taken in Canada and other common law jurisdictions in relation to the concept of tradition has been the so-called 'frozen rights' strategy, in which the concept connotes a substantial degree of identification between contemporary and pre-colonial indigenous practices.

In her discussion of the *Delgamuukw v British Columbia* case, Culhane (1998, p. 302) notes that Chief Justice McEachern, who heard the initial case (which went on to successful appeal), had taken the view that Aboriginal claimants had to demonstrate continuity between their activities and those their ancestors practised before the arrival of Europeans in their country. In Australia, a similar demonstration of continuity is required. Claimants have to demonstrate that the laws and customs they currently practise, and which give rise to rights and interests in land and waters, are the same laws and customs their antecedents practised at the time of the acquisition of sovereignty by the British Crown. This is what is meant by the formulation 'traditional laws acknowledged, and the traditional customs observed' which appears in Section 223(a) of the Native Title Act. In the Australian configuration of 'tradition', the effects of colonial history on a people's ability to sustain pre-colonial forms of law and custom are not taken into account. The onus is on groups claiming native title to demonstrate continuity; the question of how colonial policies of the nation-state may have made that a difficult task is not one that courts must ask.

All native title claims in Australia have to deal with the requirement to demonstrate cultural continuity. The issue of cultural continuity has several related aspects: how this can be demonstrated given the inherent dynamism of culture; under-standings of 'culture', which inform appraisals of culture as showing either cultural continuity or demonstrating culture 'loss'; the challenges posed for some Indigenous groups to demonstrate cultural continuity in the face of apparent change; questions of cultural revival and re-invention; questions of cultural and legal translation. These are issues that have preoccupied anthropologists (amongst others) since native title's inception (e.g., see Keen 1999; Macdonald 2001; Merlan 2006).

State governments have approached the issue of continuity from the perspective that they can ascertain what Indigenous traditions and customs were like at or close to the time of colonisation. For this they rely on written accounts, with those from the early colonial period being considered particularly useful as they are temporally closest to the time of the acquisition of sovereignty by the British Crown. This is a date that varies according to state. In Western Australia, where the Sampi claim is located, the date sovereignty was acquired was 1829. Differences between the contemporary traditions of Indigenous groups and earlier reported traditions are typically read by governments and others who oppose native title claims as evidence of discontinuity. Some anthropologists too have argued that, in terms of anthropological accounts, 'earliest sources are best' (Sansom 2007, p. 79), while others have chosen to interrogate these sources and the conditions of their production (e.g., Burke 2007; Glaskin 2007a; Keen 2007; Morton 2007; Palmer 2010; Sackett 2007; Sutton 2007). Native title in Australia has, consequently, produced many contests over history, and over whose account is to be relied upon. Similar contests over the interpretation of historical accounts have occurred in Canada (e.g., Ray 2011).

What is distinct about the Australian approach to native title in terms of the 'frozen rights' strategy is the addition of the potent word 'society' into the mix of what must be demonstrated to be continuous. This arose as a consequence of the High Court's decision in Yorta Yorta, which had a substantial impact on how courts approach issues of tradition and cultural continuity in native title cases. In Yorta Yorta, Justices Gleeson, Gummow and Haynes formed the conclusion that the term 'traditional', in the native title context, needed to be understood as referring to the age and continuity of the laws and customs that give rise to native title rights and interests in land or waters:

> The origins of the content of the law or custom concerned are to be found in the normative rules of the Aboriginal and Torres Strait Islander societies that existed before the assertion of sovereignty by the British Crown. It is only those normative rules that are 'traditional' laws and customs (*Members of the Yorta Yorta Aboriginal Community v Victoria* [2002] HCA 58, at paragraph 46).

The legal clarification that 'tradition' refers to the laws and customs acknowledged and observed prior to the acquisition of sovereignty by the British Crown has increased the difficulty many Indigenous groups have had in demonstrating their native title. The other significant tenet of Yorta Yorta, though, was its introduction of the concept of a 'society' into native title jurisprudence:

> Law and custom arise out of and, in important respects, go to define a particular society. In this context, 'society' is to be understood as a body of persons united in and by its acknowledgment and observance of a body of law and customs (ibid., at paragraph 49).

This emphasis on a rule-bearing society means that, in looking at applicant groups in subsequent native title cases, courts have asked questions about whether a claimant group forms a 'whole' society or 'part' of a society, and considers whether that society has had 'continuous existence and vitality since sovereignty'.[7]

'Society' is a term that has also appeared in Canadian native title. In the Baker Lake case,[8] Justice Mahoney said, in order to establish native title, claimants had to show that an 'organised society' had exclusively occupied the claimed area at the time British sovereignty was proclaimed (Young 2009, p. 5). Ray's

(2011, p. xxiv) parenthetical comment about this doctrine highlights the problems with its underlying assumptions; he says, 'rather than [that they lived] in what…Packs?' In comparison to the Australian focus on 'society' following Yorta Yorta, Young (2009, p. 15) says that Canada's emphasis on 'society' has now diminished, as evidenced in both the 1997 Delgamuukw and the 2007 Tsilhqot'in Canadian cases.[9] Writing of the Tsilhqot'in case, Young (2009, p. 13) additionally notes that, in contrast to Australian native title, 'a close reading of the case reveals that there was in fact very little attention to or interest in specific continuity…And there was certainly no concern about post-sovereignty cultural change'. This is in direct contrast to the way Australian courts have approached the continuity requirement in conjunction with the issue of society in native title claims.

In native title, requirements about continuity of law and custom and the society from which these stem raise further issues that need to be considered. Native title does not simply recognise pre-existing land entitlements; rather, it elicits the customary in particular forms. In order to be a group capable of the kind of recognition afforded by legislation such as the Native Title Act (1993), those making claims are required to present themselves in a certain way. This is a process that comes to influence not only the outward presentation of the group, but relations within those groups (e.g., Glaskin 2002, Weiner & Glaskin 2006, 2007; Smith & Morphy 2007; Glaskin & Dousset 2011). Anthropologists working in other colonial contexts have similarly shown that customary law is always in a 'dialectical relation with state law, during the colonial period, and secondly, that this fact is crucial for the analysis of law, as a plural phenomenon, in post-colonial countries' (Fuller 1994, p. 10; and see Chanock 1985; Moore 1986). Writing about the Canadian Subarctic, Nadasdy (2002, p. 258) too has argued that the process of bringing claims in terms of Western ideas of property and ownership requires people to engage with 'a very different set of cultural assumptions' that obliges people to articulate their claims in specific ways (the requirement to draw

14

'boundaries' around territories and peoples is one aspect of this; see Glaskin 2014). For these reasons, claims are often inherently transformative.

In order to understand what a native title claim really represents, then, it is necessary to move beyond 'judge and judgment oriented accounts' to consider the entire process in social context (Ubink 2008, p. 26).[10] This necessarily includes the processes of colonisation experienced by claimants and their forebears, from which claims to indigenous status and associated rights arise in the first instance. Native title is, after all, the legal recognition of indigenous property rights based on their existence prior to colonisation and their continuation now. As a legal concept, it is enmeshed in history: the arrival of the British and their declaration of sovereignty over Australia; the interactions between coloniser and those they colonised that embodied or contradicted this larger act, and the relationships amongst and between indigenous and non-indigenous people with respect to the area claimed over time. In ideal terms, native title holds forth the promise of restorative justice, a recognition of the pre-existing rights of indigenous peoples whose property rights were legally usurped through the Crown's declaration of sovereignty. What a historical and processual examination of a native title claim shows, though, is that asymmetrical relationships of power that characterise the colonising experience remain unambiguously present in the very processes that purport, at some level, to rectify the imbalance colonisation precipitated. A claim to native title cannot, then, be considered simply as a self-contained legal case but, rather, as a more recent phase in the manifestation of a colonial relationship.

Numerous considerations have shaped the way this book has been written. Many of the people who were influential participants in this case, both Aboriginal and non-Aboriginal, are no longer with us. I have hoped to honour the contributions of those who gave so much to the case without glorifying them, and to discuss some of the real issues that emerged in the case without partisanship. This is especially important, for in the political world of native title it is often the case that participants find themselves on one side or the other, and this political positioning can create a silo effect that can prevent serious scrutiny and analysis of the interaction between these different positions. There are considerations around confidentiality, privacy and necessary detail. There are also limitations imposed by my capacity to investigate, understand and describe the many facets that make up such a complex context, and which, in the process of description, necessarily reify and objectify a human sociality that is constantly in motion. Much of what occurs in a native title case is opaque, even to many of those who may be participants in it and of course each of the participants, because they are positioned differently, are likely to see things in different ways.

My understanding of the claim spans the period from 1994, before it was lodged, until its final resolution in 2010. When I have spoken with people in the Dampier Peninsula about their case being of interest to others because of the way in which the law was applied at a time when native title was still quite new, responses have varied, but not much. Amongst those with whom I have spoken about this, discussion about the technicalities of their native title case has not been something that has garnered special interest. What actually happened on the ground is more compelling, as is what has happened since. When I have said to people I planned to write a book about their native title claim, some complained that native title has not lived up to its promises anyway, and that in fact the technicalities of its recognition have not yet been properly implemented. In many instances agencies and people still act as though native title has not been recognised, they say. They also speak of the old people they have lost along the way, the people who fought so hard and so long to have their native title recognised. These are the people I had the privilege of working with, and it is because of them that I wanted to write this book.

Chapter Two

When Whiteman Came In

Speaking of native title in general, Uju bemoaned the
fact that people had to fight for their own country. That
'when whiteman came in, Aborigine was minding their
own business'. Went on to relay the story of the massacre
at Galan (Skeleton Point), and spoke of retaliatory killings.
Identified one of the men from Nilagun who had been
killed in one of these expeditions (extract from journal
entry, One Arm Point, 8 March 2003).

Country

From the port town of Broome, known for its pearls and
multicultural population, the drive to Cape Leveque at the
northern tip of Dampier Peninsula is about 200 kilometres. Until
relatively recently most of the road to Cape Leveque was gravel
or sand that required regular grading. Between gradings various
parts of the road became either bone-crunching corrugations or
one-car-width sand gullies lined with steep banks that meant,
when confronted with oncoming traffic, having to drive along the
sides of the gully at a forty-five-degree angle with enough speed
that your four-wheel drive would not slide into the vehicle going
by. The Kimberley region has a tropical monsoonal climate and,
in the wet season, from November to April, impressive rains can
turn these roads into floodways: amongst some Bardi, a standing

joke was that a hovercraft would be a more effective means of travelling to Broome when the road was in such a condition. Nowadays half the 200 kilometre stretch has been bitumised, but this does not prevent the other half from being closed when substantial summer rains come. Rains during the wet season also make driving on the dirt roads to the many outstations in the peninsula difficult to impossible at different times.

The first major community along the Cape Leveque road is Beagle Bay, a former Pallottine mission, established in 1890. Somewhere around the northern edge of the Beagle Bay Reserve boundary, some 60 kilometres from Cape Leveque, one passes invisibly from Nyul Nyul country into Bardi country. After some distance, the turn-off to the two major communities on the western side of the peninsula appears. Lombadina and Djarindjin both emerged from the former Pallottine mission at Lombadina founded in 1910, and many of those resident in these communities have links, or their forebears had links, to the mission. A short way on lies the right-hand turn-off to One Arm Point (now also known as Ardyaloon) on the eastern side of the peninsula, an Aboriginal community established in 1972. Its population is primarily Bardi and Jawi people whose antecedents were associated with Sunday Island mission, a Protestant mission begun in Jawi country on Sunday Island in 1899, which closed in the 1960s. While a number of older people at One Arm Point were born at Sunday Island during mission times, and have memories of the mission, the deaths of many older people has meant the numbers of living people who grew up at the mission is significantly smaller than when I first visited the communities in 1994.

If you continue northwards rather than turning off, you reach Cape Leveque, a promontory at the far northern end of the peninsula. The view upon arrival is stunning: aqua-blue waters, red cliffs on the western side of the cape, and white sand beach. On the eastern side are two large reefs, Niwurndun and Mulurrman, with the Twin Islands visible to the north-east. Bardi know these as Murrudulun (South East Twin Island) and Juwarnan (North West

18

Twin Island). The northernmost tip is crowned by Anbarrngani (Leveque Island), which is connected to the cape by exposed rock and reef at low tide. In 1911, a lighthouse was built on the promontory. The lighthouse was manned from 1938 to 1985, and older Bardi have memories of lighthouse keepers and their wives who lived there. The signage at Kooljaman indicates that during World War II, from 1938 to 1941, Bardi man Robin Hunter took responsibility for the lighthouse. In 1986 the lighthouse was automated, and the Aboriginal Development Commission purchased the area on which it stands. It vested the land in a corporation held by local Bardi people, the Bardina Corporation, on the proviso that the corporation would run tourism there. This has become a successful enterprise, with Kooljaman at Cape Leveque, as it is called, having won various Indigenous tourism awards over the years. From a humble camping ground with basic facilities, the enterprise has grown to include different levels of tourist accommodation. High-end safari tents now carry the Aboriginal names of Bardi and Jawi forebears, including now the names of people I once knew.

Also encapsulated in the history of Kooljaman are traces of the pre-European visitors to this coast. South-east Asian fisherpeople sailing through the port of Macassar (now Ujung Pandang) in the Celebes (today Sulawesi and part of Indonesia) are likely to have been visiting northern Dampierland in search of trepang (bêche-de-mer or sea cucumber) since at least the 1700s (Crawford 2001, p. 70). Because they came through Macassar (or Makasar), these people tend to be referred to as Macassans, although they came from various parts of the Indonesian archipelago (Crawford 2001, p. 74). Occasional tamarind trees (*Tamarindis indica*) on the coast indicate their old campsites, while dense coastal vine thickets said to have mainly originated from Indo-Malaysian plants are found amongst the remnant monsoonal rain forests that fringe some areas of the peninsula's coastal dunes (Keneally, Edinger and Willing 1996, p. 21). Macassans called the Kimberley coast 'Kayu Jawa' (Macknight 1976, p. 33).

Figure 2: Cape Leveque. Photo: Katie Glaskin (1994).

To the immediate east of the northern Dampier Peninsula lie the many islands of the Buccaneer Archipelago and of the King Sound region. None of these islands have permanent populations today. Archaeological evidence points to the Dampier Peninsula having been separated from the mainland to its east by the marine transgression of the King Sound around 9,000 to 10,000 years ago, with current sea levels stabilising 'in the mid Holocene (around 6,000BP)' (Smith 2000, p. 13). In other words, the peninsula was formed as rising sea levels inundated the area now known as the King Sound. Nautical charts indicate that the depths and contours of the seabed in the region vary dramatically. The region boasts numerous islands, rocks, sandbanks and reefs and has a diurnal tidal variation that is amongst the largest in the world, with tidal variations of between 5.5 metres to 8 metres. The force of the incoming and outgoing tide travelling across a sea floor contoured by varying depths creates numerous whirlpools, eddies and tidal overfalls, areas where the incoming and outgoing tides create rough patches of water on the downside of a shallow area on the seabed. The huge tidal variation also means the intertidal zone is constantly in flux. It means you could anchor a boat offshore at an island to go ashore and find yourself having to wait for hours for the tide to come back in so as to be able to float the boat again. The many tidal currents of the King Sound are another feature of the marine geography with which seafarers must contend. It is possible, for example, to stand at Jindirron (Round Rock) at One Arm Point and to identify three currents travelling at speed (12–14 knots) in different directions. Gibson (1951, p. 2) described the King Sound this way:

> King Sound can be treacherous. When the Nor'Westerners blow this vast sheet of water 75 miles long and various widths up to 50 miles becomes a danger spot for small craft. But the greatest difficulty is with the tidal currents. This body of water, say 70 by 40 miles falls and rises 30–35 feet twice a day. This volume pours into and out of the Sound through the many islands at its mouth and creates numerous rips. On a calm night one on Sunday Island can hear the roar of the ingoing tide passing through the Sunday Straits at anything up to 15 knots.

Close to One Arm Point are a number of islands, including Julum (Middle Island), Biyana (the Waterlow Islands), Jalan (Tallon Island) and Jayirri (Jackson Island). During the native title hearing in the Sampi case, the question of whether these islands were associated with either Bardi or Jawi peoples at the time of colonisation became a matter of contention, with the applicants arguing they were Bardi, and respondent parties arguing they were Jawi. Other islands, such as Ralral (Salural Island), Bulnginy (Poolngin Island) and Iwanyi (Sunday Island) were also included in the claim area, but were presented as Jawi islands. This was not contentious. Islands to the east of Sunday Island, including Unggaliyun (Long Island), Ulal (High Island) and Karrar (Mermaid Island) are subsumed within the adjoining Mayala native title claim, which is still in progress.

Ferret Reef
Urrundun

North West Twin Is.
JUWARNAN

South East Twin Is.
MURRUDULUN

N

Anchor Shoal

Swan Is.
GARDIYN

Gammon Bank

Karrakatta Bay

Dickie Rock
Nyayini

URRULJUN

West Roe Is.
BELAYN

East Roe Is.
GARNDALAYN

Howard Is.
NGAYJIN

RALRAL
Salural Is.

Poolngin Is.
BULNGINY

Rees Is.

GARDADIN

Talboys Is.
IRRABARDAYN

Apex Is.
NGULMINJIN

UNGALGUN
Leonie Is.

Rat Is.

Tallon Is.
JALAN

Allora Is.
NGOLORRON

IWANYI
Sunday
Island

East Sunday Is.
UMBINARR

Curlew Bay

NARDA

MILAMIL

Escape Passage

Hadley Passage

Dingo Rock
Kalmbarr

ILNGUDA
Waterlow Is.
BIYANA

Jackson Is.

JAYIRRI

Hancock Is.
GANIRRING

ONE ARM POINT

Middle Is.
JULUM

Tyra Is.
MUNBURRAN

MUNU

Lalowan Is.
LALAGUN

Holtnam Is.

Catamaran Bay

2.5 km

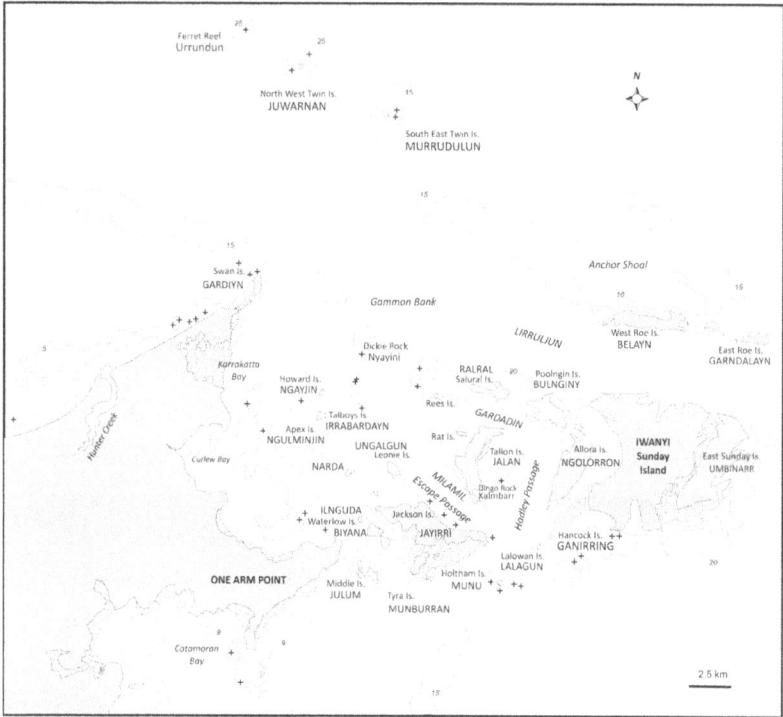

Figure 3: Islands in the Bardi and Jawi claim area.

To the south of Bardi country, at James Price Point, lies the site where a proposed gas hub had been the subject of a great deal of controversy, with some Aboriginal people, supported by environmentalists, musicians and activists, arguing the area should be preserved. Other Aboriginal people represented by the Kimberley Land Council had been in favour of the development going ahead, because of the material benefits and opportunities the agreement between Woodside and the traditional owners represented. Between those conflicting positions lay a complex local history. Those supporting the agreement with Woodside, too, did so with the spectre of the compulsory acquisition of their land over their heads, meaning that, even if they did not agree to the proposal, this would not have prevented the project from going ahead. While in 2013 Woodside withdrew its interest in building the gas hub at James Price Point, this did not prevent the Western Australian government from subsequently acquiring the area through the compulsory acquisition process, which occurred in November 2013. The wider Dampier Peninsula area is presently the subject of several overlapping native title claims.

While James Price Point lies south of Bardi country, the area in which it lies is importantly connected to it. In local cosmology, ancestral beings traversed the western coastline, beginning in Bardi country in the north and travelling down to Karajarri country, today centred on the old La Grange mission (now called Bidyadanga) in the south. As the beings travelled, they left in their wake a series of interconnected sites of significance. The sites and the track are connected through an important ritual complex practised by all those groups associated with the track, from Bardi in the north extending to include other language-named groups to their south. This is known as 'Bardi Law'. Some aspects of Law are celebrated through ritual activities, such as those associated with male initiation. Some of these activities are highly secret and participation in these, and knowledge about them, is subject to restrictions based on gender and initiation status. Others have a public dimension. Bardi refer to the time when ancestral beings gave them the Law as *milonjin* (a long time ago) or *milamilonjin* (from a long time ago). The deeds of the ancestral beings may be read from the shape of the country or from features, both terrestrial and marine, that bear their imprint and their essence. A rock, for example, can embody a being and their associated story. It might also be intrinsically connected with associated social conventions or prescriptions. The Law is understood to have come from various beings who laid down a complex mosaic of rights, obligations and reciprocal responsibilities that place people within networks of kin instantiated in place. What the connections between sites of significance mean, for example, is that any development at James Price Point that might impact on these sites of significance would also have likely consequence for Aboriginal groups elsewhere who are connected to that particular ritual complex and set of sites, including Bardi.

In Bardi and Jawi cosmology, there are a number of supernatural beings who gave humans the Law to follow. One of them, Galalung, can be spoken of publicly. He gave people laws about marrying the right way, and is responsible for moral injunctions about sharing, amongst other things. Information concerning others, who brought aspects of male initiation, is restricted.[11] Galalung is the oldest of these beings (e.g., see Worms 1952, p. 545); applicants gave evidence to this effect in the Sampi case.[12] The beings who are associated with Law are travelling beings whose travels and activities created networks of interlinked sites traversing large areas that go beyond the domain of particular language named groups.

Along with these travelling creator beings are other beings whose activities might also be considered creative or generative but who are more localised. While the degree of localisation varies (for example, some of the narratives are regionally known), others tend to be associated with particular estate-owning groups, whose members have the knowledge of them and the right to speak about them. These narratives associated with sites in particular estates, for which senior members have the right to speak, is an aspect of estate-group identification members of that estate share. These narratives simultaneously encode moral dimensions about expected behaviour as well as intimate knowledge about place. For example, Jungalbil (a man who became a grasshawk) and his two wives lived at Jackson Island and are now recognisable to those who have knowledge of the country and the narrative as particular rocks at a site called Bulngurr, and at one of the Waterlow Islands to its east. But the story itself concerns the fact that Jungalbil refused to share his firestick with other people. This led to others attempting to steal the firestick and, when he chased them, they turned into birds and spread the fire (an avian behaviour exhibited by some species – including the brown falcon – which has only recently come to the attention of ornithologists).[13]

According to the man who told the story, his wives 'felt shame about him keeping that fire to himself', so 'they shift away from shame, what he was doing to other people', hence explaining why Jungalbil (the rock) is on one island and his wife (another rock) is located on another nearby island (Bagshaw & Glaskin 2000, p. 50). So, estate-specific mythological narratives such as these index particular geographical features of a person's estate. Notwithstanding his appearance in other parts of the country, Jungalbil is not a travelling being in the way the law-givers are.[14]

In 1994, when the research for the Sampi native title claim was just beginning, there was no indication that any large-scale development in the area was imminent. Indeed, from 1994–2010 (throughout the years of the claim), proponents of possible large-scale development projects, whether in Bardi or Jawi country or in the immediate vicinity, were not discernible. Native title has a process in which, once Aboriginal claimants have registered their claim, groups with an interest in the land (or sea) under claim can apply to the Native Title Tribunal to become an interested party to the legal proceedings.[15] In the Sampi case, fifty-two groups notified the National Native Title Tribunal and gained the status of interested party.[16] Principally, though, there were three main interested parties with which claimants would have to contend: the State of Western Australia, the Commonwealth of Australia and WAFIC (the Western Australian Fisheries Industry Council). The presence of the Commonwealth and fisheries (along with the Blue Seas Pearling Company) as interested parties was a consequence of the claim extending offshore.

The First Explorers

Abel Tasman sailed past Cape Leveque in 1644. He did not go ashore in Bardi country, although he did make landing further south. King (1827, p. 93) thought that the place that Tasman landed was likely to have been Carnot Bay, and he quotes Tasman, who wrote: 'their proas are made of the bark of trees; their coast is dangerous; there are few vegetables; the people use no houses'. The Dampier Peninsula is named after the English buccaneer William Dampier who landed there in 1688. Dampier's boat, the *Cygnet*, was anchored off the coast from 5 January to 12 March 1688 while the boat was careened. This provided Dampier with an opportunity to record his observations of local Aboriginal people. First published in 1697, Dampier's account is the earliest description of Australia's Aboriginal inhabitants to appear in the English language.[17] Dampier wrote,

> At our first coming, before we were acquainted with them, or they with us, a Company of them who lived on the Main, came just against our Ship, and standing on a pretty high Bank, threatened us with their Swords and Lances, by shaking them at us. At last the Captain ordered the Drum to be beaten, which was done of a sudden with much vigour, purposely to scare the poor Creatures. Hearing the noise, they ran away as fast as they could drive. And when they ran away in haste, they would cry *Gurry, Gurry*, speaking deep in the Throat (Dampier 1937 [1697], pp. 315–16).

Linguist Christopher ('Toby') Metcalfe (1979, p. 197) has argued that the words Dampier recorded as 'Gurry, Gurry' are likely to have been the Bardi words, *ngaarri, ngaarri*, as it is unlikely he would have been able to hear the initial 'ng' sound. *Ngaarri* is a Bardi term applied to various classes of malevolent spirit beings, glossed today in English as 'devil-devil' but also used to refer to the spirits of the recently dead; beings who are inherently unstable and unpredictable, since they have neither fully joined the dead nor fully departed the living. As Sutton and Veth (2008, p. 2) say, accounts from around Australia indicate that 'dominant' indigenous reactions to European strangers initially saw them as returned ghosts, which could provoke reactions of either welcome or fear. Dampier (1937 [1697], p. 313) also recorded seeing fishtraps, or, as he described them, 'Wares of Stone, across

Figure 4: *Mayurr* (stone fishtrap) at Marraljinan. Photo: Katie Glaskin (1996).

little Coves or Branches of the Sea: every Tide bringing in the small Fish, and there leaving them for a prey to these People, who constantly attend there to search for them at Low-water'. Centuries later, some parts of Dampier's published impressions of New Holland and its inhabitants would find their way into the Sampi native title claim.

Other explorers came into the region a century or more after Dampier.[18] In 1803 a French boat captained by Nicholas Baudin, the *Geographe*, sailed past the northern tip of the Dampier Peninsula. Baudin named this point Cape Leveque after Pierre Leveque, the hydrographer aboard the boat. Along with Cape Leveque other French place names along the Dampierland coast such as Cape Bertholet and others can be traced to Baudin's expeditions of 1800 and 1803. Phillip Parker King explored the area in 1821, recording his experience with the treacherous currents on the way to Swan Point at the northern tip of the Dampier Peninsula; in commemoration of Dampier's voyage, he gave the name 'Buccaneer Archipelago' to the islands (King 1827,

27

p. 88). John Lort Stokes explored the area between January and February 1838. At the Roe Islands, just north of Sunday Island, his party found:

> A native raft, the first we had yet seen. It was formed of nine small poles pegged together, and measured ten feet in length by four in breadth; the greatest diameter of the largest pole was three inches. All the poles were of the palm tree, a wood so light, that one man could carry the whole affair with the greatest ease. By it there was a very rude double-bladed paddle (Stokes 1846, p. 35).

Encountering the force of the tidal currents in the region, Stokes was reminded of King's experience at Sunday Strait. He wrote of how King 'drifted in and out of it that day…amid an accumulation of perils that will long render the first navigation of this dangerous Archipelago a memorable event in the annals of nautical hardihood' (Stokes 1846, p. 35). Of course, this was not really 'the first navigation', given that local people were evidently using rafts to travel through the area by that time. The 'perils' of moving through these waters, regardless of the craft, would have included the many partly submerged marine features (rocks, sandbanks, islets and reefs), along with the currents, eddies, whirlpools, and tidal overfalls characteristic of this region. These are the same waters in which Dampier had seen men swimming; he had recorded seeing 'a drove of these Men swimming from one Island to another' (Dampier 1937 [1697], p. 315). Grey also explored the region in 1838, though much of his exploration centred on mainland country on the eastern side of the King Sound (Grey 1841). The last of these recorded marine explorations was E. J. Stuart's Nor' West Scientific Expedition of Western Australia of 1917 (Stuart 1923). The photographer Jackson accompanied Stuart on this expedition. Jackson's footage has largely been lost or destroyed: the only known reel of the lost Jackson footage is the seven minutes preserved as *Chez Les*

Figure 5: Bardi and Jawi men at Jayirri. Photo: William J. Jackson (1917). Courtesy of the State Library of Western Australia.

Sauvages Australiens (1932).[19] Some of this footage was shown during the Federal Court hearing of the Sampi case, although not to the applicants' intended effect.

Pearling Days

Dampier, Stokes and Grey had all noted the presence of pearl shell along the northern coast of Western Australia (McCarthy 1993, p. 1). Responsive to news of the discovery of rich pearling grounds, pearling fleets, which based themselves in Broome, came into the area from the early 1880s onwards.[20] In the Dampier Peninsula, pearling luggers laid up at Beagle Bay, Pender Bay, Hunter's Creek, the Skeleton Point area and Cygnet Bay, where Dampier had allegedly landed.[21] Along with seasonal crews, the early settlers in this region were pearlers attracted to the area by the promise of the wealth these pearling grounds could potentially bring. Japanese, Malays, Filipinos, Koepangers,

29

Chinese and Europeans all came to the region to work in the pearling industry. Other resources were being sought as well: Uju described how 'these Asian people, Koepang, Manilla, they used to come from Broome and pick up man from here, Bardi, and take them all over, they used to pick up trepang and sandalwood' (in Bagshaw & Glaskin 2000, p. 28). The nearby town of Broome owes its distinctive multicultural history to these involvements in the pearling industry, and many families in Broome, both Indigenous and non-Indigenous, bear surnames that can be identified as Japanese, Chinese, Malay or Filipino.[22]

In the Kimberley, many Aboriginal men and women were nominally 'employed' as pearl divers in these early days; as early observer Bishop Gibney (1886) reported, 'the diving is performed almost exclusively by natives under the direction of white men'.[23] This 'direction' often amounted to kidnapping and enslavement, a practice that became known as 'blackbirding'.[24] Bardi have spoken about how local Aboriginal divers were incarcerated on the Lacepede Islands, which are situated about 30 kilometres off the western coast of the Dampier Peninsula and to the south of the country with which Bardi are associated. The distance between the islands and the mainland meant it was too far to swim back. Many divers died prematurely as a consequence of the risks associated with pearl diving, including drowning, shark attacks and the bends.

Some of the violent encounters between members of pearling crews and Aboriginal people are recorded, while others are preserved in oral narrative and the memories of local people. Bardi man Tudor Ejai's narratives 'Punitive expedition against the Bardi' and 'The killing of the "Bilikin" brothers' (in Hercus & Sutton 1986, pp. 141–49, 151–64) are likely to be related to the killing of the pearlers Rickinson and Shenton in 1885. Reports suggest Bardi murdered these men in retaliation for being forced to dive for pearls (Skyring 2001, p. 10). On the basis of his fieldwork with people at Sunday Island mission in the late 1940s, Gibson wrote:

The Djaui apparently were a very hostile group and despatched some whites as a reprisal for violation of their territory and the exploitation of their lubras. Paddy has vivid memories of the occasions when the white punitive expedition shot many of his tribe in cold blood (1951, pp. 39–40).

As well as detailing early hostilities between local Aboriginal people and pearlers, Tudor Ejai's accounts provide us with a sense of how strange some of these early experiences were for local people. One Bardi man who had spent time in prison in Fremantle (2000 kilometres south) indicated how numerous whites appeared, describing them as 'just like leaves down there', while donkeys, an animal with which people were unfamiliar, were described as large 'dogs' (in Hercus & Sutton 1986, p. 148). Nilili, who was born in 1919, relayed this story concerning her father's experience of encountering Europeans for the first time:

> Whitefellas came to Chile Creek one time when they had run out of water…[My father] was there…They called out *ngaarr* when they saw the whiteman…[My father] and the others gave the whitefellas water – they were communicating using signs. When the whiteman came they thought he had two heads because they could see his head and his hat. They touched him to make sure he was real, they felt his clothes, they really examined him. He brought them shirts and clothes because they were naked. They slept that night in the clothes they had put on and those people sleeping in the clothes got nightmares. They jumped up in the night and were going to spear that whiteman but he had gone. The reason they were going to spear him is because when you get nightmare, *ananiny,* it's always spirits (personal communication 4 March 1997).

This kind of exchange (clothes for water) has an analogy in Dampier's (1937 [1697], p. 315) description of how he and other men from the *Cygnet's* crew gave local men some old clothes in an unsuccessful effort to get them to carry water for them, and in which he noted the men did not seem to have 'any great liking' for the clothes.

Settlement

By 1886, the Western Australian government had decided that there was a need for special legislation governing relations between Europeans and Aboriginal Australians, and introduced the *Aboriginal Protection Act 1886* (WA). This was closely followed by the *Aborigines Act 1889* (WA), which, building on this protectionism, allowed for Crown land to be reserved 'for the use and benefit of Aboriginal inhabitants'. This was the provision under which the north-eastern portion of the Dampier Peninsula was set aside as Aboriginal reserve. In 1904 the Roth Royal Commission into the condition of Aboriginal people in Western Australia was prompted by serious allegations concerning their treatment in the pastoral industry, leading to the proclamation of the *Aborigines Act 1905* (WA) in April 1906 (Haebich 1998 [1988], p. 70). The 1905 Act, as Haebich (1998 [1988], p. 83) describes,

> Laid the basis for the development of repressive and coercive state control over the state's Aboriginal population...It set up the necessary bureaucratic and legal mechanisms to control all their contacts with the wider community, to enforce the assimilation of their children and to determine the most personal aspects of their lives.

Among the many provisions of the 1905 Act was an increase in the powers of 'honorary protectors' to intervene in and substantially regulate Aboriginal lives at the local level without any corresponding system of regulation for the manner in which these duties were performed (Haebich 1998 [1988], pp. 85, 87).

In 1883, Broome and Derby were declared townships, and from then onwards pastoral leases were issued in the northern

Dampier Peninsula. Most of the pastoral leases taken up in the peninsula were prospective. While some cattle and sheep were run to fulfil the conditions of the leases, and as 'killer herds' for a steady supply of meat, pearlers often used the leases as a means to secure shore bases for their pearling activity. Pearlers Henry 'Harry' Hunter, Sydney Montague Hadley, 'Frenchy' D'Antoine, Harry and Jack O'Grady and Thomas Puertollano all obtained such leases.

The impact of Englishmen Harry Hunter and his one-time business partner Sydney Hadley in the region was especially profound. The two men moved from Cossack to Lombadina in 1880, and gained a lease over the present-day Lombadina mission site in 1884. When they sold their lease to Bishop Gibney in 1892, Hunter re-established his pearling base at Bulgin (known as Hunter's Creek, east of Cape Leveque), where he engaged in trading pearl shell, trochus, tortoise shell and trepang with passing pearlers. A Derby-based police patrol consisting of Troopers Farrell and Armitage to the Dampier Peninsula in 1887 provides early and conflicting impressions about Hunter. In his journal dated 9 February 1887, Farrell reported that:

This afternoon a native named Toby from Father McNabs [sic] Mission Informed me that there was 5 natives who had run away from a man named Hunter with the intention of going to Derby when they were followed by Hunter and another called Fred. With 4 Horses they were caught back to Hunters place and there placed under restraint by being placed in a roome [sic]...Feb 12th 1887:...we then travelled untill [sic] we reached the homestead at Cape Leveque at 9pm. During the afternoon we saw some of the natives that was supposed to have been maide [sic] fast by Hunter and Fred but they denied any knowledge of it – saying that – Hunter was a very good master: all the natives hear [sic] look well and seem as if they are well cared for and were quite contented. We maide [sic] all the Inquiries as regards the natives without the knowledge of Hunter so that the natives could not have been Intimidated. Hunter Reported to us that the natives about Swan Point had been very troublesome amongst his sheep he having lost 200 since he came to settle here but as we could not get any direct evidence against any of them we did not deem it advisable to go after them (Farrell 1887).

Hunter's public reputation oscillated between negative and positive appraisals of his treatment of Aboriginal people. Robinson (1973, p. 153) reports that in 1908 'the Travelling Inspector of Aborigines...claimed that he [Hunter] performed a service for the Department [of Native Welfare] by keeping the Bardi away from "the coloured crews and grog"', and it was after this that Hunter was made a local Protector of Aborigines, responsible for the distribution of clothing and rations to Bardi in the area.[25] Robinson (1973, p. 154) says:

> The Bardi did not share the administration's high opinion of Hunter's treatment of them. To them, Hunter was a ruthless and materialistic employer who caused them considerable personal hardship and contributed towards the deterioration of traditional life. One of their most important grievances was Hunter's sexual relations with both Bardi and Djawi women, at least eleven of whom bore him children.

Hunter was given the Bardi nickname Malarrid, literally meaning 'many wives'. Hunter's children were usually 'grown up' by their mothers and their mother's Aboriginal husbands: in this context, where rights in country are primarily gained through patrifiliation, Hunter's children's rights in country tended to be reckoned on the basis of paternal adoption, called *andala* (Bagshaw 1999, p. 58). Bardi who congregated around Bulgin and who worked for Hunter were mainly people from the part of the peninsula that Bardi refer to as Gularrgon (west). The genealogies compiled for the Sampi claim show many of Hunter's wives were from the estate Mardudburu where Hunter set up his camp, or were the wives of men who were from that estate. Other Bardi were drawn to the camp to take advantage of rations, the possibilities of the nominal kind of employment Hunter offered and to visit kin. Like other pearlers in those days, it appears that Hunter exercised a proprietorial interest over Aboriginal people he considered to be 'his natives'. Father Nicholas Emo, a local Protector of Aborigines at Cygnet Bay, witnessed Hunter warning other pearlers 'not to take his natives away; they then produced a permit, and said they would take *as many natives as they liked*' (Emo 1907). In 1910, Hunter was convicted on the charge of cohabiting with Aboriginal women, and lost his authority in the area as a local Protector and his licence to employ Aboriginal people (Robinson 1973, p. 146). In the same year, a 'feeding depot' was established at Lombadina, with the idea that it could be run as an outstation of Beagle Bay mission, to its south. When Hunter went to prison, Bardi who lived at Bulgin were removed to Lombadina, but they returned to Bulgin of their own initiative. Hunter later returned to Bulgin, where he remained until his death by drowning in 1919. Robinson (1973, pp. 154–55) and Glaskin (2002, pp. 114–17) discuss the social consequences of Hunter having children with women from different generational moieties. It meant he had children who should have been of the same generational level but were not, and this had implications for observance of prescribed kinship behaviour and marriage. This has required ongoing adjustment amongst Bardi and Jawi people over a number of generations.

Some of Hunter's sons, Jack, Robin and Christy Hunter, along with 'Frenchy' D'Antoine's sons Tommy and Ginger, maintained a camp at Bulgin for a long time after Hunter's death in 1919. Christy Hunter left Bulgin (also called 'Hunter's station') in approximately 1925, but others remained at the camp until at least 1928, when the anthropologist Elkin conducted fieldwork in the area (Nilili, personal communication, November 1994; Robinson 1973, p. 175). Jack Hunter, Robin Hunter and Tommy D'Antoine gained exemption certificates under the 1905 Act, although Tommy's certificate was later revoked.[26] These certificates 'exempted' those who had received them from being subject to the restrictive laws that were being applied to other Aboriginal people under the Act. Being classed as non-Aboriginal from the state's perspective, though, did not necessarily reflect the views of other local Aboriginal people nor the views of departmental staff who actually dealt with such individuals.[27]

Like other early settler camps, Hunter's settlement at Bulgin played a distinctive role in the economy of the region, and in the web of social relations between Aboriginal and non-Aboriginal people. The settlement pre-existed the establishment of Lombadina mission by over twenty years. Families moved between Hunter's camp at Bulgin (in the Hunter's Creek area), O'Grady's camp at Mardnan (in the Skeleton Point area) and the lighthouse at Cape Leveque, depending on the availability of work. As one woman observed, her father would work, sometimes for Hunter and sometimes for O'Grady, in order to obtain food 'and things', exchanging labour for goods (Gardingunjun, personal communication, November 1994). At Tyra Island (Munburran), the D'Antoine camp remained until the 1930s (Robinson 1973, p. 175).

In 1890, a Catholic mission was begun at Beagle Bay at the site of one of the pearlers' lay-up bases. Set up by French Trappist monks, the German Pallottine order assumed control in 1896 when the Trappists left (Choo 2001, p. 55). Daisy Bates visited Beagle Bay mission in 1899 and observed that 'every laying up season, when the pearling boats were off shore, practically every boy who had a woman took her down to trade with the Asiatics. The women returned dying and diseased, after the boats resumed pearling' (Bates 1966 [1938], p. 12). From 1903 until at least the beginning of World War I, a police constable was stationed at Beagle Bay during the lay-up season, with the express purpose of overseeing relations between pearlers and local Aboriginal people (Durack 1997 [1969], p. 235). In 1906 one of the Trappists, Father

Figure 6: D'Antoine's camp at Tyra Island. Photo: William J. Jackson (1917). Courtesy of the State Library of Western Australia.

Nicholas Emo, founded a mission at Cygnet Bay. The bay offers shelter from big swells in rough weather, and was favoured by pearlers as a location to lay-up their luggers. That same year, Abbot Torres noted that there were up to a hundred pearling luggers and 600 crewmen at Cygnet Bay, and that in the eastern King Sound region Aboriginal people had 'sad and bitter memories of outrages committed by Filipinos and Malays' (in Bottrill, n.d., p. 2). The fledgling mission at Cygnet Bay closed in 1908.

One of the rationales for establishing missions in the area was to 'protect' local Aboriginal people from pearlers. Sunday Island and Lombadina were established at a time when governmental responsibilities towards Aboriginal people were largely delegated to the missions, beginning with distributing rations, followed by aspects of health care, welfare and education. In this sense, the missions acted as agents of the state, although they were often agents over which the government was unable to exercise full control. Lurie's (1988, p. 432) term 'denominational colonialism' is apposite to the overall context in which the missions operated in northern Dampierland, but has additional resonance given the distinctions that emerged between what became known as the 'UAM mob' (those associated with Sunday Island mission) and the 'Catholic mob' (those associated with the Pallottine mission at Lombadina). While the experiences of those who lived at Sunday Island and Lombadina missions are closely intertwined, the historical, institutional and theological differences between the two missions differentiated them from each other in particular ways. People associated with both missions maintained they were 'all one mob'. Yet mission experiences created some distinctions between people who otherwise considered themselves close kin. This mission history would, over a hundred years later, have an influence on the initial outcome of the Sampi native title case.

Chapter Three

Mission Days

We didn't know what was happening really. Only missionaries know it. We had no money, we had to work for bread and tea. We just get the ration, we just the ration people...Walking from Beagle Bay to Lombadina, walked. No money, I just been running, I walk for my bread and tea. It was not for the money (Joe Rock, 30 June 1998 in Barker 1998).

In *To The Islands*, Australian novelist Randolph Stow writes about an old missionary who has lived on a remote Kimberley mission for many years, working with its Aboriginal inhabitants, and the crisis of faith that leads him to try to reach the islands. In his preface to the revised edition of the book, Stow (1982 [1958], p. ix) says that his inspiration for the novel is drawn from his experiences of working at a Kimberley mission for 'a short time' in the 1950s. There are striking similarities between the situation Stow describes of this remote mission in the East Kimberley region, and Sunday Island mission, situated on the Jawi island called Iwanyi. Both missions closed down in the 1960s, and it was after this that former mission residents were relocated to towns, with the subsequent emergence of problems relating to social dislocation and access to alcohol (Stow 1982 [1958], p. x).

The Jawi island of Iwanyi, Sunday Island, is often simply referred to by both Bardi and Jawi people in English as 'the Island'. The use of definite article is significant, for there are many islands off the northern tip of the Dampier Peninsula and in the King Sound region: but locally, everyone understands 'the Island' as Sunday Island. Iwanyi occupies a distinct place in local cosmology. It is mythologically connected to the much smaller island Julum (Middle Island), just off the coast of One Arm Point; Galalung, an important ancestral being, left his footprint sedimented into the rock there. Afterwards, he travelled across to Iwanyi (Sunday Island), from which he ultimately ascended into the sky. So, while you cannot see Sunday Island from One Arm Point, you can see Julum, and, for those who know Galalung's story, Julum is a mnemonic that reminds those who stand at the point and look across the currents there of its connection to Iwanyi, Sunday Island, about 10 kilometres distant.

Beyond these much longer-term associations, Sunday Island is also of considerable importance in the recent history of Bardi and Jawi because of the mission established there. Following his religious conversion, Hunter's ex-business partner Hadley, who had been pearling in the region since the 1880s, sought permission from the Aborigines Protection Board to found Sunday Island mission as a non-denominational Protestant mission. Sunday Island mission was founded in 1899, at a place on the island Jawi call Ilon. Those people who were at Sunday Island mission say they lived in family groupings in huts in the valley while mission staff lived on the hill. Not all the Aboriginal people on Sunday Island lived at the mission site, though. When Elkin visited Sunday Island in 1928, Gargi and his two wives, Ninya and Lamburrgu, were living at Guwarngun in his own estate, Nilagunbur. Rituals were 'normally' held in this area (Gibson 1951, p. 21).

Sunday Island Mission in the Hadley Era (1899–1923)

People from throughout the King Sound region were drawn to Sunday Island mission. They included Bardi from the northern and eastern regions of the Dampier Peninsula, especially; Jawi from Sunday Island and other Jawi islands; and some people from the eastern side of the King Sound region, who are collectively referred to as Mayalayun (people from the Mayala region) by those on the western side of the King Sound. Some Mayalayun who came to Sunday Island were Jawi. Others were Uggarangu (also pronounced Uggarang, and Ungarang), Umide or Uwini; a few were Arbidej or Yawjibaya.[28] According to Khaki Stumpagee, the seasonal departures of pearling crews on the eastern side of the King Sound influenced Mayalayun (eastern King Sound people) to come to Sunday Island mission in search of 'stores' or to visit family at the mission:

> Well they come here [to Sunday Island], all this mob here, not long way, this mob been come in here for ration, from whiteman, white bloke. Missionary been here and they know it, everybody know it from Dugong Bay side, all that. That's why I got mother, Jawi man, Jawi my own father been get Uggarang, ah, Umide woman, my mother…they know half of their family was here, that's why they coming, only for their family…Like my mummy been come here and then, and she been settle down. Then, all her relatives coming, to look by my mother (personal communication 15 November 1994).

The widespread presence of pearlers in the region is likely to have affected local hunting of game such as dugong and turtle, which require stealthy approaches to catch. So while people may have come to the missions in search of goods such as flour, tea and tobacco, which they had acquired tastes for through trading with pearlers, they may equally have come because they were hungry. In 1904, Wace, the Resident Magistrate of Derby, reported that Aboriginal people stayed at the mission because of the secure food supply the mission offered, although rations were only available to those who worked (Marks 1960, p. 75). A Jawi man from Unggaliyun (Long Island) explained to me why Bardi 'came in' to Sunday Island. His perspective was that the missionaries were there trying to get Jawi to work for them, 'but Jawi was lazy people, Jawi wouldn't work' – they would rather go fishing, he said – so, he argued, the missionaries brought Bardi over from the mainland to work for them instead (Wotjuluwarr, personal communication, 5 July 1997).

During Hadley's time at Sunday Island, 1899–1923, the main financial support of the mission came through the collection and sale of trochus shell, bêche-de-mer, tortoise shell and pearl shell, all of which was collected by local mission residents under Hadley's direction.[29] Hadley experimented with growing tobacco, bananas and rubber, but this was unsuccessful (Bain 1982, p. 191). The mission received a government subsidy in 1911, but even then Hadley still met most of the mission's expenses (Marks 1960, p. 75). Bain (1982, p. 191) suggests the mission's relative autonomy worked well for Hadley, whose activities were not particularly scrutinised by the Aborigines Department. She points out that in 1904 Hadley travelled extensively overseas; he also visited America and Japan in 1913, indicating the mission was not as financially precarious as Hadley portrayed it to be (Bain 1982, p. 191).

Wiringar was eight or nine years old when he went to Sunday Island in about 1919. For him, 'coming in' to the mission was in the latter years of Hadley's time there. He recalled coming to the mission this way:

> I went with the owner of Sunday Island Syd Hadley. He came there, put up Presbyterian mission, came over from England. Picked me up, me and my stepfather was round there, on the coast, picked me up for schooling in Sunday Island. Mostly all the Jau [Jawi] and Bardi was around there...When he first came, Syd Hadley, he was a young boy. He went through the

Law. I don't know who put him through that Law, might be old Jau man (personal communication 21 September 1998).

Hadley's conversion to Christianity and his development of the mission at Sunday Island were not without controversy. From the earliest days of the mission, Hadley was subject to much outside criticism, based on mistrust of his commitment to evangelism, his motives for setting up the mission and claims of misconduct. One aspect of this alleged misconduct was the 1901 claim by a mission employee that Hadley had taken two girls as wives; the claim that Hadley was having relations with two women was corroborated by Hadley's Japanese cook on the island (Omerod 1901; Shigaro 1901). In the early 1970s, Robinson (1973, pp. 161–62) writes that Sunday Islanders told him that, while Hadley had relationships with Aboriginal women before establishing the mission, he did not have 'wives' at Sunday Island. Wiringar, who remembered Hadley, told me categorically that he 'didn't have any wife' (personal communication 21 September 1998).

In 1901 the Resident Magistrate of Derby described the attitudes of Sunday Island mission residents towards Hadley in the context of these allegations. In his letter to the Chief Protector of Aborigines he discussed 'the business of getting rid of him' (Hadley), and stated 'we must bear in mind that the natives almost worship him and he might take it into his head to make trouble or again he might go quietly' (Harwood-Brown 1901). Hadley's response to the Department's attempts to remove him from the island was similarly instructive. Hadley wrote that 'the natives are with me in saying that if I am to be dismissed and turned out that they one and all [will] go with me and we will settle down elsewhere' (Hadley 1901b). In 1903, Constable Napier reported having 'questioned a number of Natives on the Island and also others on the Mainland who had been on the Island and they all spoke very highly of Mr Hadley and seemed to have every confidence in him' (Napier 1903). Much later, Bain interviewed Bardi man Locki Bin Sali who reflected on Hadley this way:

> When I was young I was there. He [Hadley] was a good man that fellow, knew all the black fellow law. I grew up and went dry shelling in shallow water up to Long Island, Bedford Island, Tide Rip Island and Blue [sic: Brue] Reef – hundreds of them. What did he get out of it? I reckon that fellow a millionaire when he left us. But he a good fellow that Hadley (Locki Bin Sali, cited in Bain 1982, p. 34).

In these accounts of Hadley, two features emerge: the extent to which people at Sunday Island mission recall working for Hadley in the shelling industry, and their generally positive appraisal of him, despite speculation about how much money he may have made from their labour. Hadley's general lack of interference in Aboriginal culture and his own apparent willingness to participate in some ceremonial activity is likely to account for the general positive view Bardi and Jawi had of him in those days. Among those views are reports Hadley went through initiation.[30] In the 1990s, stories of Hadley going through Law continued to circulate. Austin-Broos (2009, p. 12) has argued in a different context, amongst Western Arrernte, that such reports might be understood as evidence of the way the past is re-imagined in order to make sense of the present. What is evident is that Hadley made little attempt to seriously proselytise or implement deliberate policies of change at Sunday Island: his primary goal was protection. His attitude toward indigenous culture was sympathetic and non-interventionist. Marks (1960, p. 75) argues that 'Hadley was not, like most missionaries, offering the native material benefits linked with an informal obligation to change his pattern of living. Rather, he was offering the native material benefits while continuing in his traditional life'. While children growing up at Sunday Island mission received some education, Marks (1960, p. 77) says that 'generally little attempt was made to provide adult education or to teach trades other than the management of boats used for getting shell', a focus reflecting the economy that underpinned the mission's existence. Hadley's efforts were often at odds with Department of Native Welfare objectives and those of other missionaries, including his own staff.

Hadley's twenty-four-year administration of the mission at Sunday Island did not bring about overwhelming changes for Aboriginal mission residents. There was a gradual incorporation into a different economy, in which people worked for Hadley, exchanging their labour for rations and other goods. Imperatives for change, while present, were not dramatic. This contrasted with the Pallottine mission at Lombadina, founded eleven years after Sunday Island mission.

Lombadina and 'Correct Mission Method'[31]

German Pallottine missionaries founded Lombadina as an outstation of Beagle Bay mission in 1910, locating it on the western side of the Dampier Peninsula near the place locally known as Lumedinar. Nilili estimated that she would have been approximately 6 or 7 years old when she came to the mission, in around 1925 or 1926. She described how children slept in dormitories in the mission compound, while their parents and other family members lived in paperbark huts on the hill above the mission. Visiting the mission in 1928, Porteus (1931, p. 57) described how Aboriginal people there had 'pitched their camps, not together as in a village, but each camp surmounting its own little hillock.'

Nilili recalled how it was that she 'came in' to the mission at Lombadina. She talked about how her brother had left one of the 'stations' (pearling camps) in 1925 to come to the mission, and of how her father's brother 'worked with Cape Leveque people' (at the lighthouse):

And he'd get something and we'd take some fish or whatever papa would get. And he'd give us a little bit of his food, what he used to get, rations, and then ah, we found it hard you know to stay like that, and probably they talked – mama and

papa – between themselves that best to come here, Lombadina…
because their families like you know, sisters and cousins were
here, brothers, and we did come in, and I stayed at the camp
there for a while, getting used to the place…there was a Sister
here…she used to coax me into the kitchen and refectory with
milk and rice, so that I could go into the dormitory. Slowly I
went in. I couldn't really, you know, settle for a while, either,
mum had to come in, oh well a week, if not few days, and
stay with me until I got used to it…So I settled in, and mum
went back to the camp [on the hill above the mission] (personal
communication 9 November 1994).

Nilili's account of 'coming in' to the mission at Lombadina
resonates with the Sunday Island experience. People came into
the mission in search of a reliable food supply, and the presence
of relatives was often a determining factor. In speaking with
older Bardi and Jawi men and women about their respective
experiences of the missions at Sunday Island and Lombadina,
though, differences between the two also emerge. At Sunday
Island, children were not separated from their relatives, whereas
at Lombadina they were put together in a dormitory, as Nilili's
account demonstrates. One of the Lombadina women contrasted
growing up in the dormitory at Lombadina with the Sunday
Island experience:

When we were little kids we were brought into the dormitory.
Some of us did have the sense to question our parents, some
parents died early so kids couldn't learn much. One Arm
Point people were free to live with their parents, but we had
little time to live with our parents (Garndingunjun, personal
communication, November 1994).[32]

The dormitory system used by Catholic missionaries of
the Pallottine Order at Lombadina was a central facet of their
approach to the missionary endeavour. Father Georg Walter, who

was at Beagle Bay mission between 1901 and 1908, provides an exposé of this, which he referred to as 'correct mission method'. Walter advised that:

> For Aborigines, correct mission method is to let them get used to a settled life-style and regular work without using force or restricting their freedom...As soon as possible, children can be removed from the adult camp and the nomadic ways of their parents, and be housed in dormitories on mission premises to be educated in schools and trades...The earlier the children came to the Mission and the less they know of bush life, the more receptive they were for a Christian education. After they have spent several years in the bush, and been indoctrinated in tribal law and lore, they are almost unfit for schooling (Walter 1982 [1928], p. 124).[33]

Similarly, Alroe (1988, p. 34) says the key to 'the method' – which was predicated on the 'success' of New Norcia mission to the south – was 'control of the children'. Gaining such control was only possible if 'the missionary had the power to co-erce [sic] or materially reward his converts', that is, if the intended converts could see they would gain some 'tangible benefit' from the missionary (Alroe 1988, p. 35). Access to food supplies provided the inducement for settlement, which was seen as a necessary pre-condition for conversion; where traditional food sources were depleted, as was the case in the Broome-Derby area, this strategy was more effective than in others where the imperative was not as great. A widely used missionary strategy throughout the Kimberley was the use of tobacco to foster acceptance of, and dependency on, particular missionary regimes (Alroe 1988, p. 36).

The Pallottines, like the Trappists before them and the Lay Missionaries and St John of God nuns who joined them, rejected materialism and were 'celibate, poor and obedient' (Alroe 1988, p. 32). Alroe describes the fundamentals of 'the method' they used as 'establishment of control through dependency,

Figure 7: The church at Lombadina. Photo: Katie Glaskin (2011).

intervention in transmission of culture from parents to children, church monopoly of education' (1988, p. 37). The daily routine at Lombadina, as at Beagle Bay, was strictly regulated by Catholic religious observances, work and, for the children, school. The 5.30 am bell summoned mission residents to mass, meditation and communion. Masses were conducted in Latin at first, and were later conducted in English. Christian songs sung in the local dialect (Bard) later came to form part of the service. Breakfast at the dining hall followed and then the 'working bell' called adults to work. For the children, school began every day with religious instruction, followed by reading, writing, arithmetic, drawing and singing (Raible 1938, p. 275). At 11 am a lunch break was followed by a period of rest until 2 pm when work resumed until the sounding of the church bell at 5.30 pm. Dinner followed the afternoon service. Some of the older people who experienced these mission days understood the strict religious basis of the

Pallottine mission at Lombadina to have been augmented by German cultural traits, which in their view emphasised discipline. This view is represented in Jimmy Chi's popular musical, *Bran Nue Dae*, where he depicts these traits in the character Benedictus, a German priest (see Chi and Kuckles 1991). When World War I broke out, a number of the German priests from Lombadina and Beagle Bay were interned as a consequence of national-level concerns about Germans living on an unprotected coastline (Father Kreiner, personal communication 15 December 1994).

Janganbirr's impressions of 'correct mission method' highlight the active interference of the missionaries at Lombadina with Bardi cultural practice – both in terms of segregating children and their parents, restricting contact between them – and by prohibition on ceremonies:

> We were kept in dormitory. Our parents were up on sand dunes, living up on the sand dunes. And if ever we wanted to go and talk, see our parents, we'd have to get permission from the priest, and the priest would give us certain times, give us an hour or so, when you hear them ring the bells you have to be down, you have to be back in dormitories. Because it was very hard, you know, we had to go according by the rules, and of course we were all brought up by Germans, and the rules were very tough...we weren't allowed to even talk about ceremonies in those days because Christianity was so strong in those days, especially Catholics. You know, we weren't allowed to even sing or dance in those days. We'd be allowed to see corroborees coming from Beagle Bay or often, certain, Sunday Island, but that was all. We weren't allowed to practise our own ceremony, initiation ceremonies, anything like that (interview with Geoffrey Bagshaw 14 December 1994, my transcription).

The dormitory, the imposed rules and Catholic interference with transmission of cultural knowledge are the features of mission life at Lombadina that people who grew up at the mission most often cite when describing their time there. These were the dominating and central facets of the Pallottines' 'correct missionary method'. This contrasts with Sunday Island mission residents' experiences during the Hadley era in the early days of that mission. When Hadley retired in 1923 and Sunday Island was taken over by the United Aborigines Mission, though, the new missionaries' evangelical commitment produced a stronger impetus for local people to change.[34]

UAM at Sunday Island (1923–62)

As a fundamentalist non-denominational organisation, the United Aborigines Mission (UAM) missionaries actively sought to transform mission residents into Christians, and this included discouraging them from engaging in traditional practices. The emphasis on evangelism was, as Marks (1960, p. 84) argues, at the expense of 'practical training', since 'Christianity did not necessarily demand a knowledge of Western techniques of production'. Nor was the mission accepting of Aboriginal culture, as Hadley had largely been. Wilf Douglas, a missionary linguist who was at the island between the years 1947–49, credits a request from Jimmy Ejai to translate the Bible into Bardi with his own decision to leave the island in order to study linguistics, literacy methods and translation procedures. He produced a Bardi word-book for the One Arm Point community in 1992, and in it he says that, following his departure, 'the authority administering the Sunday Island mission at the time forbade my return after training on the ground that by learning "this heathen language" I would be "taking the people back to heathenism"' (Douglas 1992, p. 28).

The UAM regime continued the shelling and bêche-de-mer operations begun by Hadley, but financial and other problems such as rapid staff turnover significantly impacted the mission (Robinson 1973, p. 167). Throughout the UAM era (1924–65) the mission was plagued with financial difficulties, and these problems underlay the 1934–35 relocation of the mission to a mainland site, Wotjulum on the Yampi Peninsula, where it was thought that agricultural prospects might provide a better economic base for the mission. The move was unsuccessful, as many Bardi and Jawi preferred to remain at Sunday Island or go to Lombadina. Of those who went to Wotjulum, all had returned to Sunday Island by their own means by 1937, and were subsequently followed back by UAM staff themselves (Robinson 1973, p. 168). Jinju described the move back from Wotjulum to Sunday Island to me this way:

> They [the mission residents who had been shifted to Wotjulum] didn't like it out there, they moved back to Sunday Island, and the missionaries look like, eh, everybody gone away, they said, they couldn't boss them around or anything like that. When those blokes used to move, they used to move, if they didn't like the place. When missionary looked that, ah well, they not gonna stay here, we may as well follow them, follow them to Sunday Island see. They [missionaries] had lugger. But they [the mission residents] had their own raft, and *barrawarr* [canoe] and all, all them people (personal communication 30 September 1997).

Marks (1960, pp. 90, 92, 93) says that Sunday Island 'made commendable progress for the first six years of UAM operation', but this initial 'progress' was 'doomed' by the shift to Wotjulum, since the administration lost the confidence of 'the islanders' during this time. He writes that 'most native customs were still in use at the end of his [Hadley's] period. But under the new UAM regime many of these were replaced in five years' (Marks 1960, p. 83). The 'customs' he refers to were overt cultural practices that conflicted with missionary values. Despite this, the missionary perception of when these practices ceased was frequently earlier than their actual cessation.[35] The discrepancy between missionary accounts and what was occurring on the island perhaps reflected missionary optimism about their own progress, but may also indicate that mission residents had begun to hide certain activities from the missionaries. For example, based on his fieldwork in 1968–69, Robinson (1973, p. 220) wrote that certain rites associated with the Ululung ritual were still practised, but that Bardi exercised caution to ensure that the missionaries were not present and did not learn that they were still performed.

Other more prosaic activities were also hidden. Bateman (1948, p. 7) reported that 'another cause of complaint [by Aboriginal people at Sunday Island] is the fact that no tobacco is allowed on the island by the superintendent which means that the natives are debarred from tobacco except when they pay occasional visits to Derby on the barge or lugger'. Baaji told me that, when the mission lugger went to Derby for supplies, whoever was manning the lugger would pick up tobacco for others at the island. As he described it, the old people were particularly adept at secreting these tobacco supplies, burying them and hiding them under rocks, and more often than not appeared not to have tobacco when other people asked for it. Although people had such clandestine supplies, nobody smoked in front of the missionaries (personal communication 27 September 1997).

World War II brought significant changes to the West Kimberley region. German priests from Lombadina and Beagle Bay were again interned, while Cape Leveque and the Champagney Islands became bases for the Army and the Royal Australian Air Force. When Lombadina and Sunday Island missions were closed, army personnel from the regional bases distributed rations to local Bardi and Jawi people (Robinson 1973, pp. 170–71). Locki Bin Sali was amongst a number of Bardi men who operated boats for the Royal Australian Airforce through this period. Aboriginal residents of Broome were evacuated to Beagle Bay, representing a huge influx of people into the region who required assistance. The bombing of Broome and Drysdale River Mission in 1942 exacerbated fears of a Japanese invasion and led the Army to burn all boats along the coast, an event that left an indelible impression on the generations of Bardi and Jawi alive in that time. In the 1990s, the names of boats and luggers belonging to the missions and to others in the area – Hunter and his descendants, O'Grady and others – were well remembered; some Bardi men had been actively engaged in their construction. The travelling inspector McKnight reported in 1942 that many of the previous occupants of Sunday Island were living in camps, especially in the Bulgin area. In these camps he found 'the occupants very wary and rather sullen. I attribute this to the fact that they cannot understand why the military authorities found it necessary to blow up so many luggers' (McKnight cited in Gibson 1951, p. 76). It was not until after World War II that 'the bulk of the Bardi and Djawi population became associated with Lombadina or the Island' (Robinson 1973, p. 175).

Throughout this period Lombadina's financial difficulties remained. From its inception in 1910 up until at least the 1960s a significant portion of its funding came either from Germany, from the Pallottine order itself, or from donations (Father Kreiner, personal communication 15 December 1994). Prior to the 1960s, the government subsidy amounted to a penny a day per Aboriginal person (ibid.). In addition to the subsidy and overseas donations, the mission used various means to augment its income: during the Commonwealth Games in 1960, Lombadina sent over 200 boomerangs to Perth for sale there, receiving 15 shillings for each boomerang. In 1963 the mission cut dead trees and transported the firewood to Broome where it was sold for about $5 a bag as fuel for wood stoves. The mission grew tobacco and raised cattle, but neither proved to be economically viable. Father Kreiner, who was at the mission in the years 1960–68 (and again in 1991–92), told me that, when Lombadina's financial situation was grave, Lombadina would go to Beagle Bay mission for assistance. He explained:

We had no money then, we couldn't give the Aboriginal people any money. Slowly came the child endowment and pension. When they first got the pension we managed it for them, got them blankets and food, until they learnt to manage money. They also gave the mission some money because the mission was looking after them (Father Kreiner, personal communication 15 December 1994).

Sunday Island mission also struggled financially. Their difficulties were compounded by the collapse of the trochus shell market in 1960 and the closure of their airstrip in 1961 (Robinson 1973, p. 187). Native Welfare staff in Derby, critical of the mission, mounted efforts to have it closed (Robinson 1973, p. 188). In addition, UAM missionaries felt that 'attempts to Christianise the Bardi had failed', and in 1962 UAM withdrew its staff from the mission (Robinson 1973, pp. 187, 188). Most people who had been formerly associated with Sunday Island mission were subsequently relocated to Derby.

Many Bardi refused to leave the island. They told Department of Native Welfare staff that, should food shortage or illness require it, they would shift to Cygnet Bay where Dean Brown's new cultured pearl farm was situated; a Department of Native Welfare officer reported that 'questioning revealed that they held Brown in some esteem' (in Robinson 1973, p. 188). When Department of Native Welfare staff removed school-aged children and housed them at the Amy Bethel hostel in Derby, many Bardi families followed their children to Derby and were settled on the town reserve at the edge of the marsh. Others went to Dean Brown at Cygnet Bay (Robinson 1973, p. 189). Some older people refused to leave the island until May 1964 when all delivery of food supplies to the island ceased and they were taken to Lombadina. Robinson (1973, p. 192) observed that by 1968 most people who had been living at Sunday Island were living in Derby.

The people who shifted to Derby were not happy with their new surrounds, and from their arrival onwards agitated to return to Sunday Island (see Robinson 1973, pp. 191–92). Derby is situated at the mouth of the King Sound on a small peninsula surrounded by tidally inundated mudflats, and the outlook from the Derby jetty is of an earth-coloured sea. Compared to the aqua-blue waters surrounding the northern Dampier Peninsula and islands in the King Sound, Derby was both foreign and vastly different country. I heard older people refer to Derby, drawing on their experiences there, as 'rubbish country', a 'horrible place' and 'too hot', since temperatures there are consistently higher than by the coast. At the time when Bardi and Jawi had shifted to Derby, people from sixteen 'tribal or linguistic groups' representing most major groups in the Kimberley were living there, but Bardi involvement with other Aboriginal people in Derby was kept to a minimum (Robinson 1973, p. 200). Bardi refusal to mix with other reserve people was viewed by Department of Native Welfare staff 'as evidence of Bardi resistance to change and "assimilation"' (Robinson 1973, p. 208).

Award wages in the pastoral industry came into force in the Kimberley in 1970 and drastically affected Aboriginal people who worked on cattle stations (Coombs et al. 1989, p. 25). Station owners were unwilling or unable to pay award wages, and Aboriginal refugees from the stations came in to townships such as Derby where they lived in fringe camps and later on reserves created to deal with the influx. While the award wages did not affect ex-Sunday Island residents in this manner, financial autonomy in the form of social security payments (in the Kimberley often referred to as 'social') followed award wages, and were a contributing factor in their return to country.

Bardi and Jawi men and women who were at Sunday Island have identified the time in Derby as detrimental to the community as a whole. For senior people, in particular, their sense of the damage occurring amongst their people increased the impetus to return to their own country. It was in Derby that alcohol first became a real issue for people who, by virtue of their isolation at the mission, had previously had very limited or no access to it. In the first instance, men were more affected by drinking than women. As one woman described it to me, it was once they shifted to Derby the 'trouble' began; as she put it, 'our sons were drinking, our husbands were drinking' (Daan, personal communication 22 November 1998). The troubled times of Derby are in stark contrast to the remembered trouble-free times at Sunday Island. Most people who were at Sunday Island would recall it with a great deal of affection, a time in which the community had greater cohesion and pressures from the outside world were few. Indeed, Rouja (1998, p. 19) says that 'the problems experienced in the community [One Arm Point] today cause some Bardi to reflect on Sunday Island as being the last place where there were "real Bardi people"'. In their attempts to return to Sunday Island, Bardi enlisted the aid of sympathetic Europeans: Frank Renehan, who lived with Jawi woman Rosie Bulam in Derby; and, when Renehan's attempts to assist them failed, David Drysdale, a retired UAM missionary who had worked at the island in the 1920s (Robinson 1973, pp. 262–4). Ingrid Drysdale described how a small group decided to return to Sunday Island in 1969:

> At last two of the elders, Billy Ah Choo and Tommy Thomas, decided to return to Sunday Island and live as best they could… The people set off in old dinghies, travelling by short hops from island to island until they returned home (Drysdale & Durack 1974, p. 186).

By mid-1970, forty-nine Bardi had returned to the island (Coombs 1974, p. 14). Drysdale and his wife Ingrid moved to the island, selling their house in Perth to assist financing the struggling community (Drysdale & Durack 1974, p. 189). Logistical and financial difficulties associated with life at the island caused the group to shift to the mainland to a site called Malumb, near One Arm Point, in 1971. Coombs (1974, p. 15) reported that the group survived during this period 'largely on Social Service payments, sea-foods…and the assistance of sympathetic persons and organisations'. The first government aid to the group came through the Commonwealth government, which assisted the community to establish a green-back turtle hatchery at Algunumar in the One Arm Point area in 1972 (Drysdale & Durack 1974, p. 192; Coombs 1974, p. 15); the Commonwealth also began turtle-farming projects on a number of the islands in the Torres Strait in the same year (Beckett 1987, p. 182). One Arm Point community was officially founded that year, and most Bardi and Jawi who had been living in Derby, former Sunday Island mission residents, became associated with this community.

Cosmology and Aboriginal Tradition

The Pallottine regime at Lombadina accepted certain 'cultural' activities (such as 'bushcraft', see Walter 1982 [1928], p. 124), but attempted to regulate others. According to oral accounts, the Pallottines' prohibition on initiation ceremonies resulted in a hiatus in ritual practice in the Lombadina vicinity during a particular period of the Pallottine administration. During this period Law continued at Sunday Island, and many Lombadina residents managed to travel to Sunday Island in order to participate in ceremonies there.

In discussions about this with many of the older people at Lombadina and One Arm Point, there were different views about who had been responsible for reinstating the mainland practice of Law following this break. Some people at Lombadina asserted it was they who 'brought the Law back', while those who had been associated with Sunday Island mission claimed it was they who had done so. In the view of an elderly woman who grew up at the Catholic mission at Lombadina, it was the Catholic priest, Father Kreiner, who enabled people at Lombadina to practise Law again. She said previous missionaries had attempted to 'squash' the Law and in those times people would travel from Lombadina to Sunday Island to go through Law. She described how Kreiner had taken drums of water out to boys in the bush near Lombadina, thus facilitating the business of them being made men. 'He was really good in that way', she said. A One

Arm Point man synthesised the three views about the Law being 'opened up' again at Lombadina. In his view, it occurred when Kreiner came and got the old people left at Sunday Island after the UAM mission had closed. It was these old people who 'opened the Law up' when they came to reside at Lombadina. The small discrepancies in accounts about this matter are indicative of the different perspectives people associated with each of the missions developed.

Yet despite their opposition to some aspects of Aboriginal culture the Pallottines sought to evangelise by a process of integration of local beliefs rather than through their renunciation. They sought to 'acquire a full and authentic knowledge' of Aboriginal culture, in order to 'explore all possible avenues of approach to the blacks' mind', and viewed that culture as containing 'remnants of an original revelation that were handed down from their ancestors' (Raible 1938, p. 274). At Lombadina, hymns were translated into local language, and Galalung's name was transposed where references were made to 'God'. Perhaps unsurprisingly then, various Lombadina people have described Galalung to me not simply as 'like God' but as being 'God himself'. After performing certain feats on earth Galalung 'went up' to reside in the Milky Way and is visible in the shape of an emu during the months of June and July. Worms and Petri (1998, p. 153) describe Galalung as living now 'in the dark spot between the constellations Centaury and Scorpio'. Marrawiny described the place where Galalung resides as *gandayun* ('from above') and translated it to me as 'heaven' (personal communication 18 November 1994).

Pallottine practice sought similarities between Christianity and Bardi cosmology, and encouraged syncretism far more than UAM style teachings at Sunday Island that emphasised the incompatibility between them. Reflecting on his experience at Sunday Island, for example, Khaki Stumpagee elaborated the relationship Jawi have with their Law, and the inability of mission influence to stop them practising their Law:

Geoffrey Bagshaw: Before white people came to Sunday Island, did people still practise that Law?

Khaki Stumpagee: Nobody stop Jawi people, they don't, only one, one *gardiyas* [non-Aboriginal people] been stop, well church people, because we can't serve, they said – you can't, you can't serve two master, God himself and other master might be devil...you understand what I mean.

Geoffrey Bagshaw: I do. And so did that stop the Law?

Khaki Stumpagee: No. We was, they didn't want the Law, but we can't stand we belong to Law. We never take notice of missionary.

Geoffrey Bagshaw: You kept it going?

Khaki Stumpagee: Missionary come [to] Island, go. Another year might be another one come. Well so many years here, might be six years, another one change over. They talk, well, cut out that, you can't have two master but we can. We belong to Law, we gotta keep going Law (Khaki Stumpagee video transcript 2001, p. 36).

In the 1990s, when work on the Sampi claim was beginning, Bardi and Jawi people distinguished between those from the different missions as the 'Catholic mob' and 'the UAM mob'. But the differences between the two missions were more than nominal. The Pallottines' evangelical method was more societally based, predicated on a separation of children from their parents, and with a much stronger emphasis on discipline and regimentation in daily life. At Sunday Island, UAM-style evangelisation took an inflexible approach to Aboriginal cosmology and certain related practices, and this fostered a greater resistance from Bardi and Jawi at the island than the Pallottine missionaries' more integrative approach towards many (though not all) facets of Aboriginal culture at Lombadina. There was greater continuity in the mission regime at Lombadina than at Sunday Island, most graphically illustrated by the closure of Sunday Island mission in the 1960s and the relocation of many of its residents to Derby, but also in more general terms as alluded to by Khaki Stumpagee in the transcript excerpt earlier.

In meetings about their native title claim during the 1990s, Bardi and Jawi often said they were 'all one mob', regardless of whether they or their families had been primarily associated with the mission at Lombadina or at Sunday Island. This encapsulates the fact that they practise Law together, have close genealogical connections and intermarry. Notwithstanding this, different experiences at the two missions created a layer of difference between those who had grown up in them. It meant, for example, that some mythological narratives were better known in one community than they were in the other, and vice versa. But, as described previously, the corpus of beings in Bardi cosmology include localised beings whose activities are recounted by those who have the right to speak about them – senior people whose *buru* (estates) are imprinted with the activities of those beings. In other words, there are distinctions in knowledge amongst Bardi and Jawi people that have their basis in a cosmology and a social system that distributes rights and interests in land and sea and their associated narratives according to that cosmology. There are also distinctions in knowledge arising from different experiences in a post-contact, mission-influenced environment. In a litigated setting, such distinctions – regardless of their provenance – could be used by respondent parties to argue that those who were at Sunday Island had gained their knowledge of certain matters post-sovereignty through their association with Jawi at Sunday Island mission, and hence that such knowledge was not 'traditional'. As the conduct of the Sampi case amply demonstrated, this perspective played into the key question of whether Bardi and Jawi were one or two societies at sovereignty that would emerge so distinctively in this case.

Chapter Four

A Land and Sea Claim

Bardi and Jawi are putting in this claim in the interest of
their culture, to teach the kids their culture, how to spear
fish, how to use the tide to cross waters, like our ancestors
did, which island to go for water and bush tucker, and
to keep our language going...That's why we're very
strong on native title on the land and on the sea (Baaji,
6 March 1997)

Claiming Country

I first travelled to the communities of the northern Dampier
Peninsula in 1994 to set up a meeting of those people who had, in
1993, formally instructed the Kimberley Land Council to pursue
a native title claim on their behalf. The people whose signatures
appeared on the sheet of paper recording the minutes of the 1993
meeting were largely unknown to me at that time, but many
of them would become principal witnesses in the Sampi case.
Those who had instructed the land council to pursue the claim
were middle-aged and older. Most of them were elders who had
specific ritual and other responsibilities in relation to country.
Collectively they represented estate groups from nearly every part
of the larger territory that would become the Sampi claim area.

On the drive along the northern end of the Cape Leveque
road to the tip of the Dampier Peninsula, numerous small dirt

roads lead into the pindan (scrub) on both sides of the road. These roads (often little more than bush tracks) lead to small outstation communities located close to the coast. These outstations are, in many cases, material embodiments of some aspect of people's connections to country, indicative of named areas called *buru* (estates) that are part of the pattern of land tenure in this region. These named estates have freshwater sources (coastal soaks called *umban*, or permanent rock pools called *bidiyn*), and within each estate are named sites or places. Each named site is also referred to as *buru* because of the polysemy of the term; it can refer to 'ground, camp, site, estate, and broader country', depending on context (Bagshaw 2001a, p. 23). Estates extend into the intertidal zone and beyond, encompassing specific named marine features such as reefs, islets and currents. Estates tend to be focused on the coast because this is where the water sources are: most of the interior of the Dampier Peninsula does not have permanent freshwater sources. Bardi characterise the scrubby hinterland area between west and east coastal estates as *bulngurru* (in-the-middle or central), *bindana* (woodland-scrub) and as *nimidiman jugara bur* (country that is shared, or possessed-in-common) (Bagshaw 1999, p. 48). This kind of shared country is not especially unusual: Sutton (2003, p. 122) refers to 'observations from widely different parts of the Australian continent' indicating that 'in the absence of local resources or remarkable features, areas on the periphery of local estates or Dreaming track areas are typically shared by adjoining landed groups, or perhaps regarded as the property of all the locally linked groups'. Bardi used well-trodden paths to 'footwalk' through this area of the central peninsula to visit kin, for ceremonial reasons, and to collect resources such as hard woods, bush honey, bush foods and medicines, the root *(barnjut)* used to stun or 'poison' fish in *mayurr* (stone fish traps that hold fish when the tide goes out), and for hunting kangaroo, flying fox and lizards for meat. Analogous to this shared hinterland as a common resource zone is the sea that lies beyond the marine features included within estates.

Offshore, some of the islands are wholly identified with a single estate, while others contain multiple estates. The Jawi island of Iwanyi, Sunday Island, has three estates: Nilagunburu, Bilinybilinyburu and Umbinarr (East Sunday Island). Jayirri has two: Jayirriburu (Jackson Island) and Munburran (Tyra Island). From a European perspective, the islands comprising these two estates are named and thought of as separate islands, Jackson Island and Tyra Island. But because at low tide they are joined by exposed reef, Bardi and Jawi understand them to be a single entity, albeit one containing two estates. This can be confusing, as the island in general terms is referred to as Jackson Island or Jayirri, but – contingent on context – this name may also be used to include Munburran (Tyra Island). The identity of Jayirri itself as Bardi or Jawi was disputed throughout the Sampi case, and conclusions about its identity became implicated with how the judge would approach the question of native title offshore.

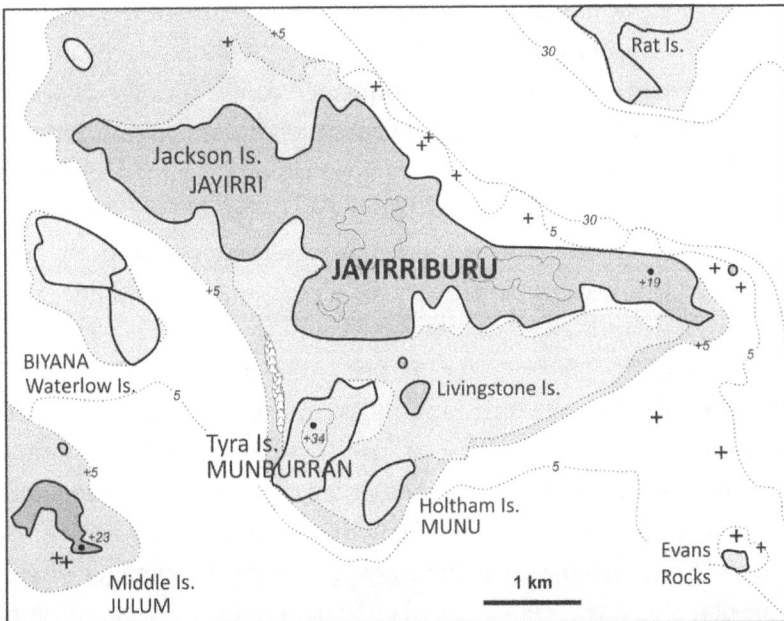

Figure 8: Map of Jayirriburu, showing Jackson and Tyra islands connected by reef.

In one of the reports written for the native title claim, Geoffrey Bagshaw (1999, p. 19) described 'the basic units of local organization among both [Bardi and Jawi] peoples' as 'exogamous patrifilial groups' identified with named estates *(buru)*:

> The members of each such aggregate are regarded as the traditional owners of the estate with which they are identified, and are often collectively known by the name of that estate. Among both peoples, important individual rights are also recognised in maternal estates *(ningarlm)* and in spousal estates *(gurirriny)* (Bagshaw 1999, p. 19).

In this region, then, the main way that people trace their country is through their relationships with others who are identified with specific *buru*: connections to country are inherited. Over many years, Bardi and Jawi have consistently stated that father's country is the most significant in this regard; that people should 'follow father for country'. But they also have rights in their mother's country and in their spouse's country. This means a single estate will have people connected to it in a range of ways; through their father, through their mother and through marriage. People may also be connected to an estate through their *rayi* (or *raya*), a pre-existing spirit that has been in the country since the creative epoch (often glossed in English as 'the Dreaming'), when ancestral beings performed various deeds that gave shape and form to the land.

In English, people refer to *raya* in a number of ways: as 'kids', 'small kids' or 'spirit kids' (Glaskin 2005, p. 302). *Raya* may become instantiated in human form, first appearing to the father in a dream.[36] *Raya* inhabit particular locations within estates, and when a child is born he or she may be consubstantially identified with the sites from which their *raya* came (for example, a white pipe clay site, a waterhole, a tidal current, a tree). This relationship with the place the person carries within them is called *barnman* (or *jarlng/a;* in English, people may describe this as their 'totem').

Raya can also appear to a man as an animal that, if he spears it while hunting, will also result in that *raya* becoming instantiated in human form.[37] In this case, the child who is later born has that particular species of animal for their *barnman* (their 'totem'). Examples of this kind include those whose *barnman* is a species of fish (such as an ocean mullet), *gurlil* (green turtle), and a species of shark. In rare cases, a person's *raya* may be said to be from a country other than their father's estate, usually because the father himself was travelling and encountered the *raya* in that country.[38] In such cases, a person's primary affiliation remains with their father's estate but their identification with another estate through their *raya*, assuming this is broadly recognised, allows them special (non-transferrable) rights in that country. When a person dies, their *raya* returns to its place of origin, usually their father's country, in accordance with the Bardi and Jawi ideology of patrifiliation, and in exceptional circumstances the same *raya* may be re-instantiated (Glaskin 2005, p. 303; Glaskin 2006a; but also see Glaskin 2015 for a more complex view on this).

At the time the Sampi claim was being prepared, there were nineteen extant Bardi *buru*, four Jawi *buru* and six deceased estates (estates without any living patrifiliates or matrifiliates) within the Bardi and Jawi claim area (Bagshaw 2001a, p. 17). The land area of estates is not large (estimated at around 6 and 4.5 square kilometres in two particular examples), but the offshore components can be much larger (Bagshaw 1999, p. 49). Tidally exposed areas contiguous with the land are considered part of an estate, as are nearby offshore features such as small islands, rocks, sandbanks, reefs and shallow waters. Proximate currents may also be associated with particular estates. An example of this is Iwalajalajala, a current and whirlpool associated with Gambarnanburu. Deep water *(jarrayn jarrayn)* may also lie within an estate; this may arise from especially deep channels or from *nimir* ('holes in the sea'), associated with subsurface rivulets of freshwater that emerge offshore (Semeniuk 1983). According to Bain (1982, p. 152), such 'deep holes in the sea floor camouflaged with gently moving seaweed' were a 'source of accidents' amongst pearl divers. Deep sea or distant offshore waters (also called *jarrayn*) beyond estate boundaries are characterised similarly to the interior of the peninsula, as *bulngurru jarrayn* (in the middle; between deep waters associated with particular estates). Like the interior of the northernmost tip of the Dampier Peninsula, *bulngurru jarrayn* is considered to be held in common and similarly may be referred to as *nimidiman jugara bur* (shared country) (Bagshaw 1999, p. 48).

Making a Claim

Bardi and Jawi people today live in many places other than the Dampier Peninsula. Some people live in Perth, Katherine and Melbourne or other towns or cities; many people live in the townships of Broome and Derby much closer by, or move between these towns and the major communities or outstations in the peninsula. During the 1990s, though, genealogies indicated that most Bardi and Jawi people lived in the Dampier Peninsula, either in the three major communities of Lombadina, Djarindjin and One Arm Point, or at outstations that, for the most part, were located on their country, their respective *buru*. When I first visited the area in 1994, many people were preoccupied with the processes associated with setting up their outstations. Such processes included incorporating their groups under the Commonwealth *Aboriginal Councils and Associations Act 1976*, securing funding in order to establish the rudimentary infrastructure, and setting up projects that would provide economic support for outstation living, such as ecotourism ventures. At the time, these issues were the focus of many people's engagement with the bureaucratic arms of the state. Outstation economies in this region were based on a mixture of subsistence through fishing and hunting; social security payments (including pensions); and income derived from establishing tourist camping grounds at their outstations or from running various kinds of cultural tours.

Outstation living allows people to monitor their country. It puts them in a position to watch over nearby sites of significance and to keep an eye on how bush tucker and coastal resources in that area are being used. In my experience, outstation residents are constantly alert to vehicle tracks and footprints, depletion of resources, interference with areas of significance, and to the movements and health of terrestrial and marine species. Being vigilant to these things is all part of 'looking after' country, fulfilling one's customary responsibilities to it. People would also say that the outstation lifestyle was quieter and more removed from the 'humbug' of larger community life, especially from the more violent and disruptive elements often related to alcohol abuse. Many of the middle-aged and older people I worked with said they felt 'good' being in their own country *(ngayijinaburu)*, because of the deep familiarity and emotional attachment they had to the place. People said their health was better at outstations, partly because they could eat food from their own country, and because there was less emotional stress associated with living at the outstations compared to being in the larger communities.

Figure 9: Near Nillargoon outstation. Photo: Katie Glaskin (1994).

Nearly all the outstations within the claim area are located on the mainland. During the 1990s, there was just one outstation on one of the islands offshore. This outstation, Nillargoon, was situated in Jawi country, located at Guwarngun in Nilagunbur on Sunday Island. The existence of only one outstation in Jawi country reflected the much smaller Jawi population (estimated in 1999 on the basis of the genealogies as being about seventy people as compared to a much larger Bardi population of around 950), as well as the additional difficulties and added costs involved in establishing outstations on islands. People travelled between Sunday Island and One Arm Point mainly by dinghy, although in 1998 the outstation owned a larger boat *Nillargoon* as well as a barge.[39] The distance between the two places is approximately 10 kilometres, and involves skirting among islands and reefs, and negotiating tidal currents which run from at least three different directions when the tide is coming in or going out. Nillargoon outstation was primarily developed at Khaki Stumpagee's behest, but his aspirations were only realised with the assistance of an Englishman whose wife was one of Khaki's relatives.

The outstations were largely established by estate-affiliates (patrifiliates) within their own estates *(buru)*. The typical unit of outstation incorporation, though, tended to be the extended family group. Thus an artefact of the incorporative process was that it set up ambiguities between the customary unit of land tenure (the estate) and the outstation group (which had an externally sourced imprimatur as the authority for its creation). The structural location of these matters within a non-indigenous domain, involving various government agencies, programs, bureaucratic requirements in relation to procedure and expenditure, accountability measures, spot-checks on outstation groups and more, accentuated the politics of land tenure and resource acquisition in this area. Such mechanisms pitted outstation groups within the same region against one another symbolically, and in many instances materially as well. As outstation groups competed over control of outstation resources and, sometimes, of the corporation that held them, the groups fractured and formed further outstations within the same *buru*.

While there was a strong correlation between where a person's traditional estate lay and where they subsequently gained their outstation, this was not absolute. Not all estate-affiliates became part of a single outstation; and not all outstations were formed by estate-affiliates. 'Claims' were formulated largely on the basis of descent, mostly through 'following father for country', although some people 'followed *nyami*' (mother's father), while others may have pushed the 'claims' of their spouse (in their *gurririny* country), and so on. People with non-Bardi paternity who could not 'follow father for country' used other lines of genealogical descent in order to reckon their associations to country and to make 'claims' to that country for the purpose of establishing their outstation. In some instances, this resulted in friction between people 'claiming' rights to the same area through different mechanisms. Where estate-affiliates were unable to form an outstation within their own country because the land was alienated, they sought to emphasise other mechanisms of connection to country in order to make 'claims' within other *buru*. Where estate-affiliates gave permission *(nimalj)* to establish outstations in their country to others who did not have as strong a 'claim' to that country, conflict arose when the individuals making the initial agreement passed away, leaving the co-existence between these two kinds of rights to be negotiated by their descendants.

The outstation movement had implications for the native title claim that followed. First, people established their outstations using the language of 'claims'. These 'claims' (applications) were made to the government organisation with the power to grant outstation establishment, but they also had an intensely local significance because they were made in relation to the 'claims' others had similarly made to areas within the northern Dampierland Peninsula. Since they involved recourse to family histories and genealogies, most of which existed as part of an oral tradition, these claims were not always universally agreed upon and could become political. Politics arising through the outstation movement in this region were consistently articulated in normative statements of inheritance and tradition. Thus there was already a robust discussion about who had legitimate rights over different areas of country before the native title claim research began, although people would also often say that 'we all know where we come from'.

Second, 'claims' to country in the context of the outstation movement appear to have consolidated notions of the autonomy of these contemporary land-using groups. These transformations had implications for changing property relationships amongst Bardi and Jawi in general. For example, the notional idea of the outstation in this area with its incorporation and accountability requirements more closely resembles the idea of private property, something that can be 'acquired', as distinct from a *buru* through which one gains membership through descent. A number of *buru* have more than one outstation located within them, each associated with different 'families',[40] and a comparison of people attached to particular outstation groups and those attached to particular *buru* suggests that the outstation process contributed to ongoing realignments of relationships between people with respect to country.

By the time of the Mabo decision in 1992, numerous out-stations had already been established in the land that became subject to the Sampi native title claim, and others were being formed. The requirements of demonstrating native title differed from the kind of information required to establish an outstation.[41] For outstations, assertions about traditional attachment to the area could be augmented by supplying the local language name of the area as well as brief comments about the connections of the applicants to the area. Such requirements were neither extensive nor prescriptive, and were neither tested nor made subject to the kinds of proof of connection to country that were ultimately required by the Native Title Act. In contrast, too, their joint native title claim required those making it to come together in some fashion

70

as 'one mob', rather than acting only on behalf of their families. This was a significant difference between what native title required of people, and their experience of the outstation movement. Both, though, were couched in the language of 'tradition'.

Land Rights and Land Alienation

In Western Australia, the state government's first attempt to address the issue of Aboriginal land rights occurred in 1983 with the Aboriginal Land Inquiry, headed by Justice Paul Seaman QC. Aboriginal groups from throughout the state contributed verbal and written submissions to the Inquiry about the necessity for land rights in Western Australia, and to ideas regarding the form that such land rights might take. The Bardi Aborigines Association were among those who made submissions to the Inquiry. In their covering letter to Paul Seaman QC, they wrote that they had been 'thinking and talking about land rights for many years now' (Bardi Aborigines Association 1983). As well as wanting land that was currently under Aboriginal reserve to be transferred into freehold title and 'controlled by the community', they wanted 'all of the offshore islands in King Sounds, including Buccaneer Archipelago...to be included in the reserve under freehold title' (Bardi Aborigines Association 1983). They submitted that their cultural traditions could sustain claims to the seas, intertidal zones, reefs, sandbars and offshore islands. Sea rights, they argued, should be considered as seriously as land rights.[42]

Justice Seaman appears to have been persuaded in this regard. His recommendations included that waters be protected for 'traditional' uses, and he took the view that changes in marine technology did not alter the fact that the people concerned were undertaking traditional activities:

> Waters should only be protected for Aboriginal people for uses which are still part of traditional life. Traditional use should be defined to include access to and traditional activities connected

71

with significant areas in or associated with the sea, or customary modes of foraging or fishing near the sea. An activity should not be treated as outside tradition merely because it is pursued with the latest technology.[43]

Although the Aboriginal Land Inquiry recommended establishing land rights legislation in Western Australia (Seaman 1984), the government did not follow their recommendations. In 1994, when I began speaking with Bardi and Jawi about native title, many people had strong memories of the Inquiry and of having spoken with Paul Seaman a decade previously. In combination with the Sunday Islanders' experience of being shifted to Derby in the 1960s, the failure of the Inquiry to effect any change in the recognition of land or sea rights underlined the precariousness of their legal position in relation to their country. One Arm Point community is situated on an Aboriginal Reserve (Reserve 2097) created for the 'Use and Benefit of Aborigines'. This reserve and a Special Purpose grazing lease held by Djarindjin community covered most of the mainland area later included as part of the Sampi claim.[44] By the time of the Seaman Inquiry, the reality that Aboriginal reserve was not a secure tenure for those with traditional connections to these areas had become evident. It is likely that this underscored the Bardi Association's submission to the Inquiry that it be converted into freehold. The Western Australian government's failure to take up any of Seaman's recommendations created palpable disappointment among those Bardi and Jawi people who spoke to me about the matter. For some people, this was compounded by what was considered the 'loss' of Cygnet Bay, connected with the demise of Sunday Island mission and the long-established relationship that many of them had with pearler Dean Brown.

Brown lived on Sunday Island mission from 1946–62, where he employed Aboriginal workers in his pearling ventures (Brown 1984).[45] Writing in 1948, not specifically in relation to Brown but to the employment of Aboriginal people at Sunday Island more generally, Bateman (1948, p. 7) noted that Aboriginal workers at Sunday Island were not paid directly: he wrote that 'none of the natives have bank accounts and they mainly collect their earnings in the form of stores at the mission store'. Bateman (1948, p. 7) also observed that 'a certain discontent exists among these natives, who complain that they receive little from the mission in return for their work'. In 1962, the same year that United Aborigines Mission staff withdrew from Sunday Island, Brown obtained a pearling lease and a land lease at Cygnet Bay. The lease he obtained was excised from a Reserve (2097) set aside for the 'Use and Benefit of Aborigines'. This was unusual since excising land from such reserves was 'contrary to the policy' of the Department.[46]

When Sunday Island mission closed, some of the people who had been at the mission at Sunday Island went to work with Dean Brown at Cygnet Bay, while others, who had refused to shift to Derby, remained at Sunday Island. In 1963, the Department of Native Welfare received a petition signed by a number of ex-Sunday Island mission residents, which read:

> During the Xmas holidays all stores at Sunday Island were soon depleted and for the last two weeks we have been living with Mr Brown. Mr Brown tells us that he cannot give permanent residence and gainful employment to the majority under the present circumstances, due to the fact that he has not sufficient or suitable work available to cope with our numbers. If on the other hand he were to receive an additional grant of adjoining land from our tribal reserve, he assures us that if it is within his capabilities he will do all he can to satisfy our needs. We the undersigned agree wholly to the above and truly hope that earnest consideration be given to the petition in helping to solve our problem (in Bottrill n.d., p. 12).

I heard about this petition from a number of the people I worked with; they referred to having signed this paper in exchange for promises about assistance to them, having 'put their names down to help him get that place.'[47]

Brown's lease boundaries at Cygnet Bay were extended in 1972, the same year One Arm Point community was formed following the return of ex-Sunday Island mission residents from Derby. Although apparently contrary to government policy, this meant that further land was excised from an Aboriginal Reserve for private commercial purposes. In 1975 one of Dean Brown's sons wrote to Alan Ridge, then Minister for Lands, saying that:

> As we pointed out to Sir Charles Court [then Premier of Western Australia] and yourself during your last visit to Cygnet Bay, we are surrounded by One Arm Pt. and Lombadina, both having Native Reserve (I guess). We have already suffered a land grab by One Arm Pt. due I guess, almost entirely by Commonwealth pressure on the old Native Welfare Dept… The major factor that worries us is that maybe at a later date One Arm Pt. might express desires to control our land and this would be quite unfair as there is ample for everyone on this peninsular [sic], but if our plans are carried out our land will be very desirable because of the money and hard work poured into the project (Brown 1975).

The 'land grab' referred to in this letter is likely to have been the 99-year lease between Bardi Association and the Aboriginal Lands Trust (ALT) which began in 1975. It covers Sunday Island (Reserve 25106) and a portion of Reserve 2097; the same Reserve from which Brown's Cygnet Bay lease was excised. In 1984, the year Paul Seaman QC reported his findings on the Aboriginal Land Inquiry, the Browns of Cygnet Bay Pearls applied to have their lease at Cygnet Bay transformed into freehold title; this was achieved that year. Department of Lands and Surveys records indicate that both Bardi Aborigines Corporation (associated with One Arm Point) and the Kimberley Land Council had written to them on a number of occasions registering their concern about the land becoming freehold.[48] Bardi and Jawi people have subsequently been concerned not only about the alienation of the land at Cygnet Bay, but also the waters, since the long-lines of the pearling leases effectively prohibit access to this area. Cygnet Bay Pearls would, many years later, become one of the respondents to the Sampi claim.

A Genealogy of a Claim

In 1993, the Kimberley Land Council held meetings in the Dampier Peninsula to talk about the Mabo decision of 1992 and its implications. It was during this time that Bardi and Jawi elders gave instructions to the land council to pursue a native title claim on their behalf. Around the same time, a common law action called *Lorrie Utemorrah and others v Commonwealth and others* (F.C. S.92/004 (1992) 108 ALR 225) had been lodged in the Supreme Court of Western Australia through the Kamali Land Council and under the legal direction of Rosemary O'Grady. This was a claim to native title over 260,000 kilometres of land in the Kimberley region. Following a directions hearing in February 1993, the claim was broken up into several smaller actions: the lead action among them was known as the 'Ejai action' after the late Jimmy Ejai, who was the named Bardi applicant for that claim (Nettheim 1994, p. 25). In terms of territorial identity, Jimmy Ejai referred to himself and was referred to by other Bardi people as Inalabulu, signifying his identity as an islander. Meaning 'island people', the term is one of a number of designations used for regional groups of people within Bardi country defined according to geographic or directional terms, and represented in ritual. It was during the directions hearings for the Ejai action that the now commonly invoked adage 'the best evidence lies in the hearts and minds' of Aboriginal claimants first came to be articulated.[49]

The Ejai action had considerable symbolic and practical significance for Bardi and Jawi, even though most were not officially instructing O'Grady in relation to this matter. The Ejai action had some people from the broader Bardi group, along with some Jawi, as initial signatories to the action. The area covered by the application took in One Arm Point, all the islands throughout the King Sound region, and included a large tract of country on the eastern side of King Sound. The named applicant for the claim, Jimmy Ejai, was a Bardi man, but much of the area covered by the application covered country associated with a number of language-named groups, over areas that were later subsumed by the Mayala and Dambimangarri native title claims. The division of Bardi and Jawi people – between those involved in the Ejai action and the majority of those who were not – appears to have arisen from a complicated nexus between traditional ownership of certain resource-rich areas (islands surrounded by large, trochus-bearing reefs), the politics of resource exploitation, a mission history that saw many Bardi people move into Jawi country, where the Sunday Island mission had been established in 1899, tourism aspirations, and robust community politics, at least.

At the time of the common law action, most Bardi people resident in Bardi country had not given legal instructions in relation to this matter and many were actively antithetical to it, playing out factional loyalties to the Kimberley Land Council as against Kamali Land Council within this legal forum.[50] When other Bardi people instructed the Kimberley Land Council to begin a native title claim on their behalf, these factional loyalties also had legal consequences, with people from the same communities being legally represented by two different organisations. In October 1994, when Geoffrey Bagshaw and myself began research for the native title claim, the politics associated with this situation were evident. There were those who were loyal to the Kimberley Land Council (which, as a regional grassroots organisation had gained a considerable following after the Noonkanbah dispute in 1978), and those who were adverse to the KLC or those who supported them. In terms of how the claim would be formulated, parts of the country associated with those who were covered by the Ejai action were off-limits.

Drawing boundaries around native title claims is always complex. Social interaction between Aboriginal people is not confined to language-named identities and associated country. Multilingualism and intermarriage between people associated with different language-named groupings are common. While the boundaries of some countries are clearly demarcated in myth (usually associated with topological features of the landscape) or by other geographical features (such as creeks, or certain rocks, or trees), others are less clearly marked. Rather than the clearly marked boundaries of the cadastral map, there can be zones of transition and areas of shared country (Sutton 2003, p. 122).

Bardi and Jawi accounts of their interaction before the arrival of Europeans in the region emphasise meeting for trade and for ritual expressions of their cosmology that involved young men going through various stages of Law in order to become *mambangan*, fully initiated men. People travelled between the mainland and the islands using the double raft (called *galwa* in Bardi, *galu* by Bard speakers and *biel-biel* in Jawi) made from light mangrove logs *(julbu)*. This craft was distinct from the type of raft used on the eastern side of the King Sound (Akerman 1975; Love 1939). Both men and women used *galwa,* often referred to in English as a catamaran (locally pronounced *katamarang*); some also used canoes called *barrawarr* or *inbargun* (the latter being the Bardi term for coolamon, also used to refer to canoes). To navigate through the many marine hazards they used sea-routes called *numurr*, a term people described as referring to a marine route or 'road in the sea'. In his first report to the court, Bagshaw (1999, p. 73) said that as he understood it the term could also 'be used to refer to (a) the appropriate tidal conditions for sea travel (b) the locations at which such conditions are gauged and (c) the actual tidal currents used to effect safe travel'. As Bagshaw (1999, p. 73) said, this knowledge of *numurr* enabled Bardi and Jawi to travel 'large distances with a minimum of effort by skilfully "riding" a complex network of incoming and outgoing tidal currents'. In addition to *numurr,* which people still use when travelling by dinghy, because they still represent the most effective routes to travel between islands, other navigational aids include using stars when travelling at night, as well as the feel of the vessel in the water and the smell of the sea and exposed rocks. Rouja (1998, p. 85) describes how:

> In the King Sound the state of the tide and concurrent water movements plays a crucial role in how the Bardi find their bearings. Older, more experienced hunters know the area well and how it is affected at different tidal stages and can look down at the water and know their specific location. It is essential to possess the knowledge of how the water reacts at different stages of its tidal ebb and flow and how geographical features, be they sub or supra-tidal, affect the water. This kind of knowledge is especially useful when travelling at night. Dinghies, even under power, react differently in different kinds of water and an experienced hunter can literally feel where he is from the particular way the dinghy is behaving in the water.

Figure 10: Men and women on mangrove log rafts crossing the straits near Sunday Island (Source: Porteus 1931, p. 63).

Khaki Stumpagee told us that Bardi and Jawi were 'all mixed', from 'a long time before...[that] Jawi [were] coming to mainland to steal wives', and Bardi were coming to Jawi islands to steal Jawi wives (personal communication 11 November 1994). 'Mixed' here refers to intermarriage. Genealogies prepared for their native title claim clearly indicated that Bardi and Jawi intermarriage preceded effective colonisation of the area in the 1880s. Robinson (1973, pp. 102–3) commented that 'there are enough similarities between the Bardi and Djawi...to regard them as socially and culturally homogeneous for most purposes'. These similarities include their marine orientations and technology, cosmology, ritual practice and mythical narratives, a common system of local organisation, and a common system of kinship and social organisation. These commonalities, the joint ceremonial context, and the high degree of social relatedness between Bardi and Jawi, were all important factors leading to the formulation of a joint native title claim.

This formulation was, however, also a negotiated compromise that took into account the area covered by the Ejai action, as well as local political sensitivities concerning the Jawi island of Sunday Island. Sunday Island mission was the birthplace of many Bardi people, the site of their earliest and most formative experiences. In his draft anthropological report prepared for the Kimberley Land Council, Bagshaw said:

> While the collective membership of both groups effectively constitutes two separate possessory groups with respect to their traditional territories, the dense social, cultural and historical relations obtaining between Bardi and Jawi are such that the traditional land and sea interests of both can be accommodated in the context of a single native title claim (1995, p. 3).

Bagshaw went on to describe and map 'Sub-Area A' and 'Sub-Area B'. Sub-Area A at that time included all the mainland territory to which Bardi claimed traditional affiliations, but excluded the Bardi islands traditionally associated with Jimmy Ejai and his family, because they were pursuing their claims through the Kamali Land Council in the Ejai action. 'Sub-Area B' included the other islands that lay between One Arm Point and Sunday Island.

By the time the claim was formally lodged, Jimmy Ejai had transferred his instructions to the Kimberley Land Council, and his country was included as part of the claim. Notwithstanding this, the Jawi portion of the claim remained constricted by the Ejai action. It included only Jawi whose territorial interests lay west of the Sunday Strait. There are also Jawi islands on the eastern side of the Sunday Strait, in the region known as Mayala, which is a geographical descriptor derived from a kind of spinifex grass found on those islands, and used to refer to 'eastern King Sound people'. Today Mayala is also the name of a native title claim that adjoins the Bardi and Jawi native title claim on its eastern border, and includes all the other islands of the King Sound. It abuts the Dambimangarri native title claim (*Barunga v State of Western Australia* [2011] FCA 518), which was resolved as a consent determination (by agreement between the parties, rather than through litigation) in 2011. The artificial division between Jawi on the western side of the King Sound (up to, and including Sunday Island) and those on the Mayala side was a direct consequence of constraints on the legal representation of those Jawi whose country lay to the east of Sunday Strait at that time. Justice French would later note that this was the case when he made his 2005 determination:

> The eastern boundary of the native title claim area as it was when Mr Bagshaw's report was prepared followed the mid line of King Sound. Although traditional Jawi territory extends well to the east of this line it was not incorporated in the claim as lodged. This was due to issues about native title claim representation at the time of his initial research in late 1994. According to Mr Bagshaw these issues were resolved between

1995 and 1998 and the remaining Jawi territorial interests not covered by the claim are represented in the context of the abutting Mayala region native title claim (*Sampi v State of Western Australia* FCA 777 [2005], paragraph 809).

This exclusion of some Jawi country from the Jawi portion of the claim area would, following the Yorta Yorta High Court decision and its edicts about 'society', lead to questions about whether it was possible to include what one lawyer once ironically referred to as 'half' a society. In late 2007 (post determination and post Federal Court appeal hearing), it would become the primary reason put forward by the State of Western Australia for not being sufficiently 'satisfied' to consider a consent determination at that late stage in the proceedings.

The Road to Litigation

At any stage of a litigated case, a native title claim can be resolved through agreement between the applicants and the respondent parties, those who have expressed an interest in the claim. Some cases can go through an entire hearing only to be finally determined by a mediated consent determination, as occurred with the Karajarri native title claim (*Nangkiriny v State of Western Australia* [2002] FCA 660). In theory, this means that the claim stands as something that can be resolved at any point in time, with one implication being that mediated agreements can shorten the time it takes for a claim to be resolved. In actuality, in some cases, what it does mean is that uncertainty lingers longer than it otherwise might, as claims are steered, sometimes by inexperienced navigators, between the rocky outcrops of mediation and litigation. In the Sampi case, there were numerous attempts made to resolve the claim through mediation.

The concept of mediation and negotiation presupposes that the parties to the mediation are in equal positions of power, structurally speaking. In legal contexts, however, one party in mediation is almost always in a more powerful position than the other. Under the original *Native Title Act 1993*, once a claim was registered, native title claimants were obliged to participate in mediation through the auspices of the National Native Title Tribunal (NNTT), a body established under the Act. If an agreed consent determination could not be reached through the mediation process, the claim would be referred to the Federal Court for determination. An agreed consent determination would specify a native title determination to which all parties to the native title application could agree; the claimants and the major respondents to the claim, for example, the State of Western Australia and the Commonwealth, and in this case, fishing and pearling interests. The negotiated agreement is presented to the Federal Court; the Court must be satisfied with the agreement before it legally ratifies a consent determination, although typically this is a matter of course.

In the Sampi case, there were a number of attempts made to reach a negotiated consent determination leading up to the beginning of the evidence in 2001, but a sticking point in these negotiations was always the claim to sea. Indeed, even in their very first mediation session held at One Arm Point on 6th March 1997 (prior to the referral of their claim to the Federal Court, and before the passing of the Native Title Amendment Act in 1998, which made such referrals automatic), this was apparent. Justice French, who was then president of the Native Title Tribunal, told the claimants then that 'at the moment it doesn't appear that there'll be any agreement about native title in the sea, because neither State or Commonwealth governments will recognise your rights in the sea'.[51] Given the State and Commonwealth governments' opposition to sea rights, the claimant group considered two courses of action. One was to split the native title claim into two portions, consisting of two distinct areas: land and sea. The claimants could then negotiate with the State government over the land, while the offshore portion of their claim would be referred to the Federal Court for a determination.[52] The other option was to retain the claim as it stood, comprised of land and sea, in which case referral to the Federal Court for litigation was inevitable, since the inclusion of sea precluded any possibility of a negotiated outcome. The claimants considered the former option, concerned about the length of time the native title process would take; as one man put it, not wanting to be like Eddie Mabo, 'six feet deep', when the case was finally decided. Some saw this option as 'playing by the [whitefella] rules', choosing the most expedient option within the framework available to them to secure their interests. Ultimately, despite their cognisance of these matters, they decided to pursue their claim to land and sea as a single claim, since the notion of dividing land and sea was at odds with how they understood their country. At this very first mediation session, negotiation and mediation came to an effective standstill because the main parties were not prepared to compromise, seeing their positions as non-negotiable.

What is important to note at this point is that various forces were at play shaping the claim from its beginnings. Bardi and Jawi wanted to pursue native title in order to protect their interests in land and waters. To not attempt to protect their interest in sea country would have been anathema to them. The politics associated with trochus harvesting, which had led some Bardi and Jawi people to instruct Kamali Land Council to act on their behalf, resulted in legal constrictions on the possible Jawi component of the claim. Many Bardi people felt they had very close connections with Sunday Island mission because of having grown up at the mission, making it politically difficult to advance two separate claims. In addition, there was a robust politics over traditional ownership and over who was most properly associated with local estates that had either arisen through, or been exacerbated by, the outstation movement.

Chapter Five

The Ethnographic Archive

[The applicants' lawyer] places anthropological evidence
on too high a pedestal; anthropology is not a technical
science it's a social science – to suggest that the court
cannot make a decision about this [case] unaided by
anthropological expert evidence is ludicrous. The best
evidence is the applicant evidence and the court and
we [legal personnel] are quite capable of understanding
that and the historical evidence (respondent party
barrister addressing the court during final submissions in
Harrington-Smith v State of Western Australia ('Wongatha'),
11 June 2004, my notes)

Law, Anthropology, Experts

The sentiment expressed by the barrister acting for one of
the respondent parties in the extract above is evidently not
limited to this legal representative alone. In the Yulara claim,
the judge expressed the view that lawyers and anthropologists
risked duplicating each others' efforts and said that he could not
understand why it was that anthropologists needed to spend so
much time talking to people.[53] Part of the reason for these views
may be because anthropology, as an interpretive science, is not
bound by the rules of experimentation, control of variables, and
hence replicability of results that characterises many of the hard

sciences. But as Latour and Woolgar (1979) amongst others have argued, to suggest that the 'hard sciences' are uninfluenced by human subjectivity is itself problematic. Implicit in the judge's statement about the anthropology in the Yulara claim, too, is the view that anyone can do anthropology; there is the idea that anthropologists simply talk to people who tell them what they want to know without any apparent difficulty. What is missing from this analysis is that talking to people whose ontological foundations and experience may be radically different from our own is not a matter of straightforward conceptual commensurability; it requires us, at least, to have some awareness of how our own culture has shaped the ways that we perceive the world, and how this in turn may influence what we see and hear and comprehend. As the transcript of this case and its subsequent evaluation for determination shows, even where a discussion takes place in English, understanding is more than a matter of linguistic intelligibility.

Anthropologists have been involved in research on native title claims since the legislation was enacted. Morphy (2006, p. 136) describes the 'primary reason' anthropologists are used in native title cases as being 'their expertise in the holistic study of human social and cultural systems, in particular, the institutional structure of society, systems of kinship and social organisation and beliefs and practices'. Primarily, where research is being undertaken for applicant groups, the anthropological research task involves field research with members of the applicant group, with a focus on the applicants' connection to country, the continuity or otherwise of their associations, and the laws and customs they practise, especially as these relate to land and sea tenure. This involves spending considerable time eliciting information through dialogue and interaction, learning who the right people are to speak about certain parts of the country or other specific matters, visiting places and sites on country that are important to building up a coherent understanding of the area and how people are connected to it, and checking and cross-checking information with many different people within the applicant group. The research also involves examining ethnographic records for the area, which include published and unpublished sources: anthropological fieldnotes, unpublished theses, letters, and other relevant documents and texts. The anthropologist's findings are then condensed into reports that lay out the ethnographic basis of the claim, and these are usually accompanied by maps and genealogies, and sometimes by video. Given native title's continuity requirement, an anthropologist will usually need to address discrepancies between the archive of earlier material and the information of contemporary informants.

Burke (2011, p. 29) sees the anthropologist's task as expert witness as 'involving a deconstruction of the anthropological archive and its reassembly in terms that are relevant to the judge's task…suggestive of a fundamental triangulation' in which the claimant's evidence, the anthropological archive and legal doctrine form the three points of the triangle. This, he argues, is the same task that the applicant's lawyers undertake, creating 'an ongoing structural problem' between anthropology and law in these cases (Burke 2011, p. 29). I am not convinced it is exactly the same task, though, because, of the three points Burke identifies in the triangulation task, the starting points are different. A lawyer will begin with the law. An anthropologist will begin with ethnography, the written descriptions of various aspects of the applicants' culture, both published and unpublished. Existing ethnography may be very useful to establishing continuity in a native title claim. It may also illustrate change, both acceptable change and the kind of change that might be 'fatal' to a claim's success, as in the Yorta Yorta case, where Justice Olney concluded that 'the tide of history' had 'indeed washed away any real acknowledgment of their traditional laws and any real observance of their traditional customs'.[54] Anthropologists who do fieldwork – in native title cases, usually those who work for the applicants – will also begin with what the applicants do, and with what they have to say.

Part of the anthropological task in these cases is to elicit knowledge that may be such a part of a person's experience and everyday life that it is simply a matter of the 'way things are'; it is not necessarily knowledge that they would think to objectify. It might be part of their procedural memory, having once been learned, but now rarely brought to consciousness. A good example of this would be that no Bardi or Jawi person ever told me that they used the stars to navigate their way through the waters of the King Sound at night; and yet an incident in which a damaged engine caused four of us to travel back across the King Sound at night as the tide was going out (creating dangerous eddies, whirlpools and tidal overfalls) saw the two men (one Bardi, the other Jawi) who were on the boat effortlessly reading exactly where they were and how to get across safely using the stars as well as the feel of the boat in the water (see Glaskin 2007c). Thus part of an anthropologist's expertise is to know the right kind of questions to ask, and to build up a contextual knowledge that allows them to learn more and more about the culture of those with whom they work. Part of knowing the right questions to ask is also having an understanding of the right protocols associated with asking them, given that only certain people have the right to speak about certain matters in Aboriginal societies.

Lawyers, on the other hand, begin with law. The law they deal with is codified. It requires a positivist approach, in which law is understood as having expressly enacted rules. As one lawyer put this, 'the rule of recognition, that phrase, is used in the sense of a legal positive account of the concept of law. Now in legal positivist theory the issue of whether a particular society has law depends on whether that society has institutional structures in place for making and adjudicating their rules'.[55] Western law is accretive, with the application of legislation being subject to interpretation and refinement through the establishment of judicial precedent. Latour (2010 [2002], p. x) has said that 'there cannot be much doubt that the rule of law is one of the ways in which Western societies define themselves', and for this reason he describes law as a 'regime of truth production' that 'define[s] the hard core of our cultures'. Notwithstanding this, he says, 'it is extremely difficult for outsiders to characterise what is legal in legal reasoning' (Latour 2010 [2002], p. x). Lawyers in native title cases are likely to bring a positivist approach to their own deconstruction and reconstruction of the anthropological archive and the applicant evidence, detaching social phenomena from their context. By way of example, for one barrister, 'the rule of recognition' required the identification of the 'actual rules of the society'.[56] Lawyers begin with law and anthropologists begin with relationships and histories and differing perspectives. The 'structural tension' that Burke identifies is real enough, but some of it, I suggest, is because of the relative differences in the two disciplines' primary orientations within the triangulation task.

In Sampi, various people were involved in representing aspects of the Bardi and Jawi case that were relevant to a determination of native title to the court. Most visibly, they were anthropologists and lawyers working for both applicants and respondents, but historical, archaeological and linguistic evidence was also presented to the court. Along with anthropological work undertaken by Geoffrey Bagshaw and myself (Bagshaw 1999, 2001a, 2001b; Glaskin & Bagshaw 1999; Bagshaw & Glaskin 2000),[57] the Kimberley Land Council commissioned reports from other experts: historian Fiona Skyring, who submitted a preliminary and supplementary historical report (Skyring 2000, 2001), archaeologists Moya Smith (2000) and Sue O'Connor (2000), and linguist Christopher ('Toby') Metcalfe (2000). Smith, Metcalfe and O'Connor had done research in the region that long preceded native title, and had been called on to provide reports precisely because of their pre-existing expertise. Nevertheless, the anthropological reports were the primary 'expert' submissions.

The State of Western Australia as first respondent commissioned reports that were filed in the Federal Court prior to litigation on the order of Justice Lee (on 17 December 1999) who at that time had carriage of the case. Basil Sansom, former

Emeritus Professor from the University of Western Australia, authored a preliminary and a second preliminary anthropological report (Sansom 2000, 2001). The State also commissioned an historian's report (Green 2000), a linguist's report (Clendon 2001) in response to Toby Metcalfe's report for the applicants, and a preliminary archaeological report (Mitchell 2001) in response to Smith and O'Connor's reports for the applicants. The second respondents, the Commonwealth of Western Australia, retained a highly regarded anthropologist at the Australian National University, Professor Howard Morphy, to provide them with advice, but Morphy did not write any reports submitted to the Court. WAFIC retained the services of Paul Greenfield to provide them with advice but in the absence of documents in the public sphere, the content of both sets of advice remains unknown.[58]

While Sansom's anthropological reports for the State of Western Australia were filed with the Federal Court, they were not tendered as exhibits during the litigation, and did not form part of the subsequent case; at least, not formally.[59] Unsurprisingly, though, some of the contentions expressed within Sansom's reports did continue to inform the State of Western Australia's approach. Some were based on the ethnographic archive whereas some became obsolete as the case wore on; others assumed greater importance following the importation of the term 'society' into native title jurisprudence after the High Court's decision in the Yorta Yorta case.

The Ethnographic Archive

While the ethnographic archive of relevance to Bardi and Jawi people is fairly extensive and historically continuous, much of it has remained relatively obscure from public view, either in the form of unpublished theses (e.g., Gibson 1951, Robinson 1973, Rouja 1998), or as publications only available in German.[60] Some of the earliest records produced were prompted in response to the Western Australian government's production of a blank workbook that they distributed to people working with Aboriginal groups throughout the state from as early as 1904.[61] The workbook, entitled 'Native Vocabulary etc., compiled by [blank to be filled out]', largely called for vocabulary, although there was additional space at the back of the workbook [pp. 87–97] for 'questions' (see Glaskin 2007d). Sydney Hadley and W. H. Bird (a missionary at Sunday Island) filled out these workbooks in relation to 'the natives' at Sunday Island mission.[62] Bird's published accounts (1910, 1911, 1915; Campbell & Bird 1915) were based on the information he collated for these workbooks, and comprise the earliest records available for Jawi. Gerhardt Laves in 1929, Anthony Peile in around 1967, and Howard Coate in either the late 1950s or early 1960s all recorded data for the Jawi language, but these do not appear to be extensive (Bowern 2012, p. 7). The State's anthropologist pointed out in his supplementary report that there was an 'under-representation' of Jawi in the ethnographic record (Sansom 2001, p. 1).

One of the ways cultural continuity is demonstrated in native title cases is where earlier written records reflect the content or substance of contemporary claimant accounts. German Pallottine missionaries associated with either Beagle Bay or Lombadina missions provided a significant source of early ethnographic information for the northern mainland region, mainly in relation to those areas of the Dampier Peninsula with which people from the Lombadina mission were connected. Lombadina is situated in an area associated with a dialect of Bardi ('Bard') in which the final vowel of words tends to be dropped (relative to Bardi). As a consequence German missionaries working in this area referred to Bard rather than Bardi (rendering the term 'Bād' in their publications). Missionary and linguist Ernest Ailred Worms worked with the Kimberley Pallottine mission between 1931–38 and 1948–57 (Akerman 2015, p. vii). His publications about Bard ('Bād') culture were mainly published in the 1940s and 1950s; about half were published in German.[63] Altogether, they provided a more extensive corpus for this part of the Dampier

Peninsula than existed for Sunday Island and the One Arm Point region during the same period. Worms was particularly interested in Bard cosmology along with linguistic matters such as the etymology of place names and 'song poetry'. In the 1990s, older Bard at Lombadina remembered Father Worms as someone who was sympathetic to their culture, who said that there was very little difference between Aboriginal law and Christian beliefs, since both contained the same injunctions about the sanctity of human life, respect for one's parents, and so on (Alabornang and Gagajin, personal communication November 1994).

Written records do not always exist, though, and the absence of information about something may be used to cast doubt on the historical depth of specific matters. The paucity of earlier written documentation about marine tenure in the northern Dampierland region is one aspect of this. But there are good reasons to be wary of treating the lack of a written account about something as proof that it did not previously exist. Integral to what is in the archive is how (and whether) such information has been elicited, how or whether it has been recorded, and how it has been understood. The fact that 'all systematic observations of Aboriginal social life had been made on the safe side of the frontier' (Hiatt 1996, p. 26) is germane here. Where written records do exist it is often apparent that it is specific aspects of Aboriginal cultural life that were of interest to the person who recorded them that find their way into written form. Prevailing models (for example, of land tenure) or scholarly preoccupations may additionally influence what is recorded.

Worms (1940b) carried out some correspondence with anthropologist Professor A. P. Elkin, whose fieldwork in the area preceded Worms' arrival by just a few years. Based on research carried out during 1938 and 1939, Helmut Petri wrote about aspects of Bard cosmology (Petri 1938–40). He and Worms later wrote a book on Aboriginal religions (Worms & Petri 1998). Father Josef Bischofs, the 'second Pallottine superintendent' at Beagle Bay mission (Burke 2011, p. 105), published a paper on

Nyul Nyul to the immediate south of Bardi country containing some material of relevance to the boundary between Bardi and Nyul Nyul (Bischofs 1908).

Adolphus P. Elkin gained his doctorate in anthropology at University College in London in 1927 and travelled to the Kimberley region to conduct his first fieldwork in the same year. In early 1928, he spent just under seven weeks doing fieldwork with Bardi and Jawi people from various locations: at Lombadina (20 January to 8 February), in the Cape Leveque area (8 to 21 February), and at Sunday Island (21 February to 2 March) (Elkin 1928b; Bagshaw 2001a, p. 15). The legacy of his time there includes his fieldnotes, genealogies and letters, along with published articles based on his field research. His (1932, 1933) publications based on this fieldwork dealt with social organisation and totemism in the north-west Kimberley region. His fieldwork, which was of the short-term, rapid survey type, was the first to be carried out on both the mainland in Bardi country and on Sunday Island in Jawi country. Elkin's (1933, pp. 437–38) view was that 'for all practicable purposes the Djaui seem, nowadays at least, to be identical to the Bardi'. The term 'nowadays' contains an implicit reference to the possibility of change, indicative of the nearly thirty years that had passed since Sunday Island mission began.

The next significant ethnographic work in relation to Sunday Island was a (1951) Master's thesis written by Edward Gordon Gibson. Gibson did fieldwork at Sunday Island in 1950; his interest was in culture contact. Gibson (1951, p. 14) reported that, at the time of his fieldwork on the island, 'normally all conversation between the natives is in Bardi with a sprinkling of Djaui words, while here and there is an English expression'. Gibson's thesis is not readily accessible and did not find its way into the Sampi case.

Anthropologist Michael Robinson conducted fieldwork for his Master's thesis between June and October 1968 and July to September 1969 (Robinson 1973, p. 20). Most of his time was spent in Derby with Bardi and Jawi who had been shifted there following the closure of Sunday Island mission in 1962.

As Robinson (1973, p. ii) reported, 'the Department of Native Welfare had anticipated an assimilation of the Sunday Islanders in Derby, on the west Kimberley mainland'; but this was not to be and, as he went on to document, a small group of islanders managed to return in 1969 to eventually establish what became known as One Arm Point community in 1972. During the period of Robinson's research (1968–69) ex-mission residents were living in reserves at the edge of the mosquito-infested marsh lining the edge of Doctors Creek in Derby. Robinson's research, conducted under the supervision of Ronald Berndt at the University of Western Australia, focused on 'change and adjustment' amongst 'the islanders' during what was undoubtedly a period of rapid change. He described his thesis as a 'social anthropological account of the Sunday Islanders in Derby, up to the time of their attempted resettlement' in 1969 (1973, p. 9). While the majority of Robinson's fieldwork took place in Derby, he also visited Lombadina mission for two weeks, where some ex–Sunday Island residents had also relocated (Robinson 1973, p. 23). Robinson's thesis contained the most detailed data of any previous ethnographic work about Bardi and Jawi land tenure. It was inevitable, therefore, that both applicants and respondents would refer to the work and rely on it in certain ways in the native title proceedings. Linguist Toby Metcalfe conducted research for his doctoral thesis around the same time that Michael Robinson was in the field (e.g., Metcalfe 1970–71) and produced a thesis that focused on Bardi verb morphology.

Following Robinson, other researchers examined various aspects of Bardi and Jawi culture. Archaeologist Kim Akerman (n.d., 1975) paid particular attention to the double raft and the ways Bardi and Jawi used these in conjunction with the tides, to what he (1979) referred to as the 'cultural conservatism' of Bardi, and to the engraved pearl shells that are used in ritual and are ritually exchanged along vast trading networks throughout Australia (Akerman & Stanton 1994). Archaeologist Nic Green (1988) wrote about Bardi affiliations with the sea and, with anthropologist Jan Turner, co-wrote the Bardi Aborigines Association's submission on sea rights for the Seaman Land Inquiry (Green & Turner 1984). Moya Smith, Head of the West Australian Museum's Department of Anthropology, described her work on 'Traditional resource use amongst the Bardi Aborigines of Dampierland, West Kimberley' as a project that had begun in 1980 (Smith 2000, p. 3). She published a number of works on the basis of her research, including work on the stone fishtraps called *mayurr* constructed at various sites along the coast (Smith 1983, 1984–45, 1997). As Smith (2000, p. 6) noted in her report, William Dampier had observed such fishtraps in the claim area in 1688. Sue O'Connor's (1990) doctoral thesis was a prehistory of the islands in the Buccaneer Archipelago and the mainland on the eastern side of the King Sound; for this research she had undertaken many boat trips through the area with Jawi man Khaki Stumpagee, his Bardi wife Lena, and other members of their family (O'Connor 2000, p. 3). In 1994, overlapping with the period of time in which Geoffrey Bagshaw and myself began our research on the native title claim, Philippe Rouja began his fieldwork mainly with Bardi and Jawi people at One Arm Point. His (1998) doctoral thesis called 'Fishing for Culture' is a detailed exposition of Bardi and Jawi marine resource use.

These works, broadly speaking, formed the ethnographic archive at the time of the Sampi hearing. In addition to these were the Tindale fieldnotes, genealogies and maps (Tindale 1940, 1953a, 1953b, 1974; Tindale & Birdsell 1954). Norman B. Tindale worked for the South Australian Museum. He became interested in mapping the territories of Australian Aboriginal groups following a fieldtrip to Groote Eylandt in the Gulf of Carpentaria in 1921, when his main informant introduced him to the notion of 'tribal boundaries': territories 'beyond which it was dangerous to move without adequate recognition' (Tindale 1974, p. 3). Tindale undertook the extraordinary task of mapping the 'tribal distribution' of Australia; his first map (Tindale 1940) was later revised and published along with an encyclopaedic catalogue of Aboriginal tribal groups (Tindale 1974). From his fieldnotes, though, we know that Tindale did not actually venture into Bardi or Jawi country, but derived his information about these 'tribal boundaries' from a Bardi informant, Robin Hunter, in Broome. Tindale (1953a, p. 760) wrote of Hunter that 'he was able to give me an exact idea of the Ba:de boundary and place names within the tribal area. His pronunciation of the name varied from Ba:de to Ba:di and once to Barda'.

Jawi Country, Bardi Country

The historical ethnographic record is unambiguous in identifying Jawi country as consisting of islands in the Buccaneer Archipelago in the King Sound.[64] But precisely which islands? The archive contains different views about the extent of Jawi territory. Robinson's (1973, p. 103) view was that:

> The Djawi their [Bardi] eastern neighbours, were spread over
> the main islands of the Buccaneer Archipelago: Sunday Island
> (Iwanja), Tallon (Djalan), Tyra (Djaijiri),[65] Poolngin (Bulnginji),
> High (Ulala) and Mermaid (Garar) Islands.

Robinson's identification of Jayirri (his 'Djaijiri') as a Jawi island contrasted with the views of contemporary informants at the time of the native title research. Jayirri was typically considered to be a Bardi island. Jalan (Tallon Island) was a deceased estate; there were no longer living people with primary associations to the island through descent. At the time, Jalan was under the custodianship of Jimmy Ejai, the senior (Bardi) patrifiliate from the neighbouring island of Jayirri. This meant he was 'looking after' Jalan, which included speaking for it (and being the custodian of the mythological narratives associated with it) as well as representing its interests (see Bagshaw 1999, p. 65). Robinson (1973, p. 104) reported that the term 'Inalabulu' (derived from the term *inalang*, 'island') referred to 'island people', and said it was used with respect to 'the Djawi and the community at Sunday Island', also noting the term (along with those used for other named regions) was a 'geographical rather than social or cultural' descriptor. During research for the Sampi claim, though, the term Inalabulu ('islander') referred to Jackson Island and associated islands, and the region Inalabulu was represented in ritual by the people connected with those particular islands. Jawi people from Sunday Island (Iwanyi) were called Iwanyun and represented in ritual accordingly, while people from the islands in the King Sound east of Sunday Island were represented as Mayalayun (people from the Mayala region).

There are numerous small islands and islets throughout the region. Tindale's (1953a) and Tindale and Birdsell's (1954) field maps indicated that 'Djaui' territory on the eastern side of the Sunday Strait included Long Island (Unggaliyun),[66] Mermaid Island (Kararr) and High Island (Ulal), as well as the Bedford Islands (Garranarda), Tide Rip Islands (Nurnba), Margaret Island (Dungarr) and Pasco Island (Diji). Tindale (1953a, p. 853) wrote in his fieldnotes that 'there was a complete agreement with the Djau: informants at Broome as to which islands were Djau: & which we [sic] U:mede'. In addition to the islands identified above, the Jawi islands about which there was 'complete agreement' included Salier Island (Wijirral) and Leila Island (Marlbanda) (Tindale 1953a, p. 852). Given that all these islands are on the eastern side of Sunday Strait, it is not clear why, in his 'Tribal Boundaries Map', Tindale (1974) located 'Djaui' territory as only being west of Sunday Strait, excluding areas east of Sunday Strait, which he variously identified as 'Ongkarango' [Ungarangu] and 'U':mede' territories. The discrepancy between the latter map (which has received far greater public exposure), earlier versions, and his fieldnotes, remains unexplained. This is but one example of the conflicting information that anthropologists, lawyers and judges are called on to triangulate as part of the native title process.

On the western side of the Sunday Strait, the Jawi islands included in the Sampi claim were Sunday Island (Iwanyi),

Poolngin and Salural islands (Bulnginy and Ralral respectively), along with other small islands that were either associated with them or that came under the custodianship of those who were. This was an artificial division between Jawi country to the west of Sunday Strait and Jawi country to its east which, as previously discussed, arose as a consequence of the common law Ejai action that was in place at the time the claim was being formulated.

In a letter home to his wife Sally, Elkin (1928b) reported that 'the tribe from Pender Bay right through Lombardina [sic] and passed [sic] the Lighthouse to the north of the peninsula is all one, the Bard, and I have certainly got to know them in a remarkable way'. Robinson's (1973, p. 103) view was that 'the Bardi traditionally occupied the northern tip of Dampierland, a crescent-shaped area extending from a base-line drawn between Pender Bay and Goodenough Bay.' The south-western and south-eastern boundaries of the claim area would come under a great deal of scrutiny during the Sampi native title claim.[67] While contemporary Bardi informants asserted that Imbalgunbur (the estate immediately south of Pender Bay in the Bell's Point region) and Borlk at the head of Kelk Creek nearby were also part of Bardi country, this conflicted with many ethnographic reports locating the southern boundary of Bardi country slightly north of this at Pender Bay.[68] An exception was a map that came to light after the case had been heard. It was a microfilmed hand-drawn map appended to Bischofs (1908) publication in German. The map showed the name 'Gnalaráwan' south of Pender Bay with the words 'name for country around Pender Bay [illegible] a border horde mixed Nl-Nl [Nyul Nyul] + Bad'. Bischofs thus indicated that the 'Gnalalaráwan tribe' (as he refers to them) were 'a border horde', of 'mixed' Nyul Nyul and Bardi. While Burke's (2011, p. 105) caution about Bischofs' observations is apt – based as it is on us knowing very little about his methodology and in the absence of formal anthropological training – this designation is tantalising. It would help to explain the discrepancy between evidence given in the Sampi case of Bardi country extending beyond the southern bank of Pender Bay, and why other ethnographic descriptions have placed the boundary at Pender Bay. Justice French ultimately took the view that the weight of the evidence established Pender Bay as the south-western boundary, excluding the estate Imbalgunbur (Bell's Point), on the southern side of Pender Bay, from the determination.[69] Bischofs' map also located Bardi country as extending south down the eastern coast of the peninsula to include Goodenough and Disaster Bay, areas variously associated with Nimanbur, Nimanbur-Bard and Bard people.

In addition to the mainland, Bardi claimed a number of small islands just off the coast of One Arm Point. These included Middle Island (Julum), Tallon Island (Jalan), Jackson and Tyra islands (Jayirri and Munburran), along with associated islets, reefs, sandbanks and offshore waters. Bardi and Jawi share a mythological narrative associating Brue Reef (Juljinabur), some 23 nautical miles offshore, with Jalan (Tallon Island). The reef, like distant offshore waters, and like the interior of the peninsula, was considered to be shared country (between Bardi and Jawi), since it did not fall within the territory of a specific estate-owning group.

At the time of initial claim the Jawi population was a small population of about seventy people.[70] Most Jawi were intermarried with Bardi and lived in communities in Bardi country on the mainland. An exception was the outstation Nillargoon at Sunday Island, where Khaki Stumpagee, accompanied by various members of his family, spent much of his time. In the 1990s, some of the older Jawi spoke some Jawi, but all were more proficient in Bardi. According to Metcalfe (2000, p. 18), the two languages are more 'closely related' to each other than to other nearby languages, having much of their vocabulary in common. Interestingly, Bowern (2012, p. 5) indicates that the Bardi dialect was spoken in a number of regions in the north and east of the Dampier Peninsula, including the region she records as 'Iinalabooloo' [Inalabulu], which she describes as 'the close-in islands'. In relation to the decline of Jawi as a language, Bardi and

Jawi expressed the same view in very similar terms; that 'Bardi was too strong, it killed that Jawi language'. Part of the language's 'strength' was likely to have been the number of its speakers compared to the number of Jawi speakers, although today Bardi is also considered an endangered language. When writing his report for the Federal Court in 1999, and based on the genealogies, Bagshaw (1999, p. 12) estimated that the Bardi population was approximately 950 people. The number of Bardi speakers around this time, though, was considerably less. Metcalfe estimated there to be 350 Bardi speakers in 1975; in 2001, Bowern (2012, p. 5) estimated that there were 'no more than about 40' speakers, and in 2010 this had fallen to 'fewer than 5 fluent speakers', although a number of others 'have some familiarity' with Bardi.

More than a century ago, Campbell and Bird (1915, pp. 55, 58) referred to the Sunday Island population as 'Sunday Islanders' and described them as 'the furthest north-westerly branch of the "Barda" tribe that live on the Western side of King Sound'.[71] Robinson (1973) used various terms: 'Sunday Islanders' or 'the Islanders' to refer to Bardi, Jawi and others who came in to the mission at Sunday Island; 'Bardi and Djawi'; 'Bardi' as a gloss to indicate Bardi and Jawi; and 'Lombadina Bardi'. Based on his fieldwork with Sunday Islanders after the mission shut down in the late 1960s, Robinson's (1973, pp. 102–03) view was that 'there are enough similarities between the Bardi and Djawi...to regard them as socially and culturally homogeneous for most purposes'. As he described it, 'both share a similar cosmology and ritual, an identical kinship system save for minor differences in terminology, a like method of local organization into named patrilineal descent groups and a common maritime economy' (1973, p. 106). The high degree of social relatedness between Bardi and Jawi combined with historical factors derived from their shared experiences at Sunday Island mission were important factors leading to a native title claim being brought on behalf of both peoples. In his report for the court, Bagshaw (1999, p. 12) described Bardi and Jawi as 'peoples with distinct social, territorial and linguistic identities' who also 'view themselves as being closely linked by an extensive range of socio-cultural, economic and historical factors, many of which are regionally specific'.

Anthropological Contentions

Anthropologists contracted by respondent parties in native title cases do not have the opportunity to conduct fieldwork with the applicants. Rather, they rely wholly on the ethnographic record in providing their response to the applicants' anthropological evidence. In litigated cases, if they are present at the hearing, they will also have an opportunity to hear from the applicants directly. Of the anthropologists contracted by respondent parties in the Sampi case, only the State of Western Australia's anthropologist, Basil Sansom, was present in the Court for all of the applicants' evidence and the expert evidence. He was also the only one of the respondent's anthropologists who provided reports that became available to the applicants because they were filed in the court.

Sansom's (2000) preliminary report for the State of Western Australia was a response to Bagshaw's first anthropological report, dated February 1999. One of Sansom's primary arguments in this report was that landownership was vested at the level of distinct *buru* (estate groups), rather than at a larger jural, communal or societal level.

Elkin's (1933, p. 437) figure on the number of Bardi estates was forty-two; Robinson (1973, pp. 113–15) recorded forty-six Bardi estates, although he said that only fourteen of these were still associated with living people at the time of his research. Robinson (1973, pp. 113–15) also identified twelve Jawi estates, of which only eight were associated with living people, although three of these lay beyond the claim area. The number of extant estates identified in Bagshaw's reports differed from both of these. His conclusion was that there were nineteen extant Bardi *buru* and four extant Jawi *buru*, with a further six deceased estates

(estates without any living patrifiliates) within the Bardi and Jawi claim area (Bagshaw 2001a, p. 17). Bagshaw (1999, p. 54) thought that the discrepancy between his figures and those of earlier researchers was possibly a consequence of estate group names being 'inadvertently conflated' with the names of sites within them. The term *buru* is polysemic and can refer to a broader estate, a specific named site, or more generally to a camp, home or country, thus suggesting this as a possible explanation. Indeed, Bagshaw (1999, pp. 54–5) provided examples of where such conflation had occurred.

Sansom's argument about recognising landownership at the level of the estate appeared to be an argument the State of Western Australia and other respondent parties adopted. As Strelein (2006, p. 136) points out, it is a strategy often used by respondent parties; it has a number of advantages for arguing a case in an adversarial context. If the recognition of landownership in law were to occur at this level, evidence would have to be produced about every single *buru* in Bardi and Jawi country. If successfully argued that way, it would mean that the deceased estates (estates with no living members as identified in Bagshaw's anthropological reports) would be excluded from the determination. It would also provide the effective mechanism to exclude the *nimidiman* (the shared, pindan country that lies between estate groups).

One of the problems with the estate-by-estate approach is that, while individual assertions of rights in country are likely to be expressed in normative statements at the level of *buru*, these rights are culturally reproduced within a wider system that gives form to such local entitlements. An estate group cannot reproduce itself in social isolation but is system-dependent. Sutton (1996, p. 8) describes this as a 'whole-part dependency' in which the dependency is 'between particular rights and interests and the wider system of jural and cultural practices in which they are embedded'; 'between the rights and interests held in land or waters by subgroups or individuals, and the communal native title out of which they are "carved"'. Within the wider system, there are cultural mechanisms for deceased estates to be 'looked after', often by neighbouring estate groups. Over time, these custodial arrangements may lead to succession.

Jawi and the 'Piggyback' Premise

In his second preliminary report (Sansom 2001), a brief report of just eleven pages, Sansom's main focus was a critique of how the applicants' anthropological reports had dealt with possible differentiation between Bardi and Jawi laws and customs. He noted that the ethnographic archive mainly dealt with Bardi in contrast to Jawi, and this meant there was very little documentation of Jawi-specific traditions and customs. Given this, Sansom (2001, p. 1) argued that the applicants' anthropological reports should have documented Jawi ethnography separately; that they had 'conflated' Bardi and Jawi; that there should have been a comparative assessment of 'the extent to which the traditions and customs of the Bardi and Jawi correspond with or deviate from one another'. He wrote about the 'historical neglect of Jawi that needs to be repaired in the face of the ethnographic attention the Bardi have attracted over the years', a neglect that constituted a 'historical inequality'. The crux of Sansom's (2001, p. 2) critique was that 'the case for Jawi is made to ride "piggy back" on the Bardi ethnography'. Thus, Sansom (2001, p. 2) asked a question that appeared to inform the State of Western Australia's approach to the relationship between Bardi and Jawi throughout the case: 'to what extent is Jawi custom and tradition maintained today in its own right?'

During the course of our research Geoffrey Bagshaw and I were, in fact, acutely aware of the need for Jawi to be clearly represented. As the most senior Jawi man associated with Jawi country within the claim area, Khaki Stumpagee's evidence was of considerable importance, and for this reason a video recording of him being interviewed by Geoffrey Bagshaw at Sunday Island had been made.

Khaki's outstation, Nillargoon, was situated within his estate, Nilagunbur (after which the outstation was named) at Guwarngun. The film was made on the 16th July 1997. Professional filmmaker David Battye was contracted to shoot the video. The video was time-coded in order to demonstrate that the interview had not been edited. In the interview, Khaki talked about Jawi law and custom, and indicated a number of important places in the immediate vicinity: his own birthplace, the graves of his parents, a law ground and a site of mythological significance, for which he sang the associated song. The video provided important testimony that Jawi identity, connections to country and knowledge of it continued. Khaki was not confident of his speech in front of those he did not know, especially with *gardiya* (non-Indigenous persons, also called 'whitefellas'), in part because he had a stutter, but also because, as he put it, he was not a 'school man'. He was comfortable speaking with Geoffrey Bagshaw though; he had, by then, known him for some time. Speaking about his country on country also meant he could speak with the authority this context provided. Khaki did not know when he had been born, but we thought he was born in about 1924; he was recorded as 'Jambadji' or 'Jamadji' on Elkin's (1928) genealogies. Elkin recorded that Khaki's father Gagi was living at Guwarngun with his two wives, Polly Ninya and Lamburrgu, and he referred to Guwarngun as 'Cockie's camp' (after Gagi's name). The fact that Khaki had his outstation in the same area where Elkin had recorded his father living demonstrated continuity of connection to that part of the island in a highly specific way.

In his supplementary report to the court, Bagshaw listed numerous points to counter Sansom's critique that the anthropological reports for the applicants were making the Jawi case ride 'piggyback' on the Bardi case. These included that he had directly quoted Jawi individuals, and provided details of 'certain distinctly Jawi increase songs and mythologies' and 'extensive genealogical data for all Jawi people' (including those who country lay on the eastern side of the King Sound, outside the claim area);

Figure 11: Khaki Stumpagee and Geoffrey Bagshaw with nautical chart. Photo: Katie Glaskin (1997).

that he had 'recorded the spatial extent of Jawi territory'; that he had 'mapped the names and locations' of Jawi islands, estates, sites and marine features within Jawi country including currents, reefs and sandbars; and that, as well as identifying contemporary Jawi ritual leaders, he had recorded the interview with Khaki Stumpagee, who was at that time the most senior living Jawi person associated with that part of the claim area (Bagshaw 2001a, pp. 1–2). One of Sansom's (2001, p. 3) criticisms had been that Bardi language terms were made to represent 'Bardi and Jawi alike'; as Bagshaw (2001a, p. 2) responded, 'the difficulties in obtaining terms from a language which is no longer widely spoken should, I think, be obvious'.[72] Linguist Claire Bowern (2012, p. 7) writes that 'apart from a few words which people recognise as "islander" rather than "mainland"…there are today no clear features that distinguish the languages from each other', which is also suggestive of this difficulty. Sansom's criticism overlooked both that Jawi language terms had been specified in the reports where it had been possible, along with Bagshaw's (1999, p. 14; 2001b, p. 2) observation that 'most if not all, Jawi people...depending on age, [are] either fully or partly proficient in Bardi'.

At the time Bagshaw and Sansom were responding to each other's reports, the term 'society' had not yet entered into native title jurisprudence. Rather, what was required in native title was to show that those claiming native title had native title rights and interests that were held communally, or as a group or individual, and that these were 'possessed under the traditional laws acknowledged, and the traditional customs observed' (Section 223(1a) of the Native Title Act). Sansom (2001, p. 5) had asserted that Bagshaw's characterisation of Bardi and Jawi as a closely related community of kin amounted to 'a cognatic model of and for group association' in which 'patrifilial inheritance is demoted and Bardi plus some section of the Jawi are presented as the claimant group, members of which constitute a cognatic kindred'. This critique of Bardi and Jawi jointly holding native title would be one that the State of Western Australia's barrister would, many years later, raise in the Full Court appeal. As Bagshaw (2001, p. 5) presciently stated in his response to Sansom, though:

> To conclude that the Bardi and Jawi people constitute a single, regional community of kin based on inter-marriage is not to say that, at all levels of social and territorial identity, members of both people are, *ipso facto*, unable to mutually differentiate themselves.

Words, Facts, Fieldnotes

One core difference between anthropological and legal analyses is that the former treat ambiguity and complexity as immanent aspect of all real-life situations, while the latter seek to prune away 'extraneous' details, so as to identify the abstract, general, *de*-contextualised legal principles assumed to lie within (Good 2008, p. S51, original emphasis).

Psychologists tell us that knowledge consciously acquired is associated with a kind of memory that is explicit. This kind of knowledge may become less conscious as time goes by; it may become a kind of background knowledge, something we know without consciously thinking about the fact we know it or how it is we know it, becoming part of our implicit memory. Within this category of memory is what psychologists call procedural memory, a memory of how to do things, such as how to drive a car, and associative memory, in which associational networks are unconsciously activated.

The more time an anthropologist spends in a particular place or working with a particular group of people, the more some of the knowledge that they acquire moves into these implicit realms of knowledge and memory that inform both their interactions in the field, and their knowledge of it. Things an anthropologist comes to know well may become unremarkable, and hence no longer be recorded. Fieldnotes may become more minimalist. He or she becomes better able to contextualise information and observation; they will become a more fluent participant, more able to 'hear' what people have to say. Cultural patterns may begin to emerge, and different questions arise. The reading of one's own fieldnotes, then, is contextual, and is influenced by one's own progressive fieldwork experience. For these reasons, fieldnotes cannot record the entirety of all an anthropologist learns in the field. To a large extent, fieldnotes are mnemonics that assist the anthropologist to remember particular details, and complement what Ottenberg (1990) has referred to as 'headnotes': the information an anthropologist carries around in their head. Yet an anthropologist's fieldnotes, like the transcript of evidence, can assume extraordinary significance in a native title case. Often, they will form the basis of an anthropologist's cross-examination.

In native title, it has become fairly common for anthropologists conducting research to examine the fieldnotes of ethnographers who previously worked in the same area, where possible.[73] In native title cases, it has also become quite common for the fieldnotes of anthropologists who have prepared reports based on fieldwork to be subpoenaed by the Court. This would usually occur via the request of respondent parties who state they need to 'test' the basis on which an expert's opinions have been formulated. In February 2001, prior to the hearing of applicant evidence, Justice Beaumont directed the anthropologists to 'identify the information upon which they had relied in forming the opinions expressed in their reports and the processes of reasoning which led to their opinions'.[74] 'In particular', as Justice French stated, the anthropologists were asked to identify '(a) information taken into account but not specifically mentioned; (b) information rejected as unhelpful because it was unreliable or irrelevant'.[75] In short, what was being asked of the anthropologists was to identity every single piece of information ever acquired in the course of fieldwork. As Justice French summarised:

> The response from Mr Bagshaw in a letter dated 20 March 2001 was to the effect that he could not practically comply with the directions. He referred to various opinions which he had expressed in the report and said that they were based upon 'a consideration and appraisal of the whole of the information gathered during the course of my fieldwork'. To respond to the direction would require identification of 'hundreds if not thousands of individual items of information which either directly or indirectly informed the nine opinions referred to...'. It was 'in practical terms impossible' (*Sampi v State of Western Australia* [2005] FCA 777, at paragraph 790).

In the 2005 determination, Justice French would later agree that there are 'significant practical obstacles in requiring the proof of every item of factual material upon which opinions of this kind are based', and he pointed out that the anthropologists' conclusions would, in any case, be assessed against the applicants' evidence (*Sampi v State of Western Australia* [2005] FCA 777, at paragraph 803). It has now become common for anthropological reports submitted to the courts in native title cases, along with those prepared for the purposes of consent determinations, to identify (to the extent possible) the precise information upon which a particular opinion has been based, usually via a footnote for nearly every statement made that may reference fieldnotes along with published or other unpublished sources as well. This was not common practice at the time the reports in the Sampi case were being prepared; it is still not common practice in academic anthropology that one would reference statements made to one's fieldnotes, unless one is specifically quoting something they have been told. The transformation of anthropological reports to this kind of model is a consequence of objections raised to anthropological reports in several native title cases and the Federal Court's subsequent clarification of its requirements for expert reports in 2004 (Palmer 2016, p. xv), reinforced through the instructions of state governments who issue their own guidelines for how reports written for the purpose of consent determinations should be presented as well as what they should cover (for further analysis of state government guidelines for connection reports, see Ripper 2014). It represents a level of accountability for how an anthropologist forms an opinion in relation to every piece of data that most anthropologists writing in academic contexts will never encounter. It corroborates Burke's (2011, p. 24) thesis that 'when law interacts with anthropology…it is not in a dialogue, but an act of digestion, in which law converts anthropology into what it needs for its own functioning'.

Following the response that it would not be possible to identify every piece of information on which opinions had or had not been based, Geoffrey Bagshaw's and my fieldnotes were subpoenaed. This meant that at the commencement of the applicant evidence, the respondent parties, not the anthropologists, were in possession of the original field notebooks. This was somewhat unusual; normally the expert's fieldnotes would be subpoenaed prior to them giving evidence, in order to test what they had to say, rather than prior to the applicant evidence. The possible airing of information given in confidence in a public setting (the Court) and the treatment of highly confidential gender-restricted material were potential issues pre-trial fieldnote subpoena raised.

Respondent parties retained the original notebooks for a period of more than three weeks.[76] During discussions about their return, counsel for the Commonwealth – who indicated he had the notebooks – also indicated that one of my notebooks was then in the possession of the State's anthropologist, Basil Sansom.[77] Had this exchange not taken place we would not have been apprised of the fact that at least one of my field notebooks had been passed on to a respondent party's anthropologist (and given that it was Counsel for the Commonwealth – not the State of Western Australia – who identified this as being the case, one could infer it may not have been passed on by the party who had contracted him). This is perhaps one of the many unexpected facets of the legal process one may encounter as an anthropologist.

Following the applicants' submission that the anthropologist's fieldnotes should be returned to them, Justice Beaumont made an order allowing portions of the notes to be copied by the respondent parties, thus enabling the original notebooks to be returned. The Commonwealth indicated it wished to copy about twenty pages, and the Western Australian Fishing Industry Council indicated twenty to thirty pages.[78] Concerned about what would eventually happen to these photocopied notes and the use to which they might subsequently be put, the applicants' lawyer requested that these copied portions of the notes be returned at the conclusion of the case. Justice Beaumont made an order to this effect.[79] Despite that order, the copies of the notes remained with the respondent parties until well after the Full Federal Court appeal in February 2007, with no indication of their eventual return. Then solicitor for the applicants James Tapuelulu pursued the matter, and ultimately they were returned in late 2007, over six years after the copies had been made. When they were returned, the copied pages turned out to be rather more than the respondent parties had indicated: between the

Commonwealth and WAFIC, 316 pages of my fieldnotes were copied overall (rather than the combined maximum of fifty pages as indicated) and a 'substantial' number of pages of Geoffrey Bagshaw's notes were also copied.[80] The returned copies of our fieldnotes were highlighted in places by the respondent parties who copied them, providing an indication about the portions of the notes the respondents thought were important in some way. Some of these highlighted portions were used to cross-examine the anthropologists and some were used to question the applicants during the course of the trial.

Where reports by expert witnesses have been submitted into evidence, the authors of the reports will usually be cross-examined. In the single Noongar native title case (*Bennell v State of Western Australia* [2006] FCA 1243), historians submitting reports to the court (both for the applicants and for the respondents) were subject to extensive cross-examination, and this no doubt reflects the importance of the written historical records in this case. More typically in native title cases, though, it has been anthropologists who have experienced the most prolonged cross-examination. While cross-examination is supposed to be about testing the basis of the expert's opinions, because of the adversarial (rather than inquisitorial) nature of litigation, much cross-examination is oriented towards undermining witness credibility. While I am not in a position to refer to the highlighted portions of my colleague's fieldnotes, it is evident from the highlighted portions in my own, and from the transcript, that portions of my fieldnotes were drawn on and put to Geoffrey Bagshaw in the course of his lengthy cross-examination. As the senior researcher on the case and the author of the principal anthropological reports, he sustained four days of intensive questioning. As co-author of just one of the reports concerning sea and the genealogies, I was subject to far less intensive cross-examination: only half a day. (Notwithstanding this, after the first day of Geoffrey Bagshaw's evidence, I was still prohibited from being in the courtroom during his cross-examination). In some of the respondent party's final submissions to the court, there were instances where references to material contained in the anthropologists' fieldnotes were made.[81]

An examination of the respondents' photocopies of the anthropologists' fieldnotes in the Sampi case is interesting for what it reveals about the strategies respondent parties took to the central tenets of the case; but also, for what this reveals about their approach to anthropology. The highlighted portions, in combination with how these were used to inform cross-examination, suggest too that the anthropologists' fieldnotes were being treated much as a transcript might: that certain statements could be taken as standalone 'facts', without regard to the broader communicative (and recorded) context in which such statements were (partially) represented. An example of this in relation to my fieldnotes is evident in the transcript below:

> *Counsel (Cth):* Is there any – is it any part of an anthropologist's discipline to make data, in the way – let me start – my understand[ing] of science, generally, is that a researcher will record his data in a way that another researcher can review so as to test the conclusions. From what you're telling me now, I suggest to you that this data is totally unreviewable by anybody.
>
> *KG:* Well, if it was looked at in the light of the entirety of my fieldnotes and all the rest of the data, it would be reviewable, but it is a passage just taken out of context.[82]

Rosen (2008, p. 11) has argued that 'as category-creating creatures, we are constantly forging the units of our experience', and this means that facts, 'like anything else, must be fabricated, connected, rendered obvious'. For this reason, he argues, it is appropriate to talk about the law as something that 'creates facts', rather than as something that 'discovers or acknowledges them' (ibid.). These observations are germane to considerations of the way that 'facts' may be separated from their context to become standalone entities that can be read without context intruding on their interpretation.

With the benefit of hindsight it is apparent that certain issues were especially of interest to the parties who photocopied portions of the fieldnotes (WAFIC and the Commonwealth). Broadly summarised, these issues were to do with the south-eastern and south-western boundaries of the claim; with Jayirri and Jalan islands, which they would argue were Jawi; with the extent to which Bardi, especially people from the western side of the Dampier Peninsula, traditionally used mangrove log rafts; and with issues concerning ownership, rights and interests in the sea, with a focus on *jarrayn* (deep sea) and Juljinabur (Brue Reef). These all emerged as issues over the course of the litigation.

Chapter Six

In the Court

In claims touching on native title the best evidence lies in the hearts and minds of the people most intimately connected to aboriginal [sic] culture, namely the aboriginal people themselves. Expert evidence from anthropologists and others is of significance and due regard must, and will, be afforded to it. However, it seems to me that the full story lies in the hearts and minds of the people. It is from there that it must be extracted. This is not always easy, particularly from a people whose primary language may not be English and who, historically, have depended on oral rather than written recording of tradition (Justice Owen, in *Ejai v Commonwealth*, unreported, Supreme Court of Western Australia, No. 1744 of 1993, 18 March 1994).

Evidence

In the documentary *Gulpilil: One Red Blood* (Johnson 2002), the famous Aboriginal actor David Gulpilil explains how when a director first approached him to appear in a movie he did not speak English. The director asked him his name, and, as Gulpilil recounts this incident for the camera, his response to this question was 'yes'. The director asked him again what his name was, and again Gulpilil responded with the answer 'yes'. Then, as Gulpilil describes it, the director said to him, 'really, really, what is your name?' Once again Gulpilil responded 'yes'. When I have shown this documentary to visiting Kimberley friends, it is this scene, and the scene in which the men go hunting for a fish but then shoot rather than spear the fish, that elicits the greatest appreciative response; peals of laughter. The fish shooting incident seems to spark the response because of its obvious inversion of the 'traditionality' Aboriginal people are supposed to exhibit, while Gulpilil's account of not understanding English, and responding with the word 'yes', clearly struck a chord. While an examination of the Sampi transcript does not especially reveal similar instances of what Liberman (1985) has referred to as 'gratuitous concurrence' – responding to questions that are not well understood by answering 'yes' in order to appease the interlocutor – it does show that many instances of mutual incomprehension between lawyers and indigenous witnesses occurred.

One of the most significant factors affecting Aboriginal evidence in native title cases is the formal and foreign nature of the litigated environment. The importance of trying to foster the right conditions for native title applicants to give their evidence is foreshadowed by decades of research showing that many Aboriginal people do not, generally, fare well in litigation.[83] Much of this research has referred to criminal cases, but similar communication issues have appeared in land claims litigation, as Williams (1986, pp. 166, 170) ably illustrated with reference to *Milirrpum v Nabalco Pty Ltd* (1971) 17 FLR 141, the Yolngu case that prefigured the introduction of statutory land rights legislation in the Northern Territory. The Federal Court has been aware of this, and two of its most significant innovations in recent years, directly related to facilitating Aboriginal evidence in native title cases, have been to allow the hearing of evidence 'on country' and to allow applicants to sit in groups when they give evidence. 'On country' evidence includes evidence given on site, whether in the bush, on an island, or from a boat at sea, as in the Sampi case; but it may also include giving evidence in a community hall, at a local park under a shade cloth, or at some other community locality. This is a significant innovation for, rather than have the applicants fly to the nearest capital city to appear in a courtroom, it has been possible in many cases for applicants to remain within their communities and on country during the majority of the hearing of a native title case, making them, in theory at least, more at ease with the situation.

The provision for on country evidence in Aboriginal land claims followed an imprimatur set under the Commonwealth *Aboriginal Land Rights (Northern Territory) Act 1976* (ALRA). In these cases, hearings were held before a Land Commissioner, who, along with claimants, land council representatives (the lawyers, anthropologists and others involved in the case) travelled to various sites where witnesses gave testimony about those sites and associated aspects of their tenure systems.[84] If the best evidence for native title lies in the hearts and minds of the Aboriginal applicants, then the rationale for on country evidence is that this evidence has the best opportunity of being brought out when Aboriginal claimants are in the country about which they can authoritatively speak. In the Neowarra native title case, barrister for the applicants Robert Blowes cross-examined anthropologist Basil Sansom (anthropologist for the State of Western Australia) about this very matter:

Counsel (Apps):...you regard it as an essential – you regard it as important to see Aboriginal witnesses on their country don't you?

Basil Sansom: It makes a difference.

Counsel (State of WA): I object, your Honour, unless the question is made more specific. Important in what terms? It's a relative question and has to have something that it's relating to.

Counsel (Apps): You would agree, would you not, that there is a vast difference between the story told on site and the story concerning land that's told while the speaker is away from his or her country?

Basil Sansom: Absolutely.

Counsel (Apps): In fact you've said so in paragraph 27 of your first report. Indeed you've said that anthropologists all agree with such a proposition.

Basil Sansom: They probably all do.[85]

At the Directions Hearing prior to the Sampi trial, the State of Western Australia sought to have the claim heard within the Broome courthouse, some 200 kilometres distant from the main communities in the claim area. Following their submission, then trial judge Justice Beaumont asked the lawyers representing the applicants to provide reasons as to why their evidence should be heard on country. In this case, both the state and the trial judge initially employed the rationale that, within the Federal Court jurisdiction, cases should be heard in court. As well as following 'procedure', this reasoning can be understood as reflecting a liberal democratic ideology that citizens of the nation-state should be treated 'equally'. The motion by the Western Australian government that the claim be heard within the Broome courthouse was not successful. In litigated native title cases, on country evidence is now considered a normal procedure.[86]

Another issue affecting claimant evidence is the adversarial environment. With regard to the possibilities of developing a less adversarial approach, Connolly (2010, p. 211) has observed that 'fairness concerns' to parties who 'may want to test the reliability of that evidence in the crucible of strong cross-examination currently serve as a significant constraint on reformist tendencies'. One effect of this 'testing' is that it has the capacity to create the conditions to cast doubt on the reliability of the evidence or the witness providing it, and this then feeds into submissions placed before the judge about how much weight should be given to particular evidence vis-à-vis other evidence or the overall case. The transcript in the Sampi case reveals that in some cases the cross-examination of Aboriginal applicants effectively undermined the certainty or clarity of original responses to questions earlier put to them.

The Trial Begins

The opening submissions in the Sampi case were presented in a conference room in the Mercure Inn in Broome. Many of the applicants travelled the 200 kilometres down to Broome from their communities on the peninsula to attend, staying in accommodation organised by the land council. There was a large attendance at the court on that first day; the room reserved for the hearing was full. Some of the applicants, who had no intention of going inside, waited outside to talk to others who ventured inside.

The applicants who came into the room sat solemnly through the opening submissions. As the submissions went on, some of the formality of the context began to wane. People tired, and some fell asleep. The lawyerly English of the opening submissions was alienating, and the formal requirements of the courtroom, such as having to bow towards the judge whenever one entered or left the room, were foreign. Some people began to drift in and out for a smoke. Outside the designated legal space, conversations were going on about what was occurring inside: about what kinds of people these lawyers appeared to be (amongst the men, such conversations concerned whether they seemed like a 'good bloke', for example). As various legal personnel were introduced to them in tea breaks, there was careful scrutiny of people's apparent character on the basis of acute observation of their behaviour towards others, including their interactions with the applicants themselves. In the midst of these initial observations, claimants, too, were trying to work out what 'side' the lawyers were on; who they were acting for, and whether this compromised their apparent character in any way. The judge was the most significant amongst those whose character they sought to assess on the basis of observed behaviour. For many Bardi and Jawi people, he was analogous to a senior lawman in their own society and deserved the respect attending such a status. They were intensely interested in working out what kind of a person he was. Before the trial we had heard that the judge was interested in sailing, that he had some kind of affinity for the sea. Would this assist him in understanding Bardi and Jawi relationships to sea?

During the opening submissions several maps were presented to the court. These included a land map showing the various tenures of land on the northern Dampier Peninsula and Bardi named sites and places on that land, as well as a large Royal Australian Navy Buccaneer Archipelago and King Sound Chart (Reference Aus733) showing Bardi and Jawi locations in the sea and on islands (the 'sea map'). The sea map, prepared by Geoffrey Bagshaw on the basis of information provided by a number of Bardi and Jawi applicants, documented all the indigenous names of the islands in the King Sound Area, together with the names of islets, rocks, reefs and sandbanks, and all of the names and directions of the currents that lay in between. The map also showed the *numurr* routes traditionally used by Bardi and Jawi to 'cross over' from one side of the King Sound to the other, and to travel between the islands. As Greg McIntyre (then barrister for the applicants) indicated, the sea map covered an area larger than the area of the claim because there was 'no cultural delineation defined by this line here'.[87] The 'line' he referred to was the boundary between the Sampi claim and the adjoining Mayala claim. As he described it, 'that line there was a matter of historical convenience at the time to draw a distinction between those who had chosen to be represented by the solicitors who instructed me at the time and those at the time who were not'.[88] This line separated Jawi whose territorial interests lay on the western side of the Sunday Strait from those whose country lay to its east. Even so, Jawi people from both sides of King Sound were to give evidence during the course of the hearing.

The map represented an extensive knowledge of the marine geography of the King Sound region. This map itself, minus the annotations, was treated as an Exhibit. The annotations on the maps needed to be proven during the applicant evidence before the annotated map could be tendered to the Court. While much of the evidence corroborating the named currents and islands on this map was elicited over the course of the 'first trial', the annotated map was not formally admitted into evidence.[89]

During the opening submissions video evidence was also presented to the court. The first was a video that Bardi man Frank Davey had filmed of unrestricted parts of initiation ceremonies at One Arm Point in about 1998 or 1999.[90] Specifically, it showed aspects of Anggwuy, the first part of the initiation ceremony, and Nguril, the ceremony held when the boys emerge from the bush, after their initiation. These ceremonies are 'open' and therefore could be shown in public, and contrast with 'closed' ceremonies which are restricted according to gender and stage of initiation. In the course of his evidence explaining what was happening on the video to the court, asked by the barrister whether Anggwuy was a 'Jawi ceremony or a Bardi ceremony'; Frank Davey's response was 'it's a Bardi Jawi ceremony. It's belong to both'.[91] The video showed the court how the Bardi and Jawi regional aggregates were geographically and socially positioned in relation to one another; how, when the boys emerge from the bush during the Nguril ceremony, they have to go and sit in the regional aggregate of their *jawul* (ritual guardian). The regional aggregates were represented in sequence, in the Baniol (east), Olonggon (south, sometimes called Guwalgarda), Gularrgon (west), Adiol (north), Inalabulu (islands adjacent to One Arm Point), Iwanyun (Sunday Island region), and Mayalayun (eastern King Sound) areas. This could be seen on the video, and Frank Davey provided an explanation of it to the court.

A second video shown was another Bardi production, demonstrating the customary way of butchering *odorr* (dugong).[92] As well as being screened to illustrate the continuation of the practice, the video was shown to elicit commentary about how the various (named) cuts of meat were distributed amongst kin; with the hunter's *jawul*, his ritual guardian, being entitled, before others, to his favourite portion. Julum (the island just off the coast of One Arm Point also known by the English name of Middle Island) appeared in this video and Greg McIntyre, the applicants' barrister, asked Aubrey Tigan, the witness commenting on the video, whether it belonged to any *buru* (estate group). Aubrey responded that it was 'normally connected to One Arm Point'.[93] In the third video shown, an excerpt from the Malcolm Douglas (1991) movie *Follow the Sun*, Jawi man Tommy Thomas (who had died some ten years prior to this) could be seen making a mangrove log raft at Biyana (the Waterlow Islands).[94] This video, like the one containing the ceremonial footage, showed people who had passed away, causing some people to put their heads in their hands. Seeing dead people, kin relations, made many feel 'sorry'. Another video showed the remaining seven minutes of Jackson's 1917 footage, *Chez Les Sauvages Australiens* (1932).[95] This was film taken during E. J. Stuart's Nor' West Scientific Expedition of Western Australia of 1917. Smith (1996, p. 30) draws on Stuart (1923) to identify the people in the segment as 'Sunday Island people', and writes that 'Bardi elders who have seen a copy of this film in the early 1990s felt that the images were suitable for viewing'. In proofing, Jimmy Ejai had identified the ceremony shown in this footage as a Bardi ceremony; in evidence, he changed his view, stating that it was from the eastern side of the King Sound. It is not clear why he changed his mind about the images, although one cannot discount the legal environment in which he was giving his evidence as a factor.

A further video shown during the opening submissions was the one in which Geoffrey Bagshaw interviewed Khaki Stumpagee at his outstation, Nillargoon, in 1997, four years before the commencement of the trial. The outstation's name is derived from the name of the broader estate in which it is situated, Nilagun, on Sunday Island. The video was unedited and time-coded. To assist the court in understanding Khaki's English as well as the language terms he used in the interview, I transcribed the interview and Geoffrey Bagshaw transcribed the songs that were sung during the course of the interview. Given that the court had copies of the transcript of this video, the respondent parties contended it was unnecessary to take up the court's time actually viewing the video: the video and transcript could simply be tendered as evidence. The barrister acting for the Commonwealth argued that because the video was an interview it was 'simply dialogue', and this meant the transcript was not just the 'important thing' (as Justice Beaumont put it to him), but that it was 'the only thing really. What was said is the only part of that video which is of any relevance'.[96] In response, the barrister acting for the applicants noted the video was 'not just dialogue; it is, in fact, pointing out places'.[97] What was also important was the film location itself, Nilagunbur on Sunday Island.

The discussion about whether the court needed to view the video or whether it could satisfy itself with just reading the transcript is indicative of the reliance placed upon words in legal proceedings such as these. It is the transcript of evidence, the words recorded when witnesses provide evidence-in-chief and in cross-examination, which judges refer to in making their evaluation of the evidence. Of course, communication is far more than words, and, especially in the context of evidence given on-country, where witnesses refer to particular sites, where they point out places, things, and people, the nature of the evidence given is far more than the sum of the words in the transcript. While a judge obviously relies on the transcript, it would be reasonable to suggest that their reading and comprehension of the transcript would be mediated by and through their own experience and memory, visual and otherwise, of the larger context in which the evidence was given and to which they were present. The cognitive relationship between experience and memory, and the ways humans draw upon these in subsequent experience and evaluations, is attested to in the scientific literature on memory (for example, see Solms & Turnbull 2002).

In this instance, the court was persuaded to view the video interview between Geoffrey Bagshaw and Khaki Stumpagee. In it, Khaki Stumpagee demonstrated how Jawi would rub a particular root on their feet to protect their feet when walking on the reefs; he sang songs associated with mythological sites, while

121

indicating where those sites were (for example, Bulgun hill in his own estate); he pointed out the graves of his parents, the place where he was born, the old law ground at Nilagun, which he had placed a 'do not enter' sign next to, and so on. As this indicates, the video, like much of the other evidence heard in this case, was more than simply the transcript of its words.

Once the video evidence began to be shown, and the applicants themselves began to give evidence, claimant interest in the goings on of the trial palpably increased. This was a careful surveillance as to whether others were making the right moves, saying the right things. Were they talking themselves up? Were they only representing themselves and their family? How did what the witness have to say accord with other people's understandings of the same thing? Following the evidence, at the tea and lunch breaks, there was much backstage discussion about the performances of those who gave evidence in the trial, about what they had said, and such discussions continued throughout the hearing. On the evening of the second day of the opening

Figure 12: Photo of David Battye filming Geoffrey Bagshaw interviewing Khaki Stumpagee at Sunday Island, 16 July 1997. Photo: Katie Glaskin.

submissions in Broome, the land council put on a barbecue for the applicants, as a large number of people were away from their homes on the peninsula. I attended, and later noted the reaction of one of the Bardi elders to the video of Khaki Stumpagee at Sunday Island. He said that he 'really liked' the video; he thought that Khaki might 'win' Sunday Island for them. He pointed out it was neap tide when the video was taken – you could tell, he said, otherwise the reef would have been dry.[98]

Contentions and Their Effects

As would be expected in an adversarial case, the trial began with a number of issues in contention. Respondent parties made submissions about several aspects of the case. One of these was centred on continuity of connection; it was argued that there was no evidence of people occupying their *buru* since 1971. This was the year when ex–Sunday Island mission residents who had returned to Sunday Island from Derby had shifted from Sunday Island to Malumb, near One Arm Point. At this time in native title law, continuous physical occupation was still an issue in establishing continuity of 'connection'. This issue was clarified the year after the 2001 evidence in the Sampi case. The High Court decision in *Western Australia v Ward* [2002] HCA 28 ('Ward') handed down on 8 August 2002 said it was not necessary for native title applicants to show continuing physical occupation or use of all parts of the land and waters claimed; instead, what they needed to demonstrate was continuing *connection*.[99] What applicants needed to demonstrate, then, was ongoing connection to the land, with connection itself depending on the laws and customs of the applicant group. Connection, as clarified by Ward, could include 'spiritual connection'.

At the time of the 2001 evidence, though, this issue had not yet been clarified, and an orientation towards continuity in terms of physical occupation is reflected in much of the early evidence led in the 'first trial' of the Sampi case. Greg McIntyre, counsel representing the applicants, spent considerable time talking to people about how they had built outstations in their country, or visited their country to go fishing, hunting, collecting bush foods and medicines and so on, these queries being aimed at establishing continuity of occupation. This evidence about physical occupation was in direct response to the State's contentions that continuity of connection was an issue in this case.

The other main issues in contention were the recognition of native title offshore; the ongoing existence of a Jawi community; and the identification of Middle Island (Julum), Jackson Island (Jayirri) and Tallon Island (Jalan) as Bardi islands (respondent parties contended that they were Jawi). Their contention about the islands extended the area they suggested was identified with Jawi, and was associated with the question of whether a Jawi community continued to exist. If successful, this strategy would effectively eliminate all of the offshore islands within the claim area from a determination of native title.

Before the trial began, it became evident that the Common-wealth was going to contend that Jawi, as a community, were 'extinct', a position that emerged through a pre-trial mediation offer. This assertion was linked to a small portion of transcript from another native title case, Ngarluma/Yindjibarndi (*Daniel v State of Western Australia* [2003] FCA 666), in which anthropologist Michael Robinson had appeared as an expert witness on behalf of the applicants. In that case, Robinson, who had done research amongst Bardi and Jawi for his (1973) Master's thesis, had been cross-examined by barrister Ken Pettit, who was also acting for the Commonwealth in that case. This cross-examination in 2000 preceded the opening of the Sampi trial by just under a year. The Native Title Act (S223.1) refers to 'the communal, group or individual rights and interests' held by Indigenous Australians in land or waters. As a consequence of the word 'communal', applicants in early native title cases tended to orient their cases towards demonstrating that they were a community of native title holders. Under cross-examination, Robinson was asked his opinion about how much land was required to 'sustain' a 'tribal identity', which, given Robinson's previous experience, led to a discussion about Bardi and Jawi. On being asked about the population of Jawi at the time of his fieldwork, and no doubt under the pressure of intense cross-examination, Robinson responded that they were 'virtually extinct', that they were not an identifiable community.[100] This statement appeared to have informed the Commonwealth's pre-trial position about the existence of a Jawi community.

Contentions about Jawi being extinct as a community were, in turn, closely linked to the question of whether native title rights extended into the sea. The Yarmirr case, otherwise known as the Croker Island case (*Yarmirr v Northern Territory* [2001] HCA 56), was the first native title case to be heard in relation to the existence of native title offshore, and at the time of the 2001 evidence in the Sampi case, was reserved before the High Court.[101] In other words, the case had gone to trial before a single judge of the Federal Court; the determination of this court had been appealed to the Full Court; and the Full Court decision had been appealed to the High Court of Australia. Yarmirr set an important precedent concerning the recognition of native title rights offshore. The High Court found that native title existed offshore, but since native title had to coexist with the public right to fish and the right to navigate, the common law could not recognise an exclusive possession form of native title offshore. The Croker Island decision was handed down in 2001, but this only occurred after the 2001 Sampi evidence had been heard. What this meant was that, at the time of the Sampi hearing, the question about the recognition of native title offshore had not yet been decided in native title jurisprudence.

The ethnographic literature from the region readily demonstrated that people from the northern Dampier Peninsula and King Sound region had a form of watercraft, mangrove log rafts that they used over extensive distances to travel between the islands (e.g., Stokes 1846, p. 35; Campbell & Bird 1915, p. 57;

Davidson 1935b, pp. 142–43; Akerman 1975). In his first report to the court, Bagshaw (1999, p. 127) wrote that 'other forms of sea transport included dugout canoes...floating logs and swimming'.[102] Bardi and Jawi described the dugout canoes called *barrawarr* or *inbargun* (the latter meaning 'coolamon'), as a relatively recent technology acquired through trading with people on the eastern side of the King Sound.[103] Crawford (2001, p. 87) suggests that the term *barawa* (clearly related to *barrawarr*) is derived from a Malay dialect; canoes were initially acquired from Indonesian fishermen as gifts and through exchange or theft, and were subsequently made by Aboriginal people themselves (Crawford 2001, p. 87). In a 1935 publication, Davidson drew on earlier reports to conclude that the canoe was in the process of diffusion, and that 'in less than a century' the use of the dugout canoe in northern Australia had 'diffused westward for a distance of over six hundred miles' (Davidson 1935a, p. 77). He wrote:

> I have been informed by Mr Laves that the natives of Sunday Island, King Sound, about 100 miles to the south [of the Prince Regent River, which Davidson understood to be as far west as the canoe was found at the time], know of its use. It will be interesting to learn whether this southern and western trend of diffusion will bring this type of craft into the King Sound region within the next few years (Davidson 1935a, p. 77).

Oral accounts about people leaving Wotjulum on the east coast of the King Sound in both canoes and rafts following the failed relocation of Sunday Island mission suggest that Bardi and Jawi had adapted canoe technology by at least 1937. Under the Native Title Act, the date from which Aboriginal laws and customs need to be shown to be continuous is the date on which the British Crown acquired sovereignty. Because of its recent provenance, then, the use of the canoe was not an issue in this case: it was clearly a post-sovereignty technology. Rather, attention was directed towards the mangrove log rafts (referred to as *biel-biel* in Jawi; *galwa* in Bardi; and *galu* in Bard), which Bardi and Jawi maintained have 'originated in their own territory in ancient times' (Bagshaw 1999, p. 127). As Jimmy Ejai put it, 'always had *galwa*. *Milonjunu*. From the beginning. *Galwa* story we had always, some used to swim, some had *galwa*, from the beginning' (personal communication 11 July 1997). Akerman's (1975) comparison of the double raft used by Bardi and Jawi with those used by Worrora on the eastern side of the King Sound indicates Bardi and Jawi rafts were unique. Akerman (1975, p. 22) noted the difference between the two kinds of double rafts was that Bardi and Jawi used 'wooden pins to join the two sections' of the rafts together.

Dampier had written that the people of the region 'have no Boats, Canoes, or Bark-logs' (1937 [1697], p. 315). Tindale (1974, p. 147) stated that Bardi only discovered 'mandijlal poles' (one of the light woods used for making rafts) at Goodenough Bay in

Figure 13: Paddling a mangrove log raft. Source: Porteus (1931, p. 63).

'post contact times'. But this is not the same as saying that Bardi did not have rafts prior to contact, as Tindale's earlier (1953a) notes make clear. Tindale (1953a, p. 768) wrote that Bardi 'got their rafts from the Djau: who live on Sunday Island but who have no light mangroves themselves, having to trade with people from the east'. It was in 'post-European times' that the right kind of light mangrove wood was found growing at Goodenough Bay (Tindale 1953a, p. 768). His notes thus indicate that, prior to this time, Bardi traded with Jawi who in turn traded with their neighbours to the east. Nevertheless, these statements laid the foundations for respondent parties to contend that Bardi had acquired rafts from Jawi following the establishment of Sunday Island mission. The point of this argument was to say that Bardi use of mangrove log rafts was not a 'tradition' capable of being recognised by native title, since it was a post-contact phenomenon; that only Jawi had traditionally used these rafts. When this perspective was combined with their contention that the Jawi community was extinct, evidence about the use of marine technology by either group would potentially become of little assistance in establishing native title offshore.

With these contentions in mind, it is apparent just how important the Jawi evidence in this case would be. For this reason, the video interview between Geoffrey Bagshaw and Khaki Stumpagee at Sunday Island later came under sustained interrogation during Bagshaw's expert evidence in the Federal Court.[104] Bagshaw stated the following during this examination:

> The significance of the interview to the case, your Honour, in my estimation, was Mr Stumpagee specifically talking about Nilagunbur, his connection to it, who could speak for the *bur* itself; also other parts of Sunday Island. I had deemed it not relevant, since he'd previously told me about resource usage and that turtles were, as it were, open game in the – the *jarrayn*, in the deep water, to mention that in an interview specifically focusing on Nilagunbur.[105]

In later submissions, the Commonwealth would assert that 'the video did not, as might have been expected, give all the relevant material', arguing that because of the focus on Nilagun other information that Khaki Stumpagee could have provided was being excluded, and claiming that 'only favourable material was elicited for the video' (Commonwealth of Australia 2003, pp. 16–17). The degree to which the video came under attack during the submissions and the extent of Geoffrey Bagshaw's cross-examination in relation to it is suggestive of its value to the applicants' case.

Once the opening submissions had been completed in Broome, the rest of the applicant evidence was heard 'on country'. Kimberley Land Council personnel involved in the claim, the solicitor and the field and project officers for the claim (who had the task of managing claimant logistics) stayed in a house at One Arm Point that the community had made available, as did the applicants' barrister and anthropologists. One accommodation option available to the judge and the lawyers acting for the respondents was the Bardi-owned tourist destination of Kooljaman. This would have meant being able to drive a fairly short distance to and from the hearing each day. Instead, they stayed 200 kilometres away in hotels in Broome, arriving and departing every day in small chartered aircraft. These arrangements had logistical effects on the conduct of the hearing. The chartered flight to Broome takes about fifty minutes from One Arm Point; but light aircraft such as these could not fly after dark, and so had to arrive in Broome prior to nightfall. This significantly curtailed the time available per day of the hearing, especially in the case of the evidence heard at the Jawi island of Iwanyi (Sunday Island), but also in relation to evidence heard about other offshore islands.

On Country Evidence

For many Aboriginal people, there are constraints on what can be said and in front of whom, arising from various factors including kinship, gender, knowledge and authority (along with stages of initiation). Sutton (2001, p. 11) has explained that 'the right to speak for country', the 'right to speak authoritatively for an area', is a core right that directly reflects a person's affiliation to, and rights in, country. It is for this reason that witnesses in the trial were primarily asked to speak about their own estates *(buru)* and that the court was asked to travel to the different *buru* where evidence could be given by those most closely associated with them.

Along with discomfort created through the formal legal environment, something 'on country' evidence cannot entirely ameliorate, Aboriginal evidence and how it comes to be understood is impacted by the way that questions are asked, how a witness understands the question asked, how responses are understood, and how these responses are followed up or not followed up by counsel leading the evidence, or by counsel cross-examining. For many Aboriginal claimants, there is also a disjunction between a legal context in which information needs to be provided rapidly in response to directed questions 'one time' rather than progressively revealed and accumulated as is more in accordance with customary norms.[106] In addition, while for legal representatives it is important to try to get witnesses to corroborate each other's information, because of constraints on people's ability to speak about *buru* other than their own, witnesses were often uncomfortable responding to such questions. Consistency of responses is an evidentiary issue: and the 'test' of consistency is ultimately applied across the evidence given, in total, by all the applicants. This is one of the difficulties inherent in native title litigation. In order to establish a 'system of law and custom' giving rise to rights and interests in lands and waters, it is necessary to hear from a significant array of witnesses who, because of constraints on their right to speak about areas of country for which they do not hold primary responsibility, may not be able to provide corroborative evidence about specific places mentioned by other witnesses. This important dimension of knowledge as a form of property is unlikely to be one that respondent parties are concerned with when they assemble their submissions to the judge on the basis of transcript.[107] Nor is this a matter that is always taken into consideration when judges evaluate witness evidence. Linguist Frances Morphy has noted that:

> The Australian court system has an elaborate set of rules for proper discourse, in which different actors have different roles according to their status and function…The discourse rules are well understood and are manipulated (with varying degrees of subtlety) by the actors in the court who have legal training, but they are not transparent to, nor are they explicitly laid out for, the 'lay' actors – the witnesses – who must attempt to learn the rules as they go along (Morphy 2007, p. 35).

Among the rules Morphy (2007, pp. 35–6) identifies is the fact that the applicants' barrister 'is bound by the rules of evidence to act "as if" he knew nothing, because he may not ask leading questions – that is, he may not ask questions that contain knowledge that he and the applicants know that they all hold in common'. In contrast,

> The counsel acting for the respondents are free to ask leading questions if they so wish, and are not confined to leading evidence from the witness statements. They may even, as a tactic, pose questions that are deliberately founded on ignorance or wilful misunderstanding of the facts (Morphy 2007, p. 37).

On the first day of on country evidence at Djarindjin, Counsel for the Commonwealth sought to cross-examine one of the applicants on the basis of something that one of the other applicants had said to the anthropologists.[108] One of the important things to note about the exchange that followed is that Counsel for the Commonwealth had found the information on which he wished to cross-examine recorded in the anthropologist's fieldnotes. Counsel for the Applicants, on the other hand, had not seen the anthropologists' fieldnotes and had no idea of the context from which the question had been derived. When questioned further about this, the Counsel for the Commonwealth indicated that what he was seeking to do was to establish the 'weight' that should be given to one witness's evidence in relation to another witness's evidence. Justice Beaumont's decision to allow such questions in order to establish weight meant that applicants were, on occasion, being asked about something they, or others, may have told the anthropologists as long ago as six or seven years earlier, thus adding to the already significant communicative burden posed by the adversarial and foreign legal environment.[109]

Gender-restricted Evidence

Bardi and Jawi senior ritual experts (known as 'Lawmen', 'bosses' or *madjamadjin*) hold esoteric knowledge and have defined roles and responsibilities within the ritual sphere. Certain elements of male-only gender-restricted evidence had important bearing on the Bardi and Jawi claim to offshore areas. Cognisant of the importance of this evidence for their claim, senior Bardi and Jawi Lawmen decided that they were prepared to give gender-restricted (male-only) evidence within the native title hearing, subject to certain conditions. The first and most obvious of these was that they were only prepared to speak of these matters to men. Second, and understanding that a transcript of the evidence would have to be prepared, they sought an undertaking from the court that the restricted transcript would only be accessible to those who had been present during the giving of the restricted evidence. That is, they did not want the transcript being passed on to anyone not present during the hearing; consistent with their traditions, they were only prepared to pass this information on to men whom they could see 'face-to-face'.

Early on in the trial an issue arose concerning how widely this gender-restricted transcript could be disseminated, with the Commonwealth and WAFIC seeking access to the restricted transcript for the anthropologists who were advising them. The issue arose because unlike the State of Western Australia, neither the Commonwealth nor WAFIC had their anthropologists present for the hearing of evidence. One of the senior Bardi men was called as a witness and testified that if the transcript were to be given to men who were not present at the hearing, they could get sick and die. In his words, 'well, that's breaking our Law. It's like taking away the Judge's book and ripping it up and chucking it in the fire. It's as bad as that'.[110] Balanced against the claimants' concerns was the 'convenience and cost' to the Commonwealth and Western Australian Fishing Industry Council (WAFIC) who wanted their anthropologists to read the transcript later. As counsel for the Commonwealth stated, their anthropologist was not present because it was a matter of 'simply expense, your Honour'.[111] Balancing these arguments from the Commonwealth and WAFIC against those of the applicants, Justice Beaumont issued an interlocutory order that the restricted-evidence transcript could be passed on to their respective anthropologists who would not be present during the hearing of the gender-restricted evidence.

The senior Lawmen (and other Bardi present) were visibly disturbed by this order, shaking their heads and murmuring loudly, evidently distressed that the courts could require them to do something that was against their own Law. This seemed particularly problematic given they were in the midst of a hearing about their native title claim (based on their own 'laws and customs'). In the light of this order, the senior men met during an adjournment and deliberated over whether they should abort the trial altogether, since pursuing a native title determination was not worth the damage they would incur if their Law was broken. Pragmatically, they finally decided they had come this far, and would continue with the trial; but, under these circumstances, they were not prepared to give gender-restricted evidence. If culturally restricted information could not be protected and respected in their terms, the information would not be revealed. This was a decision not taken lightly, for some of this restricted or 'inside' information was important to the offshore component of their case. It seemed to me that, from this point on, the claimants' attitude towards the hearing was significantly tempered by this event.

On appeal, Justice Beaumont eventually revised his inter-locutory order, such that the restricted-evidence transcript would not be sent to persons absent from the restricted hearings. The Bardi and Jawi men subsequently decided they were prepared to give restricted evidence under these circumstances, and did so in the course of the hearing. This reversal did not, however, lessen the degree to which the claimant group already felt betrayed by a process purporting to recognise their 'laws and customs'. At the application of the Commonwealth in the closing submissions of the second trial, some of the restricted evidence was subsequently de-restricted. While these de-restricted passages were not extensive,[112] the fact that gender-restricted evidence can be de-restricted points to its inherent vulnerability in cases such as these.

Island and Sea Evidence

One of the logistical issues affecting the on country hearings was the scheduling of the hearing. May and June are not good months to go out on boats in the north-west Kimberley, as was required during the hearing in order to reach various islands and to hear evidence about them. Those months are when the strong south-east winds blow; a time of year Bardi call *bardunu*. Because of the winds, the sea can become extremely rough. When the dates for the hearing were being set, land council staff had suggested this was not the optimum time to access offshore sites for evidence, but the court's scheduling requirements appear to have meant this could not be given full consideration.

When the time for hearing evidence about the islands arrived, the conditions at sea were exceptionally rough. On the day the applicants intended to lead a full day of evidence from Jimmy Ejai, the most senior Bardi man for Jayirri (Jackson Island), the charter boats, which were both anchored in the shelter of Catamaran Bay, had to face 3.5 metre swells rounding the point to pick up the parties to the claim. The captains of the boats described these conditions as 'life-threatening', saying it was 'touch and go' as to whether they could make it or not. Accordingly, rather than launching the boats at 8.30 in the morning, it was midday before the court was able to set off, thereby cutting short Jimmy Ejai's evidence on country by half a day. The court first travelled to Julum (Middle Island) where Jimmy Ejai gave evidence about Galalung, whose fossilised footprint is sedimented into the rock there.

In his evidence, Jimmy Ejai stated that Galalung first came to Julum (Middle Island), a Bardi place, before going to Sunday Island, which is Jawi. Under cross-examination he allowed that Julum 'might be' Jawi too.[113] Elkin similarly recorded the story

Figure 14: Jimmy Ejai giving evidence at Julum (Middle Island). Photo: Katie Glaskin (2001).

of Galalung's journey from Julum across to Sunday Island in 1928, and records how Galalung climbed up a big rock just east of 'Cocky's camp' (a name missionaries gave the place after Khaki's father, Gagi, who lived there during the mission days at Sunday Island).[114]

Given the rough conditions for getting on and off boats, and because time had been shortened by those same conditions, the rest of this day's evidence was all given from the boat. Jimmy Ejai gave evidence on the boat and pointed out various sites of significance. Among these was Bulngurr, associated with the discovery of fire and the transformation of named beings into species of birds.[115] Bulngurr is on Jayirri (Jackson Island), and it is noteworthy that it was Jimmy Ejai, a Bardi man, who had the authority to relay the story of Jungalbil associated with the site.

The combination of logistical issues and turbulent seas also had an impact on the evidence on Sunday Island. A whole day had been set aside for the trip to the island to hear evidence, and it had been envisaged that the court would have lunch at Khaki Stumpagee's outstation, Nillargoon. But on the day scheduled for evidence on Sunday Island, the difficult seas meant that the best way to travel from One Arm Point was along the north side of Sunday Island, and then down the east side of East Sunday Island before anchoring in the small bay at Nilagun on the south side of the island (rather than taking a more direct, but hazardous, route). Two boats carried representatives of nearly all the Jawi families from within the claim area and from Jawi islands to its east, as well as the court (the judge, counsel representing the applicants and various respondents, instructing solicitors from each party, court-appointed transcribers), anthropologists and land council personnel. The seas were so rough we were concerned about the boats capsizing on route, and the crew on our charter boat kept asking us to redistribute our weight to one side or the other to prevent that outcome. In both boats, the skippers were so nervous about the combination of the weather conditions and the many marine hazards present that one of the Jawi men on each of the boats ended up skippering them safely to shore. When we got to the island, we then had to unload all the passengers and go ashore by dinghy, a time-consuming process. Khaki Stumpagee and his family had spent the week before the court's arrival cleaning and readying the outstation for this event; they had even raked the seaweed off the beach for the judge's visit, with an expectation about the visit that was quickly disappointed. After finally landing, we were told by the judge's logistics assistant that we only had half an hour to hear evidence, and then we would have to leave so the judge could get back to the mainland in time to catch his plane. Talking later with that judge's assistant, he suggested one of the reasons the judge may have been content with this limited evidence on Sunday Island was because the evidence in Khaki Stumpagee's interview with Geoffrey Bagshaw had already been submitted to the court. This was not something the claimants knew at the time, though; nor, as it transpired, was this the judge who would ultimately decide the case.

The early decision about gender-restricted evidence, the evident impact of logistical arrangements on evidentiary time, and the questioning of people's identities and affiliations to country by those who were visiting it for the first time, and who often could not understand claimant responses or mispronounced their names or the names of their country, exacerbated existing tensions within the claimant group. At the time, I noted such tensions mainly centred on long-standing issues over who had primary rights in certain *buru*:

> Repercussions at present seem to include the following. [A] told me that people were concerned, and that they were misunderstanding the native title process. Since people were giving evidence about their own country ('talking it up'), everyone thinks that people are just in it for themselves. People are wary of giving evidence that touches on anyone else's country...[B] says that native title is dividing people. Many people are upholding the rhetoric that this is for everyone and

that internal matters will be sorted out later. But as various people give evidence, the mistrust and suspicion grows (extract from journal entry, 15 May 2001).

The impact of these stresses on the community is difficult to evaluate. Some tensions were longstanding, but hearing people publicly talk about their connections to country certainly accentuated a number of them. Not everyone attended all of the evidence, or took part in all the site visits, so there was conjecture about what may have been said by others. Many people felt that the judge was adjudicating their own connections to country and 'claim' on it; that the result of the native title claim would be to gain recognition and legitimacy for their own connections in the eyes of the law. The smaller, estate-group affiliations tended to dominate how people thought about the process, and this, I suspect, was partly the legacy of the outstation movement, and partly as a consequence of hearing evidence about the estate groups from people on country.

Nine days into the on country hearing a young man tragically died. With enormous sadness, some of us who knew his family well visited his grieving family, and later that night, at their request, returned to the house with land council staff to sit by the fire with them. They said even though the boy's body had been taken away for an autopsy, his spirit would return to come and sit by the fire. Lighting a fire like that, they said, is what Bardi people have always done.

The previous day there had been another suicide of a young Bardi boy in Broome, and between these two deaths many of our main witnesses in the case were too affected to proceed. Against the overwhelming and immediate grief of the families concerned, the native title claim's importance shrank. Senior people in the community advised that a break from the hearing was required. The applicants requested an adjournment, to which the judge agreed and, after much wrangling over dates, new dates for the resumption of the trial were set. During the adjournment hearing, the State of Western Australia indicated that everything was in contention: Bardi and Jawi connection to country post-1971, the existence of a Jawi community, the claim to native title offshore, and so on.

The trial resumed on the 18 June 2001, and in the interim the death and funeral of one of the senior men who had given evidence about going through law on Sunday Island had occurred. The cumulative impact of these deaths on small communities in which everyone is related in some way is not to be underestimated (see Glaskin, Tonkinson, Musharbash and Burbank 2008). The new dates were set with reference to legal availabilities, and I was unable to be present when it resumed. In Europe, I received phone calls from Geoffrey Bagshaw who kept me in touch with how things were transpiring. Since I was not present to that evidence, my understanding of the transcript in relation to this part of the trial is mediated through my previous experiences of the people the transcript recorded and the places and events they referred to. These are familiar from fieldwork and pre-trial proofing during which we had visited those places where evidence was eventually taken.

From reading the transcript, and the subsequent submissions, a number of issues the respondent parties would later argue were contentious emerged in this part of the trial. These issues concerned evidence over the south-western and south-eastern land boundaries of Bardi country on the northern Dampier Peninsula; the identity of the islands immediately offshore from One Arm Point; the extent to which Bardi and Jawi native title could be said to extend into the sea (hence there was considerable cross-examination of witnesses about the use of mangrove log rafts, about turtle and dugong hunting, and so forth); about Juljinabur (Brue Reef), which represented the furthermost seaward extremity of the claim; and about the relationship between those Jawi identified with the claim area and Jawi identified with islands to the east of the claim area, in the adjoining Mayala native title claim.

The 'Second Trial' and the Impact of Yorta Yorta

Most of the Sampi claim was heard in twenty-one days of evidence before Federal Court judge Justice Beaumont, in 2001. This was before the High Court of Australia's decision in *Members of the Yorta Yorta Aboriginal Community v Victoria* [2002] HCA 58 ('Yorta Yorta') native title case, which was handed down in late 2002. Yorta Yorta said that the only native title rights and interests that can be recognised are those derived from the laws and customs of a society that can be shown to have had continuity with the society in existence at the time the British Crown acquired sovereignty in Australia (a date that varies from state to state). Thus claimants now had to deal with the idea of 'society' and its continuity since colonisation.

Although most of the evidence in the Sampi case was heard prior to the Yorta Yorta decision, Yorta Yorta had consequences for the Sampi case in at least two respects. Firstly, the High Court's decision in Yorta Yorta prompted the Kimberley Land Council to seek leave to lead further evidence in the Sampi case to address the issues Yorta Yorta raised. The Federal Court granted the land council leave, and a further three days of evidence was heard in 2003, in what Justice French would later refer to as the 'second trial'. This evidence was heard not in Bardi or Jawi country, but in the Catholic Healing Centre in Broome. At the land council's discretion, a different legal team appeared for the applicants: Kevin Bell, assisted by George Irving, replaced Greg McIntyre as the applicant's counsel.[116] The applicant's evidence was also presented differently in the two trials: as French summarised it, in the first trial the witness evidence was led orally, while at the second trial 'statements of the substance of the evidence of thirteen witnesses were provided exhibited to an affidavit of a solicitor from the Kimberley Land Council, Ms Guest'.[117]

Frances Morphy (2007) has discussed the ambiguous nature of the 'witness statement'. She identifies issues of literal and conceptual translation, showing how a statement from an Aboriginal witness might be transposed into a witness statement

(2007, p. 39). She notes that Aboriginal witnesses (in the case she discusses, Yolngu people) are not necessarily familiar with many of the words used in witness statements which may 'sound like ordinary English words' but which often have 'particular meanings for lawyers working in native title' (p. 39). For these reasons, she suggests the witness statement is really a 'hybrid' kind of document that 'purports to be the statement by the witness about "laws and customs"...but it is to some degree actually a lawyer's statement about native title. It belongs fully to neither of its authors, and its meaning is inherently indeterminate' (Morphy 2007, p. 40). The problem with the witness statement is that these are usually treated 'according to an unstated convention "as if" they were the *actual words* of the witness, when everyone in the court knows they are not', but 'the respondents can, as a tactical manoeuvre, when it suits them, violate the unspoken convention' (Morphy 2007, p. 40, original emphasis). The advantage of the witness statement from a lawyer's perspective is they contain 'evidence' that, subject to the acceptance of the statement by all parties, may not have to be verbally elicited before the court.

The reliance on witness statements in the second trial in 2003 is one of the features distinguishing the first trial from the second. The fact that all the evidence was heard in Broome rather than on country is another, although the judge did have the opportunity for a 'view' of the country (a brief visit to sites 'on the Dampier Peninsula and surrounding waters' without taking evidence).[118] Some revisions of the claimed native title rights and interests were also made at this point, including reducing the area of sea claimed on the western and eastern sides of the peninsula from the 12-nautical-mile limit back to the 3-nautical-mile limit, excepting the areas around Brue Reef and Alarm Shoals.[119] The second trial was also distinct from the first in being prepared and run without anthropological involvement of any kind. Finally, a different judge heard the evidence in the second trial: due to severe illness, Justice Beaumont, who had heard all the previous evidence in 2001, had to retire from the case. Justice Robert

French was assigned to hear the additional evidence in 2003 and to make the determination in this case. Yorta Yorta was significant, then, both in how legal counsel decided to present and plead the case in the 'second trial', and in how Justice French subsequently applied the Yorta Yorta principles when making a determination of the case.

Confronted with the idea of the rule-bearing society as articulated in Yorta Yorta, and with a claim brought on behalf of two named Indigenous groups (Bardi and Jawi), it appears, from the record, that the legal team running the second trial made some reformulation of the case. In the first trial, barrister Greg McIntyre had begun the opening submissions on the 8th May 2001 by saying that:

> I appear here representing the Bardi and Jawi peoples, many of whom sit before your Honour, and indeed some [are] outside still. The area which they claim comprises land and waters which have been traditionally occupied by both the Bardi and the Jawi, two distinct areas.[120]

In the second trial, these 'two distinct areas', and indeed Bardi and Jawi, were to be re-cast as one.

Chapter Seven

Legal Submissions and Crosscurrents

The Bardi and Djawi believe that ancestral beings travelled the seas and created the islands, reefs, sandbanks and marine species found within the sea. The adventures of these ancestral beings are recalled in song and story. The beings named all the features in the environment including particular places on the seabed where certain ritual activities occurred which, in some cases, resulted in ritual paraphernalia being left behind metamorphosing into particular marine features. Rituals were carried out by these ancestral beings from the north through the islands where certain named ritual sites were located. These rituals passed through the Dampier Peninsula and travelled south along the coast to Broome, La Grange and south-east into the interior (Green 1988, p. 22).

One Society...or Two?

At the time the Sampi claim was lodged, it was not unusual for claims to be brought on behalf of two or more named groups. The Mirriuwung and Gajerrong claim[121] in the east Kimberley was successfully determined in 2000 and the Ngarluma and Yindjibarndi claim[122] in the Pilbara was in progress before the court. For the Bardi and Jawi native title claim, though, the Yorta Yorta decision of 2002 and the introduction of the concept of 'society' would have an unexpected effect.

Most of the evidence in the Sampi case had been heard before the term 'society' had entered into native title jurisprudence, and the notion added further complexity to the case. Could two language-named groups constitute one society with a set of shared laws and customs? Those handling the legal carriage of the second trial appeared to have some concern about two named groups associated with differentiated territories. The claim, which land council personnel had been referring to for some time as the 'Bardi/Jawi claim' – despite Geoffrey Bagshaw's and my expressed concerns that 'Bardi *and* Jawi' was the more accurate and thus preferable way to refer to the claim (e.g., see Glaskin 2002, p. 189) – became a claim in which the relevant country was said to be 'all Bardi Jawi country'. It is my view that this reorientation had an obvious impact on the outcome of the case; one that proved, initially, to be most detrimental to Iwanyun (Jawi people from Sunday Island) and to Inalabulu (islander) Bardi.

There were some early indications as to how things were going to be run. In early 2003 the instructing solicitor for the applicants provided the anthropologists with copies of the new witness substances of evidence they were planning to file in the court in the second trial. From these, it was apparent that all of the country under claim was now being formulated as 'Bardi Jawi' country. This included the interior of the Dampier Peninsula, the hinterland area lying between the coastal estates on the Bardi mainland. According to Bardi, this area is not associated with any single estate group (or *buru*), but is considered 'shared' country. But in the new formulation, it was not country simply shared between proximate Bardi estate groups; it was also presented as being shared by Jawi. This did not make sense ethnographically. Instead of the claimants being presented as Bardi and Jawi who had two 'distinct areas', the applicants were now presented as Bardi Jawi people, and the territory they claimed, as all one country:

'Bardi Jawi country'. This reorientation appeared to be a direct response to the Yorta Yorta judgment of 2002 with its emphasis on the normative society, and represented an emphasis on unity rather than differentiation amongst Bardi and Jawi peoples.

Bardi and Jawi share many aspects of their social lives: they intermarry, practise Law together and have the same systems of kinship and social organisation (the latter involving alternate generational moieties). But they also have separate territories. Throughout the period when Geoffrey Bagshaw and I were researching their claim, people consistently distinguished between Bardi and Jawi country. In other words, what they shared and had in common was not equivalent to making the country they were claiming 'one Bardi Jawi country'. We thought this reformulation was not an accurate reflection of the views most people held, whether Bardi or Jawi, and felt a professional responsibility to outline our concerns about the proposition that Bardi and Jawi jointly owned the interior of the Dampierland peninsula. We wrote a letter to the land council in which we said that 'the recently elicited proposition that Bardi and Jawi peoples jointly possess the Dampier Peninsula hinterland' was of particular concern to us, noting that it contradicted the previous ethnographic literature, 'the overwhelming bulk of the evidence' that had already been provided to the Court on the matter, and the 'statements made to us by Bardi and Jawi people over many years and recorded in our field notebooks'.[123]

The evidence in the 'second trial' was heard in Broome between 30 June and 3 July 2003 and in the transcript is considered to be 'on country' evidence, even though Broome is neither in Bardi nor Jawi country. The trial was run on the basis that Bardi and Jawi were all one 'society' of 'Bardi Jawi people' and the country they claimed was all one country, 'Bardi Jawi country'. The reorientation of the case was apparent in the closing submissions following this evidence in 2003. Written submissions included the subheadings 'The Bardi Jawi are one society' and 'Bardi Jawi have one country' (Kimberley Land Council 2003, p. 2). The submissions stated that 'the evidence of numerous witnesses demonstrates a universally held belief among the Bardi and Jawi that they are…"one people"'.[124] The submissions cited one of the applicant's views that what made the applicants one people was their shared law, language and culture along with intermarriage – a somewhat different proposition to conflating the identities of people and the countries with which they identify.

The submissions also stated that 'Bardi and Jawi witnesses described the area subject to claim as one country – Bardi Jawi country'.[125] But to understand statements such as these, context is critical. In his commentary on Sampi following its resolution in the Full Court, Redmond (2011, p. 288) argued that there are 'various levels at which Aboriginal groups coalesce and become differentiated from one another'. These contexts are important for understanding what statements about 'one country' might mean: is it a reference to shared Law, to extensive intermarriage, or to the identity of the country itself? By the identity of the country, I mean the language with which it is associated, an identity which people are also associated with by virtue of their connection with that country. In Aboriginal cosmologies, the association between country and language is one that stems from the creative period often glossed to non-Indigenous people as 'the Dreaming', when ancestral beings left tracks and traces of themselves in country along with the language that gave that country its identity. For this reason, anthropologists and linguists have referred to language-named groups as 'the language-owning group': e.g., Rumsey (1989, 1993); Sutton (2003, p. 81). This does not necessarily reflect the language or languages that people actually speak (customarily, people spoke several languages); rather, it is indicative of the language (and hence the country) with which people primarily identify. The language-owning group then reflects an association of a named language with a particular area of country. Understood in these terms – namely, that the identity of the country with a particular language-named group is considered to be of ancestral provenance – the conflation of two named language groups with one area of country is problematic, not least because at this time, in this case, this was not how people themselves thought about the identity of their countries or indeed themselves. As Khaki Stumpagee had stated emphatically, *I'm not Bardi, I'm a Jawi.*

The final submissions following the second trial were held in the Federal Court in Perth in March 2004. I attended to see the claim finally argued. The Bardi and Jawi representatives who had come down from the Kimberley were fairly upbeat. People sat patiently in the courtroom as lawyers debated the fate of their case, sometimes exchanging jokes as they were reminded about things that occurred during the trial. Many continued to be bemused or confused by the pronunciation of placenames, leading to speculation as to what the lawyers might possibly be referring to. There were sad reminders of those who had passed away since giving evidence in the first trial. There were technical legal arguments that sent people to sleep, or out of the room to smoke or talk.

Here, I consider the closing submissions presented orally in the second trial. While my initial understanding of these submissions was made on the basis of the extensive notes I took while attending the hearing, rather than on the transcript itself, I subsequently compared my notes against the transcript in order to render what was said as accurately as possible. The value of considering these submissions lies in what they reveal, not only about the legal thinking and reasoning in this case but also about the difficulties the introduction of a new term into native title jurisprudence: the term 'society', created within this legal reasoning. The submissions indicate the faultlines in the case that would impact the trial judge's reconciliation of the case concept then being put forward – namely that Bardi and Jawi were one people with one country – with the evidence before him.

The Applicants' Case

In oral submissions put to Justice French at the conclusion of the second trial, Kevin Bell, the barrister representing the applicants, stated that he wanted to focus on the 'central issue of controversy, which is the composition of the Aboriginal society which existed within the claim area at the assertion of sovereignty in 1829, and the nature of the Aboriginal society which exists now in that claimed area'.[126] In other words, the main issue he wished to address, following Yorta Yorta, was the issue of 'society', and there is little doubt that foundational to this concern was the fact that the application for native title had been made on behalf of two named applicant groups, Bardi and Jawi peoples. Bell continued: 'the applicants make the following submissions that are fundamental in character...firstly, that from pre-contact to the current date the Bardi Jawi have been the society of Aboriginal people united and governed by one system of traditional law and custom which specifies the rights and interests they have in their country'.[127] He went on to elaborate the 'essential features' of 'Bardi Jawi traditional law and custom'.[128] Bell noted that this was 'not to say that individuals within the group do not identify themselves and each other by reference to a particular connection or association with particular territory'.[129] Notwithstanding this, 'the first submission that we make is that there is one country, not two or forty'.[130] The number 'forty' alluded to the numerous named *buru* (estate groups), and was a reference to the fact that the State of Western Australia had long argued that native title should be found at this level, thereby isolating the estate group from the larger social system or 'society' that produced it.

In response to Bell's submission, Justice French asked, 'so it really is, without overstating it, its Bardi Jawi stand or fall together in your case?'[131] Bell's response was to say:

> Yes. What your Honour says is correct, but the qualification
> I place upon the proposition is that...Yorta Yorta requires the
> application of a society test which is to be applied by reference

to the dictionary definition provided in Yorta Yorta...Now, it may be that the Bardi and the Jawi have all sorts of other differences between them of a non-normative kind which distinguishes them...but our case is that the essential question is the one to which I have already referred.[132]

The 'essential question' Bell referred to concerned the composition of the 'society' in 1829, and the composition of that 'society' now. Justice French responded that '"society" does not appear in the Act of course', and noted that 'the factual issue becomes well, is the origin [of the group's laws and customs] explained by reference to the sub-group or by reference to something coming from a large group?'[133] Given the possibility of similarities between adjacent groups, French made the observation that 'it becomes a very evaluative sort of decision-making I suppose'.[134] Bell did note there was a 'non-preferred' way of formulating the case; this, he said, was to say that:

Bardi and Jawi are separate people...then admitting that those two peoples observed the same body of traditional law and custom which gives them rights in each other's country, so that the Bardi so-called can be recognised as having special attachment to particular territory within the country entire; the Jawi can be recognised as being persons who have particular attachment to the other part of the country entire.[135]

Justice French analogised that this formulation was 'sort of like the Welsh and the English', a proposition to which Bell agreed.[136] As Bell noted, this would allow 'one single native title determination that native title rights and interests are held by all'.[137] This was not the particular way, though, that Bell sought to argue the case. As he reiterated, this way of formulating the case was 'theoretically open, but non-preferred'.[138] As he put it, 'we're not here in our submission attempting to identify a society by reference to perfect social, anthropological or other kinds of descriptors; it's not an academic exercise. The exercise is a practical, legal or forensic one dictated by the terms of the Act as explicated by Yorta Yorta'.[139]

In his discussion of the relationship between anthropology and law in native title, Burke (2011, p. 29) suggests that the task of the anthropologist is to triangulate the claimants' evidence, the anthropological archive and legal doctrine. As he says, 'it should be noted that this triangulation also describes the task of the claimants' lawyer – an indication that competition between the claimants' lawyer and the anthropologist will be an ongoing structural problem' (2011, p. 29). Bell's dismissal of anthropology as an 'academic exercise' in contrast to the 'practical, legal, or forensic' task that faced the court perhaps explains why he thought it unnecessary to involve anthropologists in this part of the case, and represents one way of attempting to avert the structural problem Burke described.

The State's Submissions

In her oral submissions at the conclusion of the second trial, Raelene Webb, the barrister acting for the State of Western Australia, noted that the 'principal issue for the State is the composition of the native title holding group'.[140] Given the introduction of the society issue into native title jurisprudence following Yorta Yorta, this was not surprising. Speaking for the State of Western Australia, Webb said, 'we reject the submission of the applicants…[concerning the existence of] an identifiable society of Bardi and Jawi people as a single community at the date of acquisition of sovereignty…It is our position that Bardi and the Jawi are two separate and independent, although closely linked, Aboriginal groups'.[141] As she went on to explain, 'what we say in reliance on Yorta Yorta…if there were in fact a Bardi society which as a society, identifiable society, had a system of laws and customs that connected it with land and you had a separate and distinct Jawi society'; if in fact these groups now say they have rights in each other's territories, 'then that is where the problem lies'.[142] In other words, Webb here raised the spectre of a transformed society which, as the State would see it, would not be the 'same' society that existed at the time of the acquisition of sovereignty. Justice French's response was to indicate that it was in the context of 'abandonment' of traditional laws and customs that the judgment in Yorta Yorta concerning the continuity of the normative society had been made.[143] Webb replied that the Yorta Yorta determination indicated the society had to continue as a group, but French appeared unconvinced. As he put it, 'I just have the feeling that the generality of the proposition that you're extracting is wider than the context which the court was addressing at the time'; that it went beyond the High Court's reasoning in Yorta Yorta and the context which had underpinned their reasons.[144] He noted that 'the case that you have set up is one in which there are, as you say, two distinct societies...[that] have merged over an historical period'.[145]

Webb's submission on behalf of the State of Western Australia was unambiguous, and was consistent with the line of argument that had been adopted on the basis of Sansom's anthropological report commissioned at the very outset of the case. Although the precise terms in which this argument was made were to alter post–Yorta Yorta with the introduction of the term 'society' into native title, in essence it was the same. The State had earlier contended that they were unconvinced by the Jawi claim, which they argued was 'riding on the coat-tails' of the Bardi claim, or, as the State's anthropologist put it, 'the case for Jawi is made to ride "piggy back" on the Bardi ethnography' (Sansom 2001, n.p). Webb said the State acknowledged that Bardi people had continued to observe laws and customs, but claimed that Jawi ('as Jawi people') had ceased to do so.[146] Webb went on to emphasise the distinction between Bardi and Jawi people: 'I think it could be said that for all social and geographic purposes... that in practical terms they are a mixed community but...within that there is still a very strong adherence to traditional laws and customs that connect people to country in terms of Bardi and Jawi as separate peoples'.[147]

Justice French's response to Webb's statement was instructive, and can, I think, be clearly related to statements he would later make in the 2005 determination in the case. At this point, his Honour said: 'I seem to recollect in the oral evidence last year that there was a fair bit of emphasis on the unity of the group although you no doubt could say that it has to do with the way the issue was emerging'.[148] This reference to the way the issue was emerging appears, in my view, to be a reference to the 'one society'/'two societies' matter.

At this point in the submissions, several issues about the direction of the case had arisen, but not all were being discussed explicitly. Webb, the barrister for the State of Western Australia, signalled something of the transformation in the way the case had been put before the court, with reference to the case 'presented to us' in the anthropologist's report.[149] Justice French had commented, too, on the 'emphasis' in the evidence he had heard; evidence that would be considered against that given in the 'first' pre–Yorta Yorta trial heard before Justice Beaumont.

Webb next sought to make the point that the connection between Bardi and Jawi could not be established mythologically. Although, she conceded, there was a 'qualification' insofar as she had not been privy to the gender-restricted evidence (which would, by nature of its restriction, have made reference to important ancestral beings and some of their activities), Webb contended that 'it seems that the major culture heroes in Bardi myth did not establish specific sites of significance in Jawi territory'.[150] Given the mythological connection between Julum (Middle Island) just off the coast of One Arm Point and Iwanyi (Sunday Island) established through the ancestral figure of Galalung, such an assertion already indicated the State of Western Australia's position that Julum (Middle Island) was a Jawi island, not a Bardi island. At one point Webb softened the State of Western Australia's position that all the islands were

Jawi, stating that 'the Jawi are islanders and the Bardi are based on the mainland of Dampier Peninsula and *perhaps* some islands close to the mainland'.[151] Again, Webb sought to emphasise the difference between Bardi and Jawi orientations to sea: as she put it, 'Jawi therefore are traditionally almost wholly dependent on the products of the sea, but the Bardi do have a different zone'.[152]

At this stage the State's case can be broadly summarised as follows: Bardi and Jawi were two separate groups, and Jawi could not really be considered to have native title. Jawi might have 'secondary' rights in Bardi country by way of intermarriage, but these secondary rights were 'largely an accumulation of marriage choices over time…but this is not a product of your connection through traditional law and custom'.[153] Justice French responded to Webb's arguments, saying that 'there's no evidence that intermarriage is a modern phenomenon'; he saw Webb's proposition as leading to the proposition that 'you get a process over a period of time', in which the final result would be 'a situation that looks very much like one society'.[154] He noted that 'we're dealing with metaphor in a sense and applying it to some sort of primary facts', describing it as a 'judgement which is to be made because of the requirement of either the statute or the common law rules or a combination of both'.[155]

At the conclusion of her oral submissions, Webb summarised the State of Western Australia's case about the one society/two society issue. Taking her lead from the case put by the applicants in the second trial regarding a single Bardi-Jawi society, Webb argued that 'if a mixing did result in a combined Bardi Jawi society', then 'there's now a new society and a new system that wouldn't be capable of a determination of native title in their favour'.[156] In her view, a determination of this kind would not be in accordance with 'tradition' or with a 'traditional society'; rather, the proposition that native title vested in the Bardi-Jawi group was really a proposal stemming from 'presence and modern practice rather than any outcome of reliance on traditional ancestral principles that connect people with country'.[157] The State of Western Australia's understanding of the term 'society', not unlike the applicants' reformulated position in their submission, was closely tied to ideas of language and territory, rather than to social interaction.

The Commonwealth's Submissions

In closing submissions, the Commonwealth of Australia, represented by Ken Pettit, limited their oral submissions to five main issues. The first of these was the approach they had argued the court should take to issues of change and adaptation in relation to the question of 'traditional laws and customs' and 'society'.[158] The second point was concerned with 'errors' in the applicants' case in this regard.[159] The third point was to do with the intergenerational transmission of rights, especially in relation to Brue Reef, 'tribal borders' (as he put it), and deceased estates.[160] The fourth point was concerned with some 'recent authority' in case law, while the last of their 'main issues' concerned the territorial sea.[161] Here, I focus on the Commonwealth's submissions in relation to the question of 'society'.

Pettit began by saying the court should 'first determine, and not work backwards...the laws and customs that prevailed at sovereignty'.[162] Drawing on the Yorta Yorta decision, he argued that 'only certain laws and customs...those that are productive of rights' in land or waters were relevant to this consideration.[163] 'As to laws and customs at sovereignty', Pettit said, 'a major aspect of these submissions...is the interrelationship between various laws and customs' and he argued this set limits 'on the idea that laws and customs may change and may be adapted'.[164] With respect to the question of society, Pettit said 'our view is that the Court should have little difficulty in accepting the orthodox anthropological conclusion that there was, at sovereignty, a separate Bardi and a separate Jawi society'.[165] He further proposed that the most important criteria for determining the present society was the 'emic view', saying that 'the opinions of Anthropologists and others on the classification of groups…run a very poor second to the emic view'.[166] An emic view is the view held by those within a cultural group, and contrasts with an etic view, a view held by persons outside the group.

These submissions prompted discussion about 'this class of expert evidence', in which Justice French drew analogies with the economist defining the market place.[167] In his view, an anthropologist could offer a conclusion about whether a group was a society or not, but that conclusion would, 'in the end', be 'argumentative', a 'characterisation', a 'taxonomy', rather than a 'fact'.[168] Speaking for the Commonwealth, Pettit agreed, responding 'that it is not evaluative; it is a straight fact – straight fact as to which societies, laws and customs govern particular land'. These facts, he said, were to be determined by 'the emic view' and that 'one set of norms must apply'.[169]

While anthropologists have long distinguished between the emic view and the etic view, the importation of these concepts into the Federal Court is, I suspect, not entirely usual, and it suggests to me that at least two things were occurring here. The first of these is that, as lawyers have dealt with native title and with reading anthropological reports and articles over a protracted period of time, certain concepts from the anthropological repertoire have made their way into legal discourse at least (if not into jurisprudence, at this stage). The second is that the importation of such concepts occurs without the attendant anthropological understandings, such as, in this case, the basic fact that there may be more than one 'emic view'. In order to understand an emic view, it is not sufficient to rely on written accounts that represent a certain group in a particular way; for example, by a language label. In reality, there are multiple levels at which identity can be expressed, with reference to many different kinds of groups, of varying size and stability, and elicited in different contexts. Justice French's response recognised something of this latter point, for, as he put it, 'once you allow that there may be sub-groups within a so-called society…the question of where you draw the boundary which defines society…whilst it involves these factual elements, does also involve a question of classification, doesn't it?'[170]

Pettit's response was to persevere with his understanding of 'the emic view', responding that both criteria were necessary: 'there must be internal unity of the separate laws and customs; the second is the emic view to which society, which group of persons do the original inhabitants defer'.[171] At this juncture, it is not clear whether Counsel for the Commonwealth was suggesting that it would be possible to determine the 'emic view' about which society the indigenous inhabitants of the area felt they belonged to at the time of the acquisition of sovereignty by the Crown; but, given his reference to 'original inhabitants', it is an inference that could be drawn. While, to this point, there had been discussion about how the term society was to be applied, the term 'society' itself had not been problematised. The reason for this is likely to be because, as courts have insisted since its first appearance in the Yorta Yorta case, what is meant by the term 'society' is its 'ordinary dictionary definition'. So, for example, in the Alyawarr case, the *Shorter Oxford Dictionary*'s definition of society as 'a body of people forming a community or living under the same government' was said to be 'the *relevant* ordinary meaning of society' for native title purposes.[172] Such a definition, arguably, would allow a 'society' to be determined at many different levels.

Pettit continued to extrapolate his position on the emic view, once again contrasting this with an anthropological perspective. Referring to neighbouring Kimberley groups, the Nyul Nyul and Nimanbur, he argued that 'It would be a nonsense, for example…to say that the Jawi are united in and by common observance of laws with the Nyulnyul or the Nimanbur, and it wouldn't matter in what degree an Anthropologist could point out the similarity of identity of their laws and customs'.[173] The irony in Pettit's critique of anthropology is that at no point had the anthropologists who had been involved in the case actually been asked to comment on the question of society. In his original anthropological report presented to the court in this case, Bagshaw

(1999, p. 13) had explicitly described the formulation of the joint claim, saying that:

> The nature, density and geographic specificity of these ties [between Bardi and Jawi] are, in fact, such that many Bardi and Jawi believe that their respective territorial interests can and should be considered within the context of a single regional native title claim.

Pettit persisted in building his argument against anthropology, referring to the 'earliest appearance of the names Bardi and Jawi in the literature', noting that they were 'in no sense, a construct of the Anthropologists or other writers'.[174] This statement might be read as suggesting that 'the anthropologists' had 'constructed' a 'Bardi-Jawi' society and, in that event, it could be assumed that the respondent parties remained unaware of the fact that the anthropologists were not involved in the case for the applicants as reformulated in this manner. What is noteworthy here is the continued undermining of anthropological analysis as a kind of 'construction', a view that had also been advanced by the Counsel for the applicants in the second trial.

Pettit next moved on to what he called 'the disavowals...the statements of several witnesses to this effect, "I am Bardi, not Jawi", or "I am Jawi, not Bardi"'.[175] He noted that:

> And your Honour will see that there is a marked discrepancy between the first trial and the second trial in what people said about that. In the second trial, people had begun saying, 'I'm Bardi Jawi' or 'This is Bardi Jawi land'.[176]

This reference to the 'marked difference' in the second trial with respect to how people referred to themselves and to their country is significant, and, in my view, accurate. During the time when we conducted anthropological fieldwork for the claim, mainly between 1994 and 1999, people had usually identified themselves as either Bardi (Bard) or Jawi, not as 'Bardi Jawi'. The exceptions to this were those persons having one Bardi and one Jawi parent, who would refer to themselves as 'Bardi-Jawi' or 'Bard-Jau'. Notwithstanding the distinctions made in terms of identity, people would sometimes refer to 'Bardi-Jawi Law', or refer to the Law as 'belonging to both', as Frank Davey had done in relation to the video evidence shown in the earliest part of the trial of Bardi and Jawi performing Law together. Throughout the first part of the trial, the vast majority of witnesses had referred to themselves as Bardi or Jawi, with the exceptions being those of mixed parentage.

Justice French's response to Pettit's observation about this 'marked discrepancy' was to say, 'well, I observed that yesterday. It was my impression that, even on a number of occasions, there is some emphasis'.[177] Pettit agreed, referring to it as the 'more recent use'.[178] The explanation the Commonwealth put forward for this 'more recent use' was that it was related to the history of Bardi and Jawi 'mixing', such that after a hundred years it was 'perfectly natural for people to come to the view, latterly, that they are combined'.[179] But this, he argued, did not shed 'any light at all on 1829',[180] the year Crown sovereignty was asserted over the State of Western Australia. The term 'mixed', as used by Bardi and Jawi people themselves, was given a number of different connotations in this case, as I explore in the next chapter.

The Commonwealth went on to make a number of submissions about the differences between Bardi and Jawi people, arguing, amongst other things, that Jawi people used '*galwa*' (as Pettit put it, using the Bardi word for mangrove log raft rather than the Jawi word, *biel-biel*), whereas Bardi did not. This argument was based on early reported sightings of the mangrove log rafts that, Pettit argued, were all in Jawi country.[181] In addition, Pettit argued, because the *galwa* relied on currents, presumably between islands, they would not have been traditionally used on the western side of the Dampier Peninsula, which is open sea.[182] The relevance of arguing that only Jawi used mangrove log rafts stemmed from the Commonwealth's aim to contest and limit the recognition of Bardi native title rights and interests offshore. Pettit drew other distinctions between Bardi and Jawi as well, arguing that, according to William Dampier's observations, the mainlanders were shy but the islanders were not.[183] It is worth being reminded that many of the islands are close enough to each other to enable people to swim between them; the distance between One Arm Point and Sunday Island is only about 10 kilometres. Pettit referred to where Bardi and Jawi had traditionally placed the deceased: Bardi placed the deceased in trees, while Jawi placed their deceased on rock ledges.[184] (A reason for this is the lack of suitable trees on Sunday Island and surrounding islands). Pettit then went on to say that although 'the emic view is much more important than the academic taxonomies...I don't want to be taken to suggest...that the academics are against us on this point'.[185] He noted that, in the applicants' anthropologist's report in which the anthropologist had addressed the 'observations made by Professor Sansom', Bagshaw had said that he 'categorically' refuted a failure to represent Jawi as a 'distinct people'.[186] In summary, Pettit concluded, all of these things pointed to the fact that Bardi and Jawi were separate societies at sovereignty. As he put it, the question then was 'which of those two societies has survived'.[187] Critical to the kinds of assessments the Commonwealth and others were putting forward were the relative differences in the size of the Bardi and Jawi populations. Pettit noted that the Commonwealth's submissions 'set out' that Jawi society had not survived, perhaps because they had been subsumed within Bardi or Mayala society.[188] 'Perhaps', Pettit said, 'it all boils down to the question arising from Yorta Yorta about vitality'.[189] In further clarification of this perspective, he noted that 'all that was necessary for the decision in Yorta Yorta was the proposition that once a society disappears completely, Native Title is lost'.[190] In a final re-statement of the importance of Yorta Yorta for the present case, Pettit proclaimed:

Native Title is in its infancy, only 12 years old, there is still the pressing need for its jurisprudential foundations to be explained by the High Court, and Yorta Yorta is second only to Mabo No 2 in the explanation of those jurisprudential foundations… So we say, with respect, that nothing said by the majority in Yorta Yorta can be dismissed.[191]

Justice French's response was to remind the Commonwealth of what he had previously stated: namely, that he thought the court here was dealing with something different to that which concerned the court in Yorta Yorta. He suggested that the Court in the Sampi case was dealing with a different kind of 'evolutionary adaptation' in which there were historical influences, and the question was one of whether 'you can have an evolutionary adaptation of which two distinct societies become one within a framework that doesn't disrupt the continuity of their law and custom'.[192] The solution to this question, as Justice French described his formulation when delivering the 2005 determination in the case, would dissatisfy nearly everyone.

Chapter Eight

How Judgments Are Made

The strict applications of doctrines of procedural fairness
in adversarial hearings has the potential to transform
pleading errors into sudden death for the native title
claimants; for example, if a regional grouping is proposed
as the relevant 'society' and the judge finds that the
regional grouping did not exist in the pre-contact era.
Justice French's mysterious decision in the Bardi and Jawi
native title claim illustrates this point (Burke 2010, p. 56).

Between the 2003 evidence and the determination of the case
in 2005, it appeared as though a mediated outcome to the Sampi
claim might be possible. Mediated outcomes, developed through
negotiations and agreement between the parties, are ratified in
the Federal Court as consent determinations. In December 2003,
the State of Western Australia sent a draft consent determination
to the Kimberley Land Council, and in February 2004 the
parties reached an in-principle agreement about finalising the
claim by consent. The Commonwealth, however, indicated it
would not be able to support this agreement, meaning that the
claim could not be resolved through consent at that time.[193] In
a press release issued just prior to the determination of the claim
in 2005, the Deputy Premier of Western Australia stated he was
'disappointed the Commonwealth refused to support a negotiated

settlement, leaving it to a court decision which could be open to appeal'.[194]

Justice French handed down his reasons for judgment in *Sampi v State of Western Australia (No. 1)* [2005] FCA 777 ('Sampi No. 1'), on the 10th June 2005. At the outset, Justice French said:

> The Bardi and Jawi people brought their application, which covered what they asserted was their traditional country, on the basis that although they were distinct but closely related groups they formed one society of native title holders for the purpose of a native title determination application.
>
> For the reasons which I explain below, I was not able to be satisfied that they were one society at the time of the colonisation of Western Australia. The probability is that they were two distinct although closely related societies which held their own traditional territories under very similar bodies of traditional Law and custom...In reaching that conclusion I am satisfied that the traditional Bardi society which existed at the time of colonisation has maintained the continuity of its existence, albeit increasingly Jawi people have come to form part of it. This has been aided by intermarriage (*Sampi v State of Western Australia* [2005] FCA 777, paragraphs 3–4).

In summary, Justice French found that Bardi continued to exist as a society, and that Jawi society, which had once been a separate 'society', had been incorporated into it. Although Justice French found that the Aboriginal witnesses displayed a 'substantial body of traditional knowledge', including of 'currents in the waters around the islands to the north of the peninsula', this was not, ultimately, the basis on which his determination about the success or otherwise of claimed rights offshore would be made.[195] His finding about society meant, as he put it, that there was a 'practical consequence'; he did not 'extend that determination to the islands to the immediate north of the mainland as I am not satisfied that they were part of traditional Bardi territory at sovereignty' (at paragraph 5). This excluded islands (within the claim area) to the east of Hadley Passage, which the applicants had claimed as part of Jawi country; it also excluded islands to the west of Hadley Passage, which the applicants had claimed as part of Bardi country. On the balance of probabilities, he found that these were likely to have been Jawi islands at the time of sovereignty, and excluded them on that basis. This exclusion of all the islands from the determination had the additional effect that native title was not recognised offshore.

Along with all of the islands, sea and associated marine features, two small areas of land at the south-western and south-eastern boundaries of the claim area on the mainland were also excluded from the determination.[196] Since these excluded portions of land may become subject to other claims in the future, I do not discuss them here. Justice French did, however, recognise non-exclusive native title rights in the intertidal zone of the Dampier Peninsula. He said he was 'satisfied that native title rights and interests subsist in the intertidal zone and associated reefs and nearby reefs which are exposed and were referred to in the evidence', but he did not include Lalariny, a significant offshore site which he described as a 'rock feature', among them (paragraph 5).

Judgments dealing with issues of native title offshore usually differentiate between land, sea and the intermediate intertidal zone, being the area between the high water mark and the lowest astronomical tide.[197] The Kimberley is a region with one of the largest tidal variations in the world. In the area of the determination, average tidal variations vary between 5.5 and 8 metres, though they can be as high as nearly 9 metres.[198] Because of the enormity of the tidal variation in the region, the intertidal zone within the claim area is extensive. While the recognition of native title in the intertidal zone was significant, then, it was far short of the recognition of native title offshore which Bardi and Jawi applicants had sought. At the outset of their case, they had made the decision not to separate the claim into land and sea, because they regarded the offshore regions as an important part of their country, and this was demonstrated in the density of named marine features throughout the area.

Jawi people whose country had been excluded from the determination were deeply upset with the result. Through the Jawi Aboriginal Corporation, they responded to the decision by seeking to represent themselves independently in the case, and applied to join the proceedings. There was a lack of clarity about precisely who had given legal instructions, though, with four Jawi, including senior man Khaki Stumpagee, providing affidavits to the effect that they had not withdrawn their instructions to the Kimberley Land Council.[199] For the reasons outlined in *Sampi v State of Western Australia (No. 2)* [2005] FCA 1567 (4 November 2005) ('Sampi No. 2'), their bid to join the proceedings was unsuccessful at this late stage.[200] Robert Blowes, one of the two barristers who came to act for the applicants in the appeal, later noted that the reasons for judgment (in Sampi No. 1) 'effectively invited the parties to talk about traditional Jawi country and/or mediate about it'.[201] As Blowes explained, though, while Justice French had 'left open the possibility…of making a determination over Jawi country', 'the door wasn't very much open',[202] and the parties were unable to reach an agreement about a determination over Jawi country. Sampi No. 2, which dealt with the application to join the proceedings by the Jawi group and outlined the proposed determination of native title, thus also confirmed 'that there would be no determination of native title over any Jawi traditional territory'.[203] This was followed by the formal determination in *Sampi v State of Western Australia (No. 3)* [2005] FCA 1716 ('Sampi No. 3'), which showed precise coordinates of where native title applied and to what extent, and followed discussions between the parties and submissions to the Court about the detailed form that aspects of that determination should take. The Federal Court sat at One Arm Point on the 30 November 2005 to deliver the determination.

The determination found different native title rights and interests depending on whether the area claimed was land or the intertidal zone. It recognised exclusive possession over the land;[204] non-exclusive native title rights in the intertidal zone and 'adjacent and offshore reefs and islets together with the waters in their immediate vicinity'.[205] There was no recognition of native title rights and interests in the sea beyond.

The need to clearly differentiate between land, sea and intertidal zone arose as a consequence of the different findings in respect of each. Just how 'land' and 'sea' are defined is not as straightforward as might be expected. In the post-judgment negotiations about the coordinates of the areas to which the determination applied, the Commonwealth proposed that land should be defined as landward of the highest astronomical tide, 'the highest level of water which can be predicted to occur under any combination of astronomical conditions'.[206] Given the enormous tidal variation in the region, if this proposal had been taken up, it would have reduced the area of land over which exclusive-possession native title rights had been found. This proposal ran counter to the applicants' draft determination that identified the area where exclusive-possession native title rights existed as landward of the *mean* high tide, a proposal that Justice French accepted.[207] As Blowes described the intertidal zone, it is 'quite a lot of land or quite a lot of – technically under the Native Title Act it's waters but which becomes land, or dry land, a couple of times a day'.[208] A consequence of the intertidal zone being 'technically waters' is that only non-exclusive possession native title rights can be recognised in that zone. The current exception to this is in the Northern Territory, where the interaction between different sets of legislation has produced a different result.[209]

None of the main parties to the claim – the applicants, the State or the Commonwealth – were satisfied with the 2005 determination. When it became clear that the decision would be appealed to the Full Court, further attempts were made at mediation, but these were again unsuccessful, and the case was brought to appeal. As appeal preparations got underway, James Tapueluelu took on the role of instructing solicitor at the KLC, and new barristers, Robert Blowes and Tom Keely, were briefed to run the appeal.[210] Blowes and Keely both had extensive experience in native title. Geoffrey Bagshaw and myself were engaged to provide anthropological assistance in relation to the appeal; Bagshaw provided advice about restricted evidence and other ethnographic matters, while I was charged with preparing a number of summaries that were used to assist the legal team in preparing the appeal. These included a summary of all the evidence in transcript; a summary of evidence about sites, islands, and sea country; a summary of evidence about laws, customs and society; and a comparative analysis of witness evidence and witness summaries in the judgment (Glaskin 2006b, 2006c, 2006d, 2006e). The preparation of these documents required me to go through the entire transcript of applicant evidence, not once but several times, and it was in the course of this task that I became especially interested in two aspects of the broader legal process: first, how judges might hear, read or perceive evidence, and render it accordingly; and second, how certain evidence slips through the judicial net, apparently undetected, to drown without trace.

From Evidence to Reasons for Judgment

Following the Yulara case (*Jango v Northern Territory of Australia* [2006] FCA 318), there was some commentary concerning the relationship between the anthropology, the case as argued before the judge, the evidence and the judge's determination of the case (Burke 2007, 2011, pp. 243–61; Glaskin 2007a; Keen 2007; Morton 2007; Sackett 2007; Sansom 2007; Sutton 2007). Most native title cases, though, remain relatively unexamined in these terms, at least in the public sphere.[211]

Native title determinations are made through applying the requirements of the Native Title Act and any 'clarifications' of the Act arising through judicial precedent in relevant case law to the evidence before the court. The court thus is constrained by the legislation, the case law and the evidence in a particular case. The court can only make a finding in relation to the case put before it, hence legal submissions are an important aspect of a case, and are taken into account when the judge makes a determination. Evidence includes the transcript and exhibits, which may be film footage, scholarly articles, theses, books, photographs, expert reports, maps and genealogies. All of this evidence is subject to evaluation and interpretation by a judge and the respective parties to the case who try to persuade the judge of a particular outcome through oral and written submissions.

In general terms, applicant evidence is always, by its nature, given greater weight than any expert evidence, since it is the applicants' laws and customs that are at issue. Notwithstanding this, because judgments usually contain explicit discussion about the weight and value of the expert evidence, it is sometimes easier to identify how judges ascribe weight to expert evidence – which various parties will especially target in the final submissions of the proceedings – than it is to applicant evidence.[212] In some cases, the process through which weight is ascribed to certain witness evidence is also specifically discussed. In other instances, where such discussion is absent from the judgment, it can be much more difficult to identify how judges have given weight to individual applicant evidence. Implicit factors, too, are likely to affect the weight given to particular evidence.

While seeking to remain as objective and impartial as possible, the judge's perception of the evidence cannot be ruled out as a factor of influence in how judgments are made. Some aspects of what we might broadly call a judge's 'perception' of the evidence are not difficult to discern. A judge may prefer historical or documentary evidence of something to establish it as a 'fact', rather than witness testimony. In the Sampi case, Justice French took the view, which is an uncontroversial one in native title law, that the applicant evidence should be given the greatest weight. Strelein (2005, p. 2) identified one of Justice French's preliminary points in his reasons as being that the applicants' 'testimony about their traditional Laws and customs and their rights and responsibilities with respect to land and waters is "of the highest importance. All else is second order evidence"'. For this reason, Justice French provided extensive summaries of the applicant evidence in the 2005 determination. While these summaries are based on the transcript of the evidence, this does not necessarily mean they wholly encapsulate or reflect the evidence given.

The Sampi case is unusual in that Justice French, who made the determination, had not heard most of the evidence in the case. Justice Beaumont, who heard all the evidence in the first trial, retired from the case following debilitating illness; as a consequence, Justice French only heard the witness evidence in the second trial, the three days of extra evidence granted to address the issues raised by the Yorta Yorta decision. What this meant was that, although the witness evidence may have been 'of the highest importance', most of the witness evidence thus considered was not mediated by the judge's first-hand hearing of that evidence, but through transcript alone. The transcript is therefore an extraordinarily important document in this case. Even seemingly minor transcript errors can affect how evidence is understood, and, if they are repeated in Federal Court judgments, may come to have a life beyond the problem of transcription. As well as dealing with aural linguistic complexity and different orthographic conventions, court transcribers are often working in trying recording conditions (the evidence taken on board a boat during rough seas is surely indicative of this), and making some errors is to be expected. Donges (1999) illustrates some of the difficulties court transcribers working in such contexts may have in hearing a recorded word, even one spoken in English; as his discussion makes clear, this may be further complicated when a specific phrase does not have a literal meaning. There are usually avenues to redress transcript errors; parties can choose to identify errors to the court, although identified transcript errors are not automatically accepted and can become subject to dispute. Even where a court has accepted that certain transcript corrections should be made, it does not guarantee such corrections will be effected.

At the end of each day of the applicant evidence in 2001, the court-appointed transcribers who were recording the evidence for the court checked the spelling of Bardi or Jawi terms with the anthropologists, as is their usual practice in such cases. They were, though, only able to check those problematic words that they had managed to jot down as the evidence was being heard. One difficulty with this approach is that a number of place names sound very similar (for example, Miligun, the name of a *buru* on the mainland, and Nilagun, the name of a *buru* on Sunday Island; Bulgin, a place name on the mainland, Bulnginy, the name for Poolngin Island, and Bulgun, the name of a rocky outcrop in Nilagunbur in Sunday Island). At the conclusion of the applicant evidence in the first trial, the applicants (via their anthropologists) identified a number of transcript errors of this nature. Some transcript errors did not have a significant impact on how the overall case might be understood. For example, the place name rendered as Gawrungung (on Sunday Island) should have been rendered Gawurngun, and on checking the recording Transcript Australia agreed with this.[213] For reasons that are difficult to explain, this place was subsequently rendered as 'Gawinungunu' in the 2005 judgment itself (at paragraph 139), an orthography that appears nowhere else in the transcript or any of the reports. Other transcript errors rendered the evidence inaccurate or nonsensical. For example, Cafarelli Island was rendered as 'Chaffered Island' at least fifteen times in the initial transcript, an identified error that was subsequently 'agreed'. Some identified transcript errors were 'disputed then agreed' on re-listening to recorded evidence.[214]

Nilagun (on Sunday Island) and Miligun (on the mainland) were particularly problematic, with the applicants arguing that the term rendered as 'Nilagun' in one case should in fact be 'Miligun':

Counsel (Apps): Now as a young girl, did you ever go fishing on any craft?

Witness: Yes, on the galwa [mangrove log raft], that's one the big girls used to go out to holidays, out to Nilagun [sic: Miligun] and they, like that, and some of the big girls, my aunties…you know, they used to encourage us to go on the galwa, the raft.

Counsel (Apps): Do you know what that's made out of, that raft?

Witness: It's made out of timber from the mangrove, mangrove timber there. Very light wood (T277.26–36).

Given that the witness concerned was a mainland Bardi person who grew up at Lombadina, and that the 'aunties' she referred to were from Miligun and the adjoining *buru*, Garambany, it was clear from the context that the witness was referring to Miligun (on the Bardi mainland) not to Nilagun (at the Jawi island, Sunday Island). Indeed, this knowledge of the witness's background provided the context for the identification of this as a transcript error. The respondents, though, contested this. Soon afterwards the Counsel for the Commonwealth cross-examined the same witness about this very matter, and this time the transcript rendered the place name correctly, as 'Miligun':

Counsel (Cth): You also told us a little while ago that when you were a girl at school you went on a galwa [mangrove log raft], is that right?

Witness: Yes, galwa we call it, yes.

Counsel (Cth): That's the raft?

Witness: Yes.

Counsel (Cth): And where did you go on that galwa?

Witness: Out Miligun way, and creeks and everywhere, fishing, or just having a look, with all the girls.

Counsel (Cth): Well, that's along the coast - - -

Witness: Along the coast and the sound there, Miligun (T283.15–31).

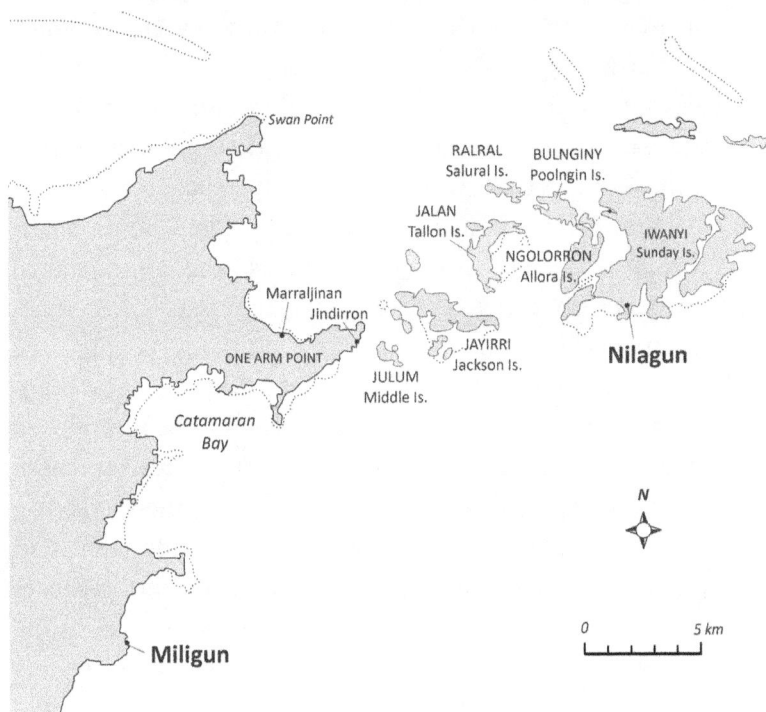

Figure 15: Map showing Miligun/Nilagun

The Commonwealth argued in this case that the name 'Miligun' should be 'Nilagun'. The significance of this dispute over the named place in the transcript is the impact it had on the meaning of the evidence. This transcript error remained disputed and, on checking the audio-file, Transcript Australia agreed that 'both interpretations are open' and that this uncertainty would be reflected in the transcript. In their 'Submissions on the Facts', the Commonwealth stated that when the witness concerned talked about their experience on a *galwa* they were referring to Nilagun (on Sunday Island), not to Miligun (on the mainland), citing this as 'inaccurately transcribed'.[215] As I have indicated, the importance of this for the case was the Commonwealth's argument that only Jawi (and not Bardi) traditionally used mangrove log rafts.

Unfortunately, the 2001 list of agreed transcript errors which had been painstakingly identified, in some cases disputed, and then reviewed by the transcribers for arbitration, were not (it seems) taken into consideration in the 2005 determination of the case, for the same errors were subsequently reproduced in the judgment itself.[216] I am not in a position to explain how or why this occurred.[217] Certainly, some of the errors were consequential for the evidence in this case. Some may be consequential for future judgments in neighbouring cases. As many people have read the Federal Court determination in the Sampi case, there is always the further possibility that these errors will be reproduced in some fashion. At least one of the claimants had read the 2005 judgment and interpreted the summaries of the witness evidence as being word-perfect versions of what had actually been said. Where place names are confused, as in some of the instances indicated above, political ramifications about who is claiming what, and who is speaking about where, become distinct possibilities. Hence, like the current legacy of historical and ethnographic documents in the native title context – themselves imperfect – these transcripts will have a considerable 'social life' (Appadurai 1986) beyond the present.

In his consideration of the 2001 evidence heard by Justice Beaumont, Justice French had to mainly rely on transcript, additionally gaining some assistance from the court's photographic diaries (Bob Shepherd, the Federal Court's logistics organiser, had taken photographs of the witnesses and most others involved in the case as an aide-memoire for the judge) and from the Court's day visit to 'sites on the Dampier Peninsula and surrounding waters' (*Sampi v State of Western Australia*, at paragraph 25). Nonetheless, Justice French's reading of much of the transcript is unlikely to have been mediated by memories associated with having heard the full range of evidence or from visiting all of the places referred to in the transcript. Although he did have the benefit of hearing from some of the witnesses in the 2003 trial, this was limited to three days of hearing in Broome. Neither

Khaki Stumpagee (the most senior Jawi man from Sunday Island) nor Jimmy Ejai (the most senior Bardi man associated with the islands the applicants argued were Bardi) gave evidence at this time. Yet the recognition of native title over the islands that these men had primary affiliations with would be most impacted by the 2005 determination. Where a trial judge is in the position of not having heard from a witness directly, but is only able to rely on transcript, the implicit factors associated with weighing up witness evidence would necessarily seem to be associated with text rather than context.

Notwithstanding his Honour's emphasis on applicant evidence, some parts of his judgment suggest that documentary evidence was given more weight: at least in relation to the issues of the traditional territorial identity of the Bardi islands at the time of sovereignty, and the identity of some of those islands now. The islands concerned included Julum (Middle Island), which lies just off the tip of One Arm Point, and Jayirri (Jackson Island), Bardi man Jimmy Ejai's country. Those issues, along with the evidence about Brue Reef and Jalan (Tallon Island), are discussed below.

The Islands

The applicants' evidence about islands within the claim area was most detailed in relation to Iwanyi (Sunday Island), Jayirri (Jackson Island), Jalan (Tallon Island) and Julum (Middle Island). Among other things, the evidence set out the claimants' connections with these islands and the relevant cultural topographies. The cultural topographies included site names, associated mythological narratives, birthplaces, burial places, and places associated with *raya* (pre-existing spirits incarnated in human form) or with the Law (Law grounds). With the exclusion of Jawi country from the determination, and with the respondents' successful strategy in arguing that Bardi use of marine resources in the area beyond the intertidal zone was a post-sovereignty phenomenon (related to their argument that only Jawi had used mangrove log rafts prior to the acquisition of sovereignty by the British Crown), much of this evidence did not make it into the trial judge's reasons for determination.

Justice French's finding that all the islands offshore were effectively Jawi limited the native title determination to the northern part of the Dampier Peninsula and the associated intertidal zone. It meant that not only were the islands excluded from the determination, but so was the sea. The causal relationship between these two exclusions (islands and sea) is demonstrated in the determination where his Honour discussed the evidence about the use of rafts in the claim area and its relationship to establishing native title rights and interests in the sea. While he considered the evidence about the use of rafts on the western side of the Dampier Peninsula to be 'scant' (where the open sea is very different from the shallower current-laden waters of King Sound to the north and east), he thought that the evidence 'could support, in my opinion, more extensive use of waters to the north of the mainland in the region of the islands and knowledge of tidal currents' (at paragraph 1109). This evidence in relation to the extensive use of waters and knowledge of tidal currents was, however, impacted by his conclusion concerning the probable identity of all the islands as Jawi, and thus had direct influence on the finding about the extent to which native title could be found in the sea. 'Given my findings about the position of the islands', he wrote, 'I am not satisfied that the evidence is sufficient to support even there a finding of Bardi native title rights and interests in the waters beyond the low water mark and exposed reefs' (paragraph 1109). His findings concerning 'the position of the islands' then had a profoundly negative impact, precluding the recognition of native title in the sea, but also, significantly, preventing native title from being found over Jackson and Sunday islands, whose senior men, Jimmy Ejai and Khaki Stumpagee respectively, had given substantial evidence in the case.

Justice French's finding that Middle Island, Jackson Island and Tallon Island (Julum, Jayirri and Jalan respectively) were Jawi at the time of sovereignty was unexpected. The finding was most comprehensible in relation to Jalan (Tallon Island) because its identification with either Bardi or Jawi was the most complicated of the three islands in evidentiary terms. Bagshaw (2001a, p. 32) identified Jalan as a deceased estate being 'looked after' by patrifiliates from the closest neighbouring island, Jackson Island (Jayirri). In contexts where there are no longer any surviving estate-affiliates, it is not uncommon for those associated with neighbouring countries to take on the role of custodian for the deceased estate; a role which, over time, may become naturalised into one of estate-ownership proper. Such succession may occur in other ways, too. Where a person is the last surviving affiliate for an estate, both they and others are aware of the impending issue of who will take on responsibility for their country when they pass away. There can, then, be active discussion beforehand about who will 'look after' an estate when that person dies, given that there are a number of people who may have a culturally sanctioned basis for doing so.

Some geographical knowledge of how close the islands are to each other and of the currents and passages separating them is useful here (see Figure 16). The passage between Jackson Island (Jayirri) and Tallon Island (Jalan) is called Escape Passage in English. Bardi and Jawi refer to the current that passes between them by the name Milamil.[218] To the east of Jalan lies an island called Ngolorron (Allora Island). Khaki Stumpagee noted that 'you can swim' from Bulnginy and Ralral (Poolngin and Salural Islands) to Ngolorron.[219] Hadley Passage, named after Sydney Hadley, who established the mission at Sunday Island, separates Ngolorron from Jalan. Jimmy Ejai identified Kalmbarr (Dingo Rock) in the middle of the passage as Bardi and part of Jalan (Tallon Island); he said to the east of Kalmbarr it was Jawi, thus identifying the rock as marking the boundary between Bardi and Jawi.[220] Between Jalan and the two islands, Bulnginy and Ralral (Poolgnin and Salural islands), there is a current called Gardadin.[221]

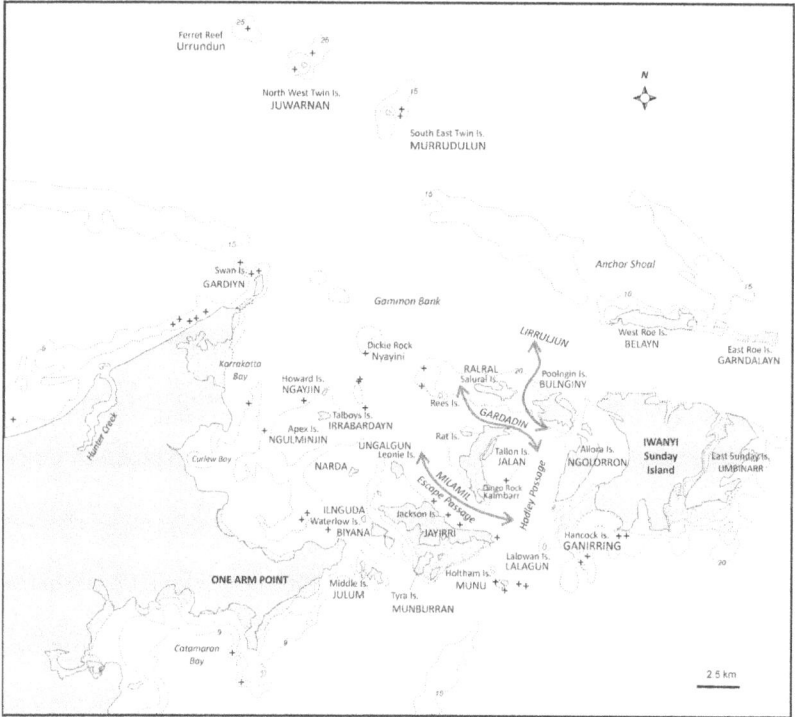

Figure 16: Map showing islands and currents between One Arm Point and Sunday Island.

As the most senior Jawi man from the Nilagunbur estate on Sunday Island, Khaki Stumpagee's evidence was important to the question of where the boundary between Jawi and Bardi country lay (and indeed, his evidence was significant to Jawi as a whole).[222] So too was Jimmy Ejai's evidence. Other Bardi and Jawi people unequivocally recognised him as the most senior man associated with Jayirri (Jackson Island), an island adjacent to Jalan. Jimmy Ejai always identified himself as a Bardi man, and he also used the term 'Inalabul' (also pronounced as Inalabulu), denoting his identity as an islander. A number of witnesses used the term Inalabulu to refer to Bardi people having primary affiliations with Jackson and Tyra islands.[223] The term Inalabul (or Inalabulu), meaning 'islander', is also used to describe this region as represented in the Nguril ritual, held when young initiates are welcomed back from a period of seclusion in the bush.[224] Jawi people associated with Sunday Island are referred to as Iwanyun, and distinguished from Inalabulu accordingly. Khaki Stumpagee's evidence clarified that Inalabul and Jawi were not the same: he stated that he was *not* Inalabul; he was Jawi.[225] In his evidence, Khaki Stumpagee said that Inalabul 'means' (refers to) Jackson Island, Tyra Island,[226] and this concurred with evidence given by Jimmy Ejai.[227]

In his supplementary anthropological report, Bagshaw (2001a, p. 28) noted that in 1997 Khaki Stumpagee identified Jalan as a Jawi island, Jayirri (Jackson Island) as a Bardi island, and the boundary between Bardi and Jawi as Escape Passage (Milamil, which lay between the two islands). He also observed that Jimmy Ejai, three days later, identified the boundary between Bardi and Jawi differently, as Hadley Passage, thus identifying Jalan as a Bardi island. Bagshaw (2001a, p. 28) relayed how, on subsequently checking Jimmy Ejai's description of the boundary with Khaki Stumpagee, the latter had concurred, and how in his initial evidence under cross-examination, he had also described the island as 'not Jawi'.[228] Towards the end of his cross-examination, however, Khaki Stumpagee also described Jalan as a Jawi Island (Bagshaw 2001a, p. 31).[229] Khaki Stumpagee's oscillating evidence in relation to the identity of Jalan was clearly an evidentiary difficulty.

In response to a question raised in cross-examination by Counsel for the Commonwealth about whether the anthropologists had considered whether 'what might have been said by a Jawi person should be compared and contrasted with what is said by Bardi people on the same issue', I noted how many of the discussions conducted with Jawi man Khaki Stumpagee also included his wife, Lena, a senior Bardi woman; and that she could (and would) contradict him on occasions.[230] Lena had also given evidence about the boundary between Bardi and Jawi.

She was closely associated with the immediate area because her mother was a Jawi woman from Bulnginy and Ralral (Poolngin and Salural islands) located between Jalan (Tallon Island) and Iwanyi (Sunday Island). She had clearly identified Jalan as a Bardi island.[231] In the court, she described Jawi country as starting from Ralral and Bulnginy islands and extending east through to Iwanyi (Sunday Island) and beyond.[232] On the basis of the totality of the evidence, Bagshaw's (2001, p. 32) opinion was that Jalan was 'located at the linguistic and territorial interface between Bardi and Jawi peoples'.

Like Khaki Stumpagee, Jimmy Ejai also identified the last two estate owners for Jalan as the brothers Nimari and Jalanbur (the latter being a name that directly identified him with the Jalan estate).[233] Jimmy Ejai added that the two brothers were Bardi men, whereas Khaki Stumpagee did not ascribe them any particular identity (as Bardi or Jawi) (Bagshaw 2001a, p. 33).[234] Jimmy Ejai identified his father as a 'close cousin' of the two men; he said they lived on Jayirri and Jalan together, that they were family.[235] He claimed a right to speak about Jalan on the basis that his father's cousin was Jalanbur, and that other Bardi people had told him he should speak for Jalan.[236] The ethnographic evidence also demonstrates that, among Bardi and Jawi people, patrifiliates from neighbouring estates usually assume custodial responsibilities (to 'look after') deceased estates until such time as succession (on their part) has taken place. Accordingly, Ejai's assumption of the responsibilities to look after and 'speak for' Jalan appears to have a further basis in traditional cultural practice.

When Khaki Stumpagee was asked about Irrabardayn (Talboys Island), and whether it was a Jawi island, he said that it was not; the 'Ejai mob' were the boss of that island, and they were not Jawi.[237] This piece of evidence was omitted from the summary of Khaki Stumpagee's evidence in the Sampi judgment.[238] The omission is significant because it clearly runs counter to the 2005 determination about the 'Jawi' identity of all the islands off the coast of One Arm Point. As Khaki Stumpagee described it, he could only speak for his island (Sunday Island), for Bulnginy (Poolngin Island),[239] Ralral (Salural Island), and Belayn and Garndalayn (the Roe Islands).[240] He did not make the claim that he could speak for Jalan, in contrast to Jimmy Ejai, who did make that claim on culturally sanctioned custodianship principles. Ejai's view was that 'Bardi as far as Jalan because my father's cousin was Harry. He Bardi and that's his country and they were together all the time in those islands'.[241]

Juljinabur (Brue Reef)

One of the mythological narratives associated with Jalan connects that island with Brue Reef, which Bardi and Jawi call Juljinabur. Brue Reef is a large tidally exposed reef located some 23 nautical miles offshore. The name Juljinabur reflects the reef's association with a central figure in the narrative called Jul.[242] Jimmy Ejai described this myth as a 'record about what happened there, story in Aboriginal way' (in Bagshaw & Glaskin 2000, p. 31). As Bagshaw (2001a, p. 35) said in his supplementary report, although there were different versions of the myth, all contained the following essential elements: that three men had drifted on a tidal current from Jalan (Tallon Island) to Juljinabur (Brue Reef), which at this time was an island; that Jul (or Julu) had intervened to save the men from the *munjanggid* (a greedy cannibalistic people who lived there, and would have killed and eaten the men); and that Jul saved the men by putting them on an *inbargun* (a large coolamon that was, in this case, made from paperbark) and sending them back on the tide to Jalan.

In the first trial, evidence was given at the reef itself. The distinctive coral outcrops on the reef were identified as the houses of Jul and his greedy sons; the name Jul referred to a fish but the fish, Jul, was a human being.[243] On approach from One Arm Point, the first parts of Brue Reef to become visible on a receding tide are the *minimbh* (a whale that turned into a rock) and the *nirrayi* (the houses of Jul and the *munjanggid*).

The *nirrayi* are micratolls, 'disc-shaped coral colonies with dead tops and live sides', which 'form on reef flats and can grow up to several metres in diameter' (Lewis et al. 2013, p. 119). These large bleached structures stand out in colour and form against the brown reefscape and are visible from some distance away. As well as preserving the knowledge of a current that, if accessed by mangrove log raft at the right time, could take people all the way out to Brue Reef and would allow them to return to Tallon Island, the narrative also provided an explanation for the topographic features of the reef.

A number of versions of the narrative also included information to the effect that it was after these mythological events that the island sank and became a reef. As Bagshaw (1999, p. 68) wrote in his original report, one version was that the powerful ancestral being Galalung had 'caused the island to be inundated by seawater in order to punish the *munjanggid*, who were drowned outright'; in another version it was the fighting between Jul and the *munjanggid* which had caused the island to sink.

In their introduction to the book *Customary Marine Tenure in Australia*, Peterson and Rigsby (1998, p. 4) say that:

> It is common for people to say, when asked how far out to sea their sea estates go, that they go 'to the horizon'…This field of vision is extended both by the distances people can see from elevated points and by the area they can see when at their farthest point of travel from land.

Bardi and Jawi people had similarly told Geoffrey Bagshaw and myself that their sea country extended as far as they could see. Their claim to an area of sea 12 nautical miles seaward of the mainland coast in the original application for native title reflected this formulation of how far they could see. As Peterson and Rigsby (1998, p. 4) suggest, 'the rule of thumb is that standing on the shore a person can see about 20 kilometres out to sea'. Peterson and Rigsby note that a definition of sea country as extending as far as the eye could see – a formulation also influenced by 'the area they can see when at their farthest point of travel from land' (by means of watercraft such as rafts) – is that such distant areas are rarely used. 'However,' they say,

> Just because parts of sea country were not used, visited or policed does not make them any less part of their sea country as Australia's difficulties with parts of its sea territory in the southern ocean, which are rarely visited and/or unpoliced and almost unpoliceable, makes clear (Peterson & Rigsby 1998, p. 4).

The tidally exposed coral reef Juljinabur represented the outer limit of the claim, and was included on the advice of senior Bardi and Jawi people on the basis that they had a story for that place. Since mission times at Sunday Island, the reef has been an important economic site that Bardi and Jawi have used to gather trochus shell for commercial sale. The fact that the reef had been exploited for shell during the mission era prompted Counsel for the Commonwealth to argue that knowledge of the reef was purely a post-contact phenomenon, and as such the reef could not be considered to lie within the traditional territory of either Bardi or Jawi people. Moreover, in the Commonwealth's opinion, the mythological narrative linking Bardi and Jawi peoples with Brue Reef had only arisen since the establishment of Sunday Island mission in 1899 (Commonwealth of Australia 2003, p. 34). Counsel for the Commonwealth therefore argued that the myth could not be construed as evidence of a continuing cultural connection to the reef predating the acquisition of sovereignty in 1829.

Yet the evidence did establish both the mythological connection to the reef, and that Bardi (particularly Ardiolan and Inalabulu Bardi) and Jawi had been exploiting the reef over some considerable time. What was also apparent in the evidence given before the court was that most people who had grown up at Lombadina mission had little or no knowledge of the mythological narrative and were less likely to have visited Brue Reef than people who had been associated with Sunday Island. Under cross-examination by Counsel for the Commonwealth, one of the women who had grown up at Lombadina described the reef as a 'men's place' that women and children were not allowed to walk upon, and said she did not know the Aboriginal name of the reef (T323.25–37). This reflects some knowledge differentiation between people who had grown up at Lombadina and those who had grown up at Sunday Island. Bowern (2009, p. 634) advances the view that 'Bardi people say it [Brue Reef] is the English name, but no one has used the old Bardi name for it in living memory'. Although she cites the mythological narrative, she does not appear to have heard the name Juljinabur, which was commonly used during the 1990s amongst people who relayed the mythological narrative at One Arm Point. Indeed, Bagshaw was given the Bardi nickname Juljinabur following his first attempt to visit the reef; some senior people today still refer to him by this name. Notwithstanding an evident differentiation in knowledge about the reef between some people associated with Sunday Island and Lombadina missions, it had been Joe Rock, a senior Bard man who had grown up at Lombadina, who first mentioned the reef to Geoffrey Bagshaw and myself in 1994.

Whether Bardi and Jawi use of Juljinabur was a post-contact phenomenon or not was not an issue his Honour specifically addressed when making his determination about the reef. Nor did he address the issue of whether or not the associated mythological narrative preceded the presence of Europeans in the area. Justice French found that the evidence about Brue Reef 'established its mythological significance'; but that 'it did not establish that native title rights and interests devolved on the applicants under their traditional law and custom' (paragraph 7). He wrote:

> There is force in the proposition that the content of the Brue Reef story is inconsistent with anyone having rights to it. The

men who were rescued by Jul were men who had drifted there. They were sent safely back to their homes by Jul. This is hardly the foundation for an assertion that the Reef is part of traditional country.[244]

Writing of Warlpiri cosmology, Munn (1973, p. 24) has observed that mythological narratives serve to memorialise 'persons and events outside the memories of living actors'. While the connection between the Brue Reef narrative and sea-level rise in this region (see Lewis et al. 2013; Nunn 2014) cannot be definitively made, it is at least suggestive that the myth may be 'of some antiquity.'[245] One elderly Bardi woman (in her late eighties or early nineties) had also told me of an *ilma* (a public genre of song, dance and associated emblems that are carried during the performance) associated with Juljinabur. She told me that the *munjanggid* sang the *ilma* and she could sing me the words. Although some older Bardi had some recollection of the existence of that *ilma*, or had heard of it, I came across few people who remembered the words with the same clarity as this woman. That few Bardi remembered the *ilma* could also be considered as indicative of the fact that the myth's inception is not as recent as Counsel for the Commonwealth would suggest.[246]

The evidence about Juljinabur exemplifies some of the difficulties associated with making claims to distant offshore areas. On appeal, the decision was made by the applicants (following legal advice) not to pursue the claim to Juljinabur. Notwithstanding this, the mythological narrative concerning Juljinabur does raise questions that may be of importance well beyond the native title context. One question is whether the myth was one of recent (post-contact) provenance or, indeed, whether it may encapsulate environmental knowledge of a time when the reef was an island before rising sea levels inundated it causing it to 'sink'. While the suggestion that an oral tradition could preserve such knowledge for such a long period of time might be met with scepticism, Nunn & Reid's (2015) research documents and correlates rising sea levels with topographical knowledge of a much earlier time, reflected in Aboriginal oral narratives from different parts of the Australian coast. This is a correlation, they argue, that should not be ignored.

Jayirri (Jackson Island)

One of the least expected parts of the 2005 determination, in my view, was the finding that Jayirri (Jackson Island) was not a Bardi island. What made it so surprising was that Jimmy Ejai was widely recognised amongst both Bardi and Jawi as being the senior man for the island. He was also recognised as a Bardi person, and most of the evidence given was to the effect that the island was Bardi. In other words, a finding that the island was not Bardi did not reflect the bulk of the applicant evidence on this matter. Justice French's finding in relation to the islands was specifically about their identity at sovereignty. As he stated, 'I am not satisfied that they were part of traditional Bardi territory at sovereignty' (paragraph 5). His view about the current identity of the islands was not apparent from the judgment.

Senior Jawi man Aubrey Tigan had testified that Jayirri was Bardi.[247] Senior Bardi lawman Dennis Davey's evidence was that Jackson Island was 'Ejai's country', and that it was Inalabul ('islander') Bardi.[248] His older brother Joseph Davey described Jimmy Ejai as the *madja* (senior ritual leader, or boss) for Jayirri.[249] Senior Jawi man Khaki Stumpagee had said that Inalabul 'means' (refers to) Jackson Island and Tyra Island; and said that while his own country (Nilagunbur at Sunday Island) was close by, Inalabul was 'really boss' for that island. Khaki also said that 'they was talking Bardi language, that one, all them mob'.[250] Khaki's wife Lena, whose mother was a Jawi woman from Bulnginy/Ralral (Poolngin and Salural islands), had said unequivocally in her evidence that Jackson Island was Bardi; her brother, Freddy Bin Sali, had also said that Jackson Island was a

Bardi island.[251] He said that Inalabulu Bardi refers to the *inalang* mob, the island mob, Jimmy Ejai and Albert Lennard; and that Jimmy's country was Jayirri.[252]

Some of the evidence in relation to the island and its identity may nonetheless have seemed ambiguous. As well as saying that Jackson Island was a Bardi island, Freddy bin Sali also referred to Jackson Island (Jayirri) and Tallon Island (Jalan) as 'Bardi and Jawi mixed,' saying they (Bardi and Jawi) were 'close together all lot'.[253] Bernadette Angus, whose father was a Jawi man from Sunday Island and whose mother was a Bardi woman from Miligunbur on the eastern side of the Dampier Peninsula, was also asked questions in cross-examination about the issue. Her father had been widely recognised as a knowledgeable Jawi man. He had passed away in early 1994, not long before the claim research began. His marriage to a woman who had grown up at Lombadina mission saw him living at Lombadina and raising his own children there, Bernadette among them. Under cross-examination, she said she was not sure whether Jackson Island was a Bardi or a Jawi island, and also described the island as being 'for' both Bardi and Jawi, saying that it was 'mixed'.[254] Under further cross-examination, she then stated that Jackson Island was Jawi.[255] This view was contrary to Khaki's testimony that Jackson Island was Inalabul and that Inalabul was not Jawi. Also noteworthy in this regard, however, is that she had said she would defer to Khaki regarding knowledge on Jawi matters.[256]

In his supplementary anthropological report, Bagshaw (2001a, p. 24) discussed the Aboriginal-English term 'mixed', commenting that the term is 'typically used to indicate or describe the nature, intensity and relative extent of various social, economic and/or linguistic relationships'. 'At least in the Bardi and Jawi case', he argued, the term 'mixed' or 'mix' was not a term used to describe territorial ownership; rather, it was indicative of some aspect of relations between people from different language-named groups; in this case, Bardi and Jawi (Bagshaw 2001a, p. 24). Where people giving evidence in the case used the term 'mixed', it usually referred to people associated with a particular area having both Bardi and Jawi forebears, or speaking both languages.

Jimmy Ejai, recognised by other senior Bardi Lawmen as the 'boss' (the most senior patrifiliate) for Jayirri, testified that his country was Jayirri (Jackson Island), and that this was also his father's country. Additionally, his father's father, Mandirr, was from Jayirri and had been born there. He stated that Mandirr's father (his paternal grandfather's father) was from Jayirri too.[257] He described Jayirri as Bardi, and said that he himself was Inalabulu, which means from the islands, a term applied to the islands from Jalan back to and including Jayirri.[258] Jimmy Ejai's evidence about Jayirri was largely given from a boat because rough sea conditions had prevented the court from going ashore. In spite of this, his evidence on the cultural topography of the island and surrounding islands and waters was substantial. None of this evidence – either from Jimmy Ejai or from the majority of other witnesses – appeared to have been considered consequential enough to identify Jayirri as Bardi.

Julum (Middle Island)

Over the course of the trial, the applicants argued that Julum (Middle Island) is a Bardi island. Julum, visible in the photograph taken from Jindirron (Round Rock) at One Arm Point, (see Figure 17), is the island where, Bardi and Jawi say, the important ancestral being Galalung had left his footprint; he had travelled from Julum to a rocky outcrop in Nilagunbur, Khaki Stumpagee's estate on Sunday Island.

During the course of the first trial, the court had travelled to Julum by boat with senior Bardi man Jimmy Ejai, who gave evidence about Galalung's footprint and the associated story there.[259] He described the island as his father's and grandfather's country. Ejai explained that Galalung had forbidden people other than old people from eating the red emperor fish, but the people did not listen to him.[260] Galalung had come to Julum

Figure 17: Standing at Jindirron (Round Rock) on One Arm Point, view across to Julum (Middle Island). Photo: Katie Glaskin (2011).

from Bulgun, a big rock at Guwarngun (in Nilagunbur) on Sunday Island, and had walked across the sea; there was a big flame moving at the same time, punishing people and burning them because they had eaten the forbidden fish. Thereafter he had returned to Bulgun and gone up into the sky.[261] Jimmy Ejai did not know what language Galalung had spoken, but said that Galalung came from Iwanyi (Sunday Island), a Jawi place, and the first place he visited was Julum, a Bardi place. He said that Galalung was going backwards and forwards (between the two islands).[262] While he originally stated that the language for Julum was Bardi, under cross-examination, he had added it was 'maybe Jawi too because he (Galalung) was there'.[263] Jimmy Ejai said that when Galalung arrived at Julum, it was a Bardi place,[264] and he pointed out Galalung's fossilised footprint on the island.[265]

Galalung is an important culture hero in Bardi and Jawi cosmology.[266] As Ejai explained in his evidence at the island, it was Galalung who gave them marriage laws which said that people from the alternate generational moieties of *inara* and *jandu* were not allowed to marry, meaning that one had to marry within their own moiety category.[267] This part of Ejai's evidence was not included in the summary of his evidence given in the determination.[268] The omission of this evidence about Galalung as lawgiver was, I suggest, consequential for how Galalung's relationship to *both* Bardi and Jawi peoples may have been understood, as I discuss below.

Reasons, Evidence and the Archive

In Sampi, unpredictably (because the term 'society' had not been introduced at the time that most of the evidence in the case was heard), judicial precedent in the form of society became implicated with the claim to sea. As it emerged through the case, the central tenet of the claim to sea came to rest on the use of mangrove log rafts that allowed people to travel considerable distances between the islands, using the currents like 'roads' in the sea. It was the evidence about the mangrove log rafts in conjunction with the impressive knowledge about the sea that, in terms of making out the native title claim offshore, appeared to be the convincing factor for the court. The knowledge about the sea was indicated, in part, through the naming of all the marine features in the area: the rocks, the sandbanks, the shoals, the reefs, the freshwater that runs underground and emerges out in the sea,[269] the currents, the whirlpools, and so on. In 2005, the mythological narrative about Brue Reef, for example, did not convince the court of any long-term association with the reef. Nor did the restricted evidence about the activities of ancestral beings and associated sites of significance offshore lead to any kind of native title right being recognised over these at the time. In the determination, evidence about the use of marine species (fish, shellfish and pearl shell) was considered as evidence pertaining to the intertidal zone (Justice French had found that the claimants had a right to take pearl shell, but this was necessarily restricted to the intertidal zone).[270] Evidence was given about the hunting of dugong and turtle from mangrove log rafts and, contemporarily, from dinghies. There was also evidence that estates *(buru)* extend offshore beyond the intertidal zone, with one applicant, for example, indicating that his *buru* went way out to 'the blue area' (or deep sea).[271] None of this evidence, however, appeared to convince Justice French that Bardi had native title offshore. A shared mission history at Sunday Island had laid the foundation for respondents to argue that Bardi use of watercraft was a post-sovereignty phenomenon acquired from Jawi and, having argued that all the islands were Jawi, the next step was to argue that Jawi had ceased to exist as a 'society'.

In his determination, Justice French stated that the evidence did not allow him 'to infer that the islands to the immediate north of the mainland were Bardi country at the time of sovereignty', saying that 'indeed the degree of inconsistency in this respect suggests that they may well have been Jawi in earlier days' (paragraph 1104). As a consequence, he wrote, 'I will not include any of the islands to the north of the Dampier Peninsula in the determination' (ibid.). While I have thus far identified some key differences between the evidence his Honour recited in the judgment and the totality of the evidence actually on record in the transcript, there are further unaccounted discrepancies which bear examination.

In making his determination on the issue, Justice French referred to the applicant evidence WAFIC and the Commonwealth had cited in their submissions. WAFIC had pointed to the evidence of Paul Sampi (a senior Bardi man from Ngamagunbur, on the western side of the peninsula) and Freddy Bin Sali (a senior Bardi man from Mardnanbur on the eastern side of the peninsula), who had both described the islands as 'mixed Bardi and Jawi' (paragraph 1103). However, what Paul Sampi had actually said in his evidence about Jackson Island was that it is Bardi, but that it is also 'mixed up', because the fathers are [Bardi] from there, the mothers are Jawi.[272] In other words, he was using the term 'mixed' to describe intermarriage; he explicitly identified the 'fathers' as being Bardi. Freddy Bin Sali had also said that the island was a Bardi island, but this part of his testimony was not included in the WAFIC account of his evidence.[273]

WAFIC also relied on evidence from Bernadette Angus that the islands were Jawi (at paragraph 1103), as discussed above. She had previously described herself and the status of her knowledge in relation to that of senior man Khaki Stumpagee as one in which she was just a 'spring onion'.[274] Jawi man Aubrey Tigan's uncertainty about the identity of Jalan and Lena Stumpagee's explicit identification of it as Bardi are also cited.[275] The applicant evidence reviewed in Justice French's determination at this point and selectively cited by WAFIC does indeed appear inconsistent (although only one of the witnesses cited, Bernadette Angus, stated that the islands were all Jawi). Yet what most stands out at this point in the judgment is that the evidence of the two men with the greatest authority to speak about the area by virtue of their traditional associations with the islands therein, Sunday Island (Jawi man Khaki Stumpagee) and Jackson Island (Bardi man Jimmy Ejai), was neither reviewed nor cited in relation to the identity of the islands. While the two men's evidence about the boundary between Bardi and Jawi and about the identity of Jalan island (Tallon Island) were not in accord (as discussed above), there was no disagreement between them about the identity of the islands to the west of Tallon Island as Bardi, including Jayirri (Jackson Island) and Julum (Middle Island). This point serves to highlight another feature of the judge's reasons; namely, that it does not appear as though an attempt was made to evaluate the evidence in relation to each of the islands in terms of who might have the most authority to speak about them under traditional law and custom. Jimmy Ejai's evidence about his own country was not included.

Other evidence cited by his Honour included submissions put forward by the Commonwealth concerning 'early accounts' which, with the exception of Elkin, were said to have identified the islands as Jawi. As Justice French stated, 'The Commonwealth submitted that all the islands east of Swan Point were traditionally Jawi albeit the Jawi had lost their connection with them' (at paragraph 1101).

From the outset of the claim, the Commonwealth had taken the view that all of the islands immediately off the coast of One Arm Point were Jawi islands. Support for this argument came from a hand-drawn map produced by resident magistrate Wace (in 1904) and a map produced by Tindale (1974). In her oral evidence, historian Fiona Skyring, who had submitted a historian's report in the case, described the Wace map as 'a very rough sketch map of – well, the particular islands at the mouth of the King Sound'.[276] As Justice French surmised it,

> According to Dr Skyring's evidence, senior Jawi men, supported by the National Aboriginal Council, wrote of the islands belonging to the Jawi in 1982. The Commonwealth again relied on Green and Turner's reliance upon Tindale in their 1984 submission. Robinson agreed with Tindale. Elkin

thought Jackson Island was mixed and was a 'stepping stone' between Bardi and Jawi (at paragraph 1100).

The Tindale (1974) map showed all of the islands west of Sunday Strait as Jawi. In their submission to the Seaman Inquiry, Green and Turner (1984) reproduced Tindale's map.[277] But Tindale's (1974) map incorrectly identified four of the islands in question (see Figure 18). During his cross-examination, Bagshaw pointed out that some of the locations of these islands were incorrect.[278] While these misidentifications of the names of

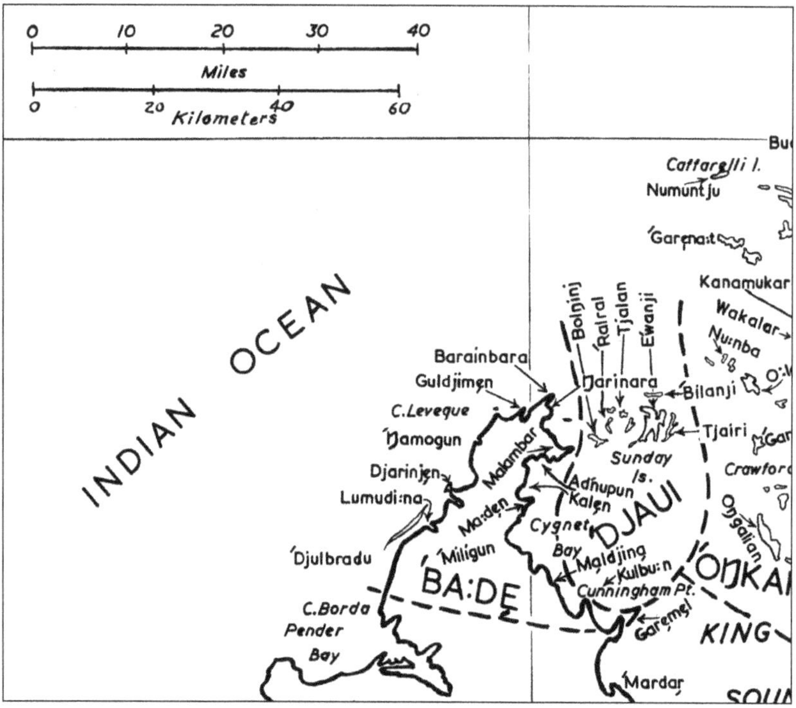

Figure 18: In the above extract, 'Bolnginj' should be Jayirri (Jackson Island); 'Ralral' should be Jalan (Tallon Island); 'Tjalan' should be Bulnginy (Poolngin Island); and 'Tjairi' should be Umbinarr, (East Sunday Island). (This map is a reproduction from N. B. Tindale's (1974, p. 146) map of Indigenous group boundaries existing at the time of first European settlement in Australia. It is not intended to represent contemporary relationships to land.) © Tony Tindale and Beryl George, 1974 courtesy of the South Australian Museum.

the islands should have led to reservations about the accuracy of Tindale's depictions, there is no suggestion that this was ever the case.

As Bagshaw also pointed out in his evidence, Tindale formulated his boundaries on the basis of speaking with a single Bardi informant, in Broome.[279] He had not visited Bardi or Jawi country, and this is likely to have contributed to the mixing up of island names evident in the map.

In his Master's thesis, Robinson (1973, p. 244) referred to 'the Djawi man Idjaji Djaijiriburu' and identified Jayirri as a Jawi island. While the orthography differs, it is clear that this is Jimmy Ejai's father, Ijay. In his supplementary report to the court, Bagshaw (2001a, p. 19) had noted that 'levels of knowledge concerning estate associations with country can and do change over time... particularly in the post-contact context', and gave several examples of mainland estates (as well as Jalan) that were subject to processes of succession. Jayirri, however, was not identified as one of these. Had there been a change in identity from Jawi to Bardi within one family in the space of a single generation, this would not have amounted to succession, for at no stage had the estate become 'vacant'. In any case, Ijay and his descendants continued to be the people that Bardi and Jawi alike associated with the island, as was another Bardi man and his family who were associated with Munburran (Tyra Island), one of the two Jayirriburu estates. Elkin's genealogies, collected in 1927–28, were divided into two sets: 'Bad' (i.e., 'Bard'/ Bardi) and 'Djau' (Jawi). Jimmy Ejai's father's father, Mandirr, ('Mander, of Djairi' – that is, of Jayirri) is in the Bād (Bard) notebook, along with other Djairi men (Elkin 1927–8a). Based on his fieldwork with Bardi and Jawi in 1968, Robinson (1973, p. 106) himself had written that 'some Bardi claim that a few (Bardi) families were occupying one or two of the smaller islands between Sunday Island and the mainland before the arrival of the first pearling fleets in the King Sound'. There is no doubt that these 'smaller islands' are those that were in contention in this case. The occupation of such islands before the first pearling fleets in the area would have meant that Bardi occupied them before effective colonisation of the area.

As I review the evidence now, more than a decade after it was originally given, the appropriate starting point in thinking about the identity of these islands remains the same: 'the hearts and minds' of the Aboriginal witnesses most closely associated with the islands in question, those persons who claimed and were recognised by the wider jural public as being the traditional owners of those islands. Of particular significance too is the relationship between Galalung the lawgiver and both the Bardi and Jawi peoples. In his Master's thesis, Robinson (1973, p. 119) described Galalung as one of the 'three main culture-heroes in Bardi and Djawi religion'. He wrote:

> Galalung was the first to travel the country in the Dreamtime, creating the natural environment and setting down the marriage laws of the Djawi and Bardi. He imposed restrictions on the eating of certain sorts of food, and when he surprised a group of men eating forbidden fish at Djulum (a small island between Sunday Island and the mainland), he sent a fire-ball across the sea to destroy them. He then threw a spear into the heavens from Sunday Island and climbed it to the Milky Way. The few men who survived the fire formed the nucleus of the Bardi and Djawi. They have maintained his laws and follow the food restrictions he imposed (Robinson 1973, p. 119).

As Bagshaw had noted in his supplementary report to the court submitted after the evidence in the 'first trial' had been heard:

> In my experience, it would be most unusual for an entire people (i.e. the Bardi) to recognize a supernatural being as a fundamental 'culture-giver' had that being not been associated (whether through physical presence or projected action) with at least part of the territorial domain (Bagshaw 2001a, p. 21, fn.13).

In a case in which native title was found over Bardi country but not over Jawi country, the boundary between Bardi and Jawi took on a significance that had not been anticipated, excluding Jawi country and Bardi islands the judge considered were likely to have been Jawi at the time of sovereignty. Writing about this with the benefit of hindsight, my view is that this result was unexpected because, given the Jawi evidence provided to the Court, it seemed inconceivable that native title would not be found to exist over Jawi country as well as Bardi country. Nor would I have envisaged that the evidence of a Bardi patrifiliate about his own country would be given less weight than the evidence of others who did not have that primary connection.

Chapter Nine

Society and Sea on Appeal

The thing that puzzles me and looms in my mind is the idiocy of an outcome whereby potentially this court says, 'No-one has native title', where in fact all the people who really know what's going on, on the ground, say these people in one or another configuration do have it. I mean, how stupid would that be, and it's not impossible (Justice North, oral statement during the Full Court appeal in *Sampi v State of Western Australia*).[280]

Technically Land or Technically Water

In 2015 the *Guardian* newspaper reported that China has been reclaiming reefs which are 'under water at high tide and therefore not considered land under international law' by covering them with enormous quantities of dredged debris from the seabed in order to create islands (Tsang 2015, p. 1). Apart from its implications for international relations, this story highlights some of the conceptual and legal issues concerning the basis of the distinction between land and sea that were also present in the Sampi case.

Justice French's comment when he delivered his judgment that he doubted whether anyone would be pleased by his decision was prescient. The applicants were unhappy for, while there was a determination of exclusive possession over the mainland,

Jawi islands and the islands claimed as Bardi had been excluded from the determination. Native title was not recognised offshore and, although non-exclusive rights had been recognised in the intertidal zone, issues about where exclusive and non-exclusive native title rights and interests were recognised had arisen due to the region's extraordinary tidal variation. One of these issues was to do with the islets and islands in the intertidal zone, features that were connected to the mainland at low tide, but separated from it at high tide. These features were treated as part of the intertidal zone; and thus as being areas where non-exclusive native title rights existed. But since they remain above the mean high-water mark, the applicants argued that these should be treated as land, where the native title rights of exclusive possession existed. Islands in this category included Leveque Island, which Bardi call Anbarrngani, located just off the tip of Cape Leveque. In response to Justice Branson's question about whether the treatment of these islets

Figure 19: Technically land or technically water: Anbarrngani, Leveque Islet, connected to land at low tide. Photo: Katie Glaskin (2011).

and islands as part of the waters rather than as part of the land had been deliberate, Robert Blowes, one of the two barristers who acted for the applicants in the appeal, suggested that it was a geographic issue that 'just seems to have been overlooked'.[281] In addition, the applicants had sought specific rights to protect two offshore features of special cultural significance – Lalariny, and Alarm Shoals – but had not been successful in this regard.

One Society or Two

The main issue for consideration in the appeal, though, was the question of society. It was this issue that led to the exclusion of Jawi country along with the claimed Bardi islands from the determination, and was additionally consequential for the recognition of native title offshore.

The State of Western Australia was not content with the determination, either. Its concerns, as stated in the appeal transcript, were to do with how Justice French had dealt with the issue of 'society'. The Commonwealth, too, had issues it wished to appeal, as did the other major respondent in the case, the Western Australian Fishing Industry Council (WAFIC). While the Commonwealth's position was one of 'general support' for the trial judge's determination, they contended that Jawi should not be included as 'rights holders' in the existing determination of native title over Bardi country simply because they were 'part of the Bardi community'.[282] In addition, they supported WAFIC's submissions that the existing determination should be amended 'to the effect that it should spell out that the native title rights which have been accorded are not of a commercial nature'.[283]

Errors of Law, Matters of Fact

Within the Federal Court of Australia, a trial judge's decision can be appealed before a Full Court constituted of three Federal Court judges. Full Court decisions (which may in turn be appealed before the High Court of Australia) typically provide legal precedent, and so are drawn on in future cases involving the 'interpretation and application' of the relevant law.[284] Appeals can only be brought on the grounds that the trial judge who originally heard the case had 'made an error of law', although there is some provision for additional evidence to be presented to the appellate court in 'exceptional circumstances'.[285] In other words, the provision is primarily to appeal matters of law rather than matters of fact. Although cases are appealed on matters of law, matters of fact are invariably raised because these provide the context through which the appeal court must comprehend how the law has been applied. At the outset of the Sampi appeal, Justice Catherine Branson reiterated that 'a ground of appeal and a ground of complaint against the original judgment or reasons for judgment are not the same thing'.[286] She said:

> A ground of appeal is a ground upon which a judgment could be set aside or varied. It will be a ground that goes to one of the fundamental elements of the case. Complaints of a more marginal nature, about how a judge reached that position, might well be a particular of a ground of appeal but won't be a ground of appeal itself.[287]

In effect, what the appeal court has to do is to come to terms with the enormous complexities of a case in which they have not heard directly from witnesses, and, having considered submissions concerning the grounds of appeal, make a determination about how the law has been applied to the facts of the case. An appeal court has the capacity to either make a different determination to that originally made, or to order that the case be re-heard.[288]

The Sampi Full Court appeal was heard in Perth from the 26 to 28 February 2007, before Justices Catherine Branson, Anthony North, and John Mansfield. Justice Branson described the appeal as 'very large and complex'.[289] As indicated earlier, the main focus of the appeal was around the question of society and the application of the concept in native title law. Given the particulars of this case, however, the recognition of native title offshore was closely associated with this. Anthropologist Geoffrey Bagshaw and Jawi applicant Vincent Angus attended the hearing. They apprised me by phone of how the appeal was progressing as I was living in Tokyo at that time. Consequently I mainly rely on the transcript of the appeal and the appeal decision for the discussion that follows.[290]

A transcript of an appeal provides insight into legal thinking in a way that a transcript of the evidence, at least in the native title jurisdiction, usually does not. In the appeal process, no one is giving evidence, so the strategies (such as asking leading questions) associated with either getting the applicant evidence onto the record in a certain form, or creating doubt about that evidence or the person giving it, are no longer in play. Here, the contest between applicants and respondents (or rather, their respective legal representatives) occurs in a realm where everyone involved understands the rules of the game, both the formal rules and the unconscious strategies required to play effectively (Bourdieu 1977). The appeal contrasts with the trial situation where non-legal personnel giving evidence are much less likely to understand the rules of the game − both the formal rules and those that are implicit − or are actively trying to work out such rules and strategies along the way. An effect of only legal personnel being involved in an appeal then is that the culture of the court, if I can put it that way, becomes not just the dominating culture of a legal interaction (as in the trial context) − it becomes the *only* culture of that particular legal interaction. And because of this, it assumes a taken-for-granted status which tends to obscure the fact that the context is one that is not simply formal but is also cultural.

This is an apt point to turn to Burke's (2011, p. 29) point about the 'ongoing structural problem' between the claimants' lawyer(s) and their anthropologist(s) in terms of their respective deconstructions and reconstructions of the ethnographic archive.

I have already argued that, because the starting points of lawyers and anthropologists are so different, the triangulation between the evidence, the ethnographic archive and native title law (to follow Burke 2011, p. 29) is inevitably quite different in both instances. In the appeal court, however, anthropologists no longer have a formal role as expert witnesses although they are likely to occupy important backstage roles at the request of the lawyers running the case. Consequently in the appeal court, the 'structural problem' between lawyers and anthropologists largely disappears since lawyers exclusively take on the task of describing the case in order to advance their arguments about the application of law. As some of the oral submissions from legal personnel representing the State of Western Australia and the Commonwealth reveal, along with their role as advocates, lawyers effectively assume the role of 'expert' in this jurisdiction as well, putting forward their views about matters one would generally expect to lie in the realm of anthropology, rather than law.

A 'Bardi Jawi' Society

The question of whether Bardi and Jawi were one or two societies at colonisation and whether they were one or two societies now became the main reference point for later commentary on the Sampi case (e.g., Brennan 2007; Burke 2010; Burns 2011; Strelein 2005; Redmond 2011; see also Glaskin & Dousset 2011). As Strelein (2005, p. 1) noted, the decision was 'significant because it is the first substantive determination by Justice French, who is arguably one of the most experienced native title Judges of the Federal Court bench'. Justice French had, as Strelein (2005, p. 2) pointed out, served as President of the National Native Title Tribunal for three-and-a-half years prior to this determination. In 2008, he went on to become the Chief Justice of the High Court of Australia, the highest ranked judicial position in Australia. Strelein's (2005) commentary, published not long after the determination was made, noted the change in emphasis between the first and second trials occasioned by the intervening Yorta Yorta decision and the need to address the notion of society; she observed that this change in emphasis 'proved to be the central point of contention in the final decision' (2005, p. 2). Strelein also argued that there were alternative findings open to the judge, and pointed out that, while Justice French 'did not make a determination that native title *does not* exist over Jawi territory', the implications were that 'the Jawi who are members of the Bardi and Jawi society…may have effectively lost any estate rights or other rights that they held in their own territory' (2005, p. 5, my emphasis). As barrister Robert Blowes noted during the appeal, however, the determination with respect to those areas of Jawi country included in the Sampi claim was 'that native title doesn't exist in those areas', and this determination was *in rem*, meaning that there could be 'no determination in favour of any society or any group over those islands, apart from the process of appeal or via North Js suggestion of agreement'.[291]

Justice French had found in favour of a Bardi 'society' into which Jawi 'society' had been incorporated. This notion was the basis upon which he had recognised native title over Bardi country with native title holders that included both Bardi and Jawi persons. Justice French's reasons for finding that Bardi and Jawi were two societies at sovereignty primarily rested on their different self-identifications as either Bardi or Jawi, along with the different languages and territories associated with each of these identifications.[292] Distinct territorial affiliations, languages and identities were thus taken to indicate that formerly there were two different societies. The applicants' emphasis on their unity as 'one people' in the second trial led the trial judge to infer that there must have been a transformation in the societies such that they had become one society in the period following settlement. The particular factors that led the trial judge to draw the conclusion that Jawi society had been subsumed by Bardi society included the much smaller population of Jawi, the decline of Jawi as a spoken language, intermarriage with Bardi, the co-residence of Bardi and Jawi at Sunday Island mission, and 'the views of early writers'.[293]

As the barrister representing the State of Western Australia, Raelene Webb, described it, there were 'three hypotheses' about the relationship between Bardi and Jawi societies at sovereignty and today suggested by Justice French.[294] She said:

> The first is that there's always a Bardi and Jawi society, one law, one culture, one country and that was the appellant's unrelenting case at trial. The second hypothesis was two societies at sovereignty which had become one because of the absorption of the Jawi people into Bardi society and that, in the end, is what his Honour found. *That's the result we complain of and the appellants complain of.* The third one is that there were always two societies, one of which, the Jawi, has considerably diminished, at least in the Sunday Island region and that of associated islands.[295]

The third possibility that Jawi and Bardi were 'always' two societies, with the contemporary Jawi 'society' being 'considerably diminished' reflected the State of Western Australia's approach to the case. As Robert Blowes, who acted for the applicants, surmised, 'as I understand the state's position throughout, your Honour, [it is] that there were two societies not one. They were prepared to accept the consequences of there being two societies. In other words, two determinations, two areas covered by separated determinations'.[296] A fourth view, not canvassed at this point, was that Bardi and Jawi as separate groups are defined by the very law they share, but that shared law did not make the country 'one country'.[297]

While the State recognised that 'native title exists and is warranted in respect of the Bardi area',[298] part of what they sought was a determination that native title did not exist with respect to the Jawi part of the claim area. As the transcript of the appeal in this case shows, the respondent parties' strategies remained fairly consistent throughout the entirety of the Sampi case, latterly being moulded to the opportunities afforded by the Yorta Yorta case and the introduction of the term 'society' into native title jurisprudence. The State of Western Australia's strategy throughout the case had been one that sought to separate Bardi and Jawi. The strategy can be understood as having continuity with their anthropologist Basil Sansom's (2001, p. 2) view that the Jawi case had been made to ride 'piggyback' on the Bardi case, and in that regard is perhaps indicative of how anthropological work might influence or shape a non-applicant's case. The next step in the strategy was to maximise the area said to be associated with Jawi (rather than Bardi) and then to argue that Jawi did not hold native title. The exchange between barrister Raelene Webb, acting for the State of Western Australia, and Justice North, who was sitting on the appeal bench, is instructive in this regard:

> *Ms Webb:* What we are now saying in essence is what we said at trial, there could be a positive resolution in favour of the Bardi, in respect of Bardi territory and those Jawi people who have rights and interests under Bardi law and custom, *but it's not our case* to say that the Jawi should have a separate determination in respect of the Jawi area.
>
> *North J:* And that's really the essence of the, sort of, practical disagreement between the parties, it's the Jawi land.
>
> *Ms Webb:* Yes. That becomes the essence of it, your Honour. I should say that the unfortunate result that would follow, if the Court accepted the findings of his Honour, of two separate societies at sovereignty which we say was clearly correct and the one Bardi and Jawi society now, would be, on our submission that there could only be a determination of no native title, but we say that was an error and there is another result, your Honour.
>
> *North J:* It would be an incredible irony if out of all of this the Court came to the conclusion that there was no native title, a result which nobody wants.

Ms Webb: Indeed, your Honour and might I say that it's always been the State's position that the case that presented the one society at sovereignty was fatal, in this particular claim. If your Honour pleases.[299]

While Webb expressed the view that presenting the case as 'one society at sovereignty was fatal', the society question was one that had only arisen following the Yorta Yorta High Court decision in late 2002. Since most of the evidence in the case was heard in 'the first trial' in 2001, Webb's reference to how the applicants had run the case in terms of the society question could only have been a reference to how it was run during the 'second trial' of 2003 when 'society' had become an issue for consideration.

In his reasons for judgment, Justice French noted a difference in emphasis between the first and second trials. He referred to 'having read the testimony of the Aboriginal witnesses given at the first trial and having heard a number of witnesses at the second trial', and said he was 'satisfied that generally they gave evidence to the best of their ability setting out their understanding of the traditional laws, customs and beliefs of the Bardi and Jawi people' (Sampi No. 1, at paragraph 1016). He referred to differences in detail between the evidence of certain of the applicants as 'hardly surprising'. He went on to say, though, that:

Having said that, it did seem to me at the hearing in June 2003 that the Aboriginal witnesses placed great emphasis upon the unity of the Bardi and Jawi people as one society and the one law. Some of their testimony seemed almost formulaic in that regard. By that time of course it was clear that the question whether there had been from the time of annexation, one society or two for the purpose of the recognition of native title rights and interests, was a matter of some importance (Sampi No. 1, at paragraph 1017).

As discussed, between 2001 and 2003 it was not simply the case that counsel for the applicants had changed. The introduction of the term 'society' into native title jurisprudence meant the way the courts approached native title had also changed. Hence Justice French's comment in his reasons for judgment that the question of whether there was one society or two at the 'time of annexation' had assumed 'some importance'. Justice French continued,

> While the emphasis on that issue at the second trial might have responded to a perceived vulnerability in the applicants' case, it does not mean that they are to be disbelieved in their statements about how they regard the current relationship between the two peoples albeit the one society proposition was put argumentatively on the basis of one law, one culture *and one country*. Their evidence, in my opinion, supports the view that the Bardi and Jawi people today see themselves essentially as one people united by common laws and customs. The contrary hypothesis would require treating the evidence of the Aboriginal witnesses as part of a wholesale coordinated fabrication about current beliefs which go to their cultural identity (Sampi No. 1, paragraph 1017, my emphasis).

In her submissions to the Full Court appeal Webb referred to the passage above, observing his Honour's comments were 'in [relation to] the way the case was – the evidence in the way the case was run'.[300] She highlighted the fact that the applicants in the case had mainly distinguished themselves as Bardi or Jawi, with the exception of 'a short spell in the 2003 evidence… when they attempt to use the terminology Bardi-Jawi'.[301] This assessment is borne out in the analysis of the applicants' evidence as between the first and second trials. In the 'first trial' where the bulk of the evidence was provided (over nineteen days of applicant evidence, followed by five days of expert evidence), the applicants had mainly referred to themselves as Bardi or

Jawi, although there are about seven references to 'Bardi Jawi'. Four witnesses had used the term: one of them had a Bardi and a Jawi parent, and the others were using the term in the context of describing relationships as 'mixed'. In the second trial, the three days of extra evidence, the term 'Bardi-Jawi' appears sixty-three times, which can only be considered a marked contrast. Webb was not the only one to point this discrepancy out during the appeal. Blowes too acknowledged that Justice French may have been facing two particular difficulties. One was that the Sampi claim did not include all Jawi country, only the islands and sea country to the west of the Sunday Strait.[302] The other was that 'his Honour noted at more than one place, I think, that there was some difference in tone between the evidence on that issue ['the assertions of unity'], at the first trial and the second trial'.[303]

Section 223(1) of the Native Title Act defines 'native title' or 'native title rights and interests' as 'the communal, group or individual rights and interests of Aboriginal peoples or Torres Strait Islanders in relation to land or waters'. These rights and interests are to be 'possessed under the traditional laws acknowledged, and the traditional customs observed' (Section 223(1a) of the Native Title Act). The terms 'communal' and 'group' used in the Act do not presuppose any particular kind of social grouping. What native title law required following Yorta Yorta was a rule-bearing *society* rather than a 'group' of native title holders. In 2001, the case had been brought on behalf of Bardi and a portion of Jawi – those whose country lay on the western side of the Sunday Strait – on the basis that they were a 'single, yet internally differentiated... community of kin' (Bagshaw 2001a, p. 5) with distinct socio-linguistic identities and territorial affiliations. They were a 'community' in that they practised the same ritual (stemming from shared Law), intermarried, shared the same local and social organisation, the same corpus of mythology and a predominantly maritime economy. In the final submissions following the 2003 evidence, this closely related community of kin was recast as a society. But there was an additional recasting of the group: the characterisation of them as 'one Bardi-Jawi people' whose territorial interests were conflated as 'one Bardi-Jawi country'. The distinction between these characterisations is not insignificant. Analogically, it is rather like saying that England and Scotland are part of the one United Kingdom, ruled by a common set of laws and thus able to be considered one society; while at the same time maintaining that there is one 'England-Scotland country' in which the long-standing distinction between the territories of England and Scotland is dissolved.

Blowes and Keely, the barristers acting for the applicants in the appeal, were the third set of barristers who had represented the applicants at different times throughout the trial process. They thus inherited these earlier characterisations as part of the case. In the appeal, Blowes obliquely referenced this in the following terms: 'Your Honours, the claim was made by people *described in a certain way* and they seek a determination of native title… ultimately the facts will determine how they can be recognised as having native title.[304] Justice Branson's response to the distinction between how a people had been described and how they could be found to have native title appeared unsympathetic:

> These people said it with the assistance of a good deal of legal advice and adhered to it for a very long time up until today. I don't think it's a time to be suggesting that what they're saying has a nuance[d] understanding not consistent with the Native Title Act. We have to assume by now the positions they are putting, they are putting in the full knowledge of the operation of the Native Title Act.[305]

As a response to the legal personnel representing the applicants in the case, this comment, on the face of it, seems justified, although it obscures the fact that these particular legal representatives had inherited the situation from two preceding sets of legal personnel. If, however, we are to read this statement as one that suggests the claimants ('these people') should have 'full knowledge of the operation of the Native Title Act', the statement then becomes more difficult to accept; with the exception of highly trained legal professionals, it is highly unlikely that many people would readily acquire 'full knowledge' of a piece of legislation, let alone one as complicated as the Native Title Act. Add to this the difficulties of communication in the Court (discussed earlier), and the fact that many of the older Bardi and Jawi people giving evidence had limited or no literacy, then it would seem unreasonable to expect such 'full knowledge'.

Blowes' response to Justice Branson was to press the connection between the 'closely related community of kin' of the 2001 evidence and the 'one Bardi-Jawi people' of the 2003 evidence, with the requirements of the Native Title Act. As he put it:

> We say that at sovereignty it was one society but Jawi and Bardi people were distinct within it. They intermarried. They had a common system of the way they allocate their identity and country. They were a community of kin. They were [an] intermarrying community of kin. That is the kind of society that they were united in at sovereignty.[306]

Blowes additionally argued that if the Court found that they were two societies then, because the formal pleadings in the case 'simply names a group of people who claim native title', it did not preclude a determination on behalf of Bardi and a determination on behalf of Jawi.[307] This was a fallback position. While it sounded similar to the State of Western Australia's argument about separate determinations, it was in fact quite different, premised on the view that there should be a determination of native title over Jawi country as well as Bardi country, and not over Bardi country alone. An additional distinction between the two positions was, as Blowes noted, that 'the state's position never included seas'.[308]

Blowes had earlier been the barrister representing the applicants in *Neowarra v State of Western Australia* [2003] FCA 1402 ('Neowarra'), a successful native title claim brought over Ngarinyin country on behalf of three named groups: Worrorra, Ngarinyin and Wunambal peoples. There were, in all, three named claims that constituted the claim region.[309] The basis upon which the three named groups were claimants in all three claims, regardless of specific socio-linguistic affiliation (broadly speaking, Ngarinyin, Worrorra, and Wunambal) was that they were members of a single society, otherwise described as a cultural bloc, who shared the same set of traditional laws and customs. Blowes drew on his experience in the Neowarra case that had been brought on behalf of three named groups to argue:

> Technically the arguments that were presented to him [Justice Sundberg, the trial judge] by all the parties would have been for any number of possibilities…it was said that native title should be recognised at the level of the language group, it was said that native title should be recognised at lower levels of regional grouping than that. It was certainly never suggested in that case that that was a matter of win or lose, it's simply a matter of at which social level will the native title be recognised as being held by a group of people.[310]

The crux of the society question, then, as Blowes put it, was that native title could be found at different social levels. If the Court found that there were two sets of laws and customs, associated with two societies, then, he argued, it was open to the court to make a determination to that effect.[311]

In response, Justice North raised the issue of the Yulara case. This was a compensation case brought by applicants in relation to the town of Yulara near Uluru (Ayers Rock). The anthropological reports (Sutton & Vaarzon-Morel 2003) had described a number of means through which the applicants were connected to the area, consistent with what many anthropologists had to say about such connections in the Western Desert (e.g. Myers 1986, pp. 129–30; and see Dousset & Glaskin 2007). This became known as the 'multiple pathways' model of connection. Earlier ethnography, though, had described the system through which people acquired rights and interests in the area as one of patrilineal descent. Contrary to the evidence of the witnesses, the judge hearing the case, Justice Sackville, had found that the system of landholding in the Western Desert was one of patrilineal descent, and that there was 'not only a lack of consistency in the evidence of the Aboriginal witnesses, but their evidence does not support the way in which the applicants have pleaded and presented their case'.[312] Justice North's reference to this case was to say, 'I thought Jango said you win or you lose based upon the case you plead. There might well be a proper basis for finding native title, but if you don't come up with the proper formulation, you lose'.[313] Blowes' response was to say 'the effect of that' amounts to 'if you don't anticipate the Court's finding before you start you lose'.[314] Given the evidence in both the first and second trials, Blowes argued that it was open to the court to make a finding in relation to Bardi country and one in relation to Jawi country 'on the basis of how the case was put'.[315]

What's in a Name?

The identification of two named groups, Bardi and Jawi, was central to the problem of society that came to dominate this case. Clearly, it motivated the reframing of the case into 'one Bardi-Jawi country'. Justice Mansfield's reference to the Ngarluma/ Yindjibarndi case (*Daniel v State of Western Australia* [2003] FCA 666) in the Pilbara region of Western Australia, in which the judge had made a determination of native title such that the Ngarluma hold native title over Ngarluma country and Yindjibarndi hold native title over Yindjibarndi country, was one possible precedent for how a claim on behalf of two named groups associated with contiguous tracts of country could be dealt with by the court.[316]

This case was determined in 2003, a year after the term 'society' had made its entrance into native title jurisprudence. At that point, Blowes referred to the Alyawarr case (*Northern Territory v Alyawarr* (2005) 145 FCR 135), in which Justice Mansfield himself had been involved. As Blowes noted, the case had established, 'at least on the evidence there, that language difference is not fatal to the claim of a single native title claim group'.[317]

What is important to point out here is that what lawyers were primarily discussing in terms of 'language difference' was not necessarily about languages spoken, but rather about what has been referred to as a 'language owning group' (Sutton 2003, p. 181). This is a term used to describe the relationship between a group, a specific area of country, and the language traditionally associated with (or 'in') that country. As the lawyers were speaking about a 'language group' in this context, they were thus really speaking about a group traditionally associated with a particular language culturally connected to a defined area of country, rather than necessarily about the languages that people are actually speaking. In Aboriginal Australia, members of language-named groups were (and in many contexts, still are) typically multilingual, speaking several languages.

The applicants contended that the necessary requirement for society arising from the Yorta Yorta decision was that the applicants needed to demonstrate that they were 'a group united by acknowledgement of traditional laws and observance of traditional customs'.[318] Given this, they argued that the differences between Bardi and Jawi that were relevant to the society question were not those of language, territory, or self-identification, criteria that had concerned Justice French. Rather, what needed to be considered was whether there were differences in laws and customs.[319]

Following the appeal, later in 2007, there were more discussions with respect to how the applicants might reach a consent determination with the State of Western Australia. The State of Western Australia – which had been willing to make a consent determination in relation to the case back in 2004 – noted that they were still not satisfied as to the existence of a Jawi society, asking that additional material be put before the Court. This remained the 'most fundamental issue at stake' in the resolution of the claim.[320] It was put to the anthropologists, Geoffrey Bagshaw and myself, through legal counsel, that if we could provide the respondent's lawyers with further information about a Jawi 'society' then they would further consider a consent determination. There was some discussion about us attending a meeting with those lawyers to answer questions. It was apparent then, however, as it had been previously, that the Commonwealth would not agree to a consent determination that included the recognition of native title rights and interests offshore. Without their agreement, there would be no consent determination. It was therefore subsequently decided that there was nothing to be gained from drawing out negotiations any further.

It would take more than three years after the conclusion of the appeal for the Full Court to hand down its decision in the case. In the meantime, in 2008, one of the judges involved (Justice Catherine Branson) was appointed President of the Australian Human Rights Commission, leaving the Full Court with only two judges, not three, to make the appeal determination. This left the Full Court appeal in a delicate situation for, if the two remaining judges did not agree, there could not be a majority decision with which to determine the case.

During the appeal hearing, Khaki Stumpagee, the senior Jawi man whose country was excluded from the 2005 determination, passed away. Between the appeal in 2007 and the Full Federal Court's determination in 2010, Jimmy Ejai, the most senior man for Jackson Island, a man who referred to himself and was referred to by others as Bardi, also died. Neither had lived to see native title over their own country; both had put enormous effort into achieving this goal.

Chapter Ten

Recognition's Paradox

I'm an ordinary man, [but] I can understand what's wrong and right. I want to speak up for my island (Khaki Stumpagee, 7 November 1994).

Law, Society, Sea

The Full Court handed down its decision (*Sampi on behalf of the Bardi and Jawi People v State of Western Australia* [2010] FCAFC 26 on 18 March 2010. The Full Court's decision, issued by Justices North and Mansfield, noted that 'whether the primary judge erred in his conclusions that the Bardi and Jawi people did not form a single society at sovereignty is the central issue in this appeal', referring to this as 'the one society or two issue'.[321] Early in their judgment, they carefully laid out the role of the appeal court, stating that the court could not simply find error on the basis of preference for 'an outcome different from that adopted by the trial judge where both were equally available or the matter was finely balanced'.[322] For an appeal court to be able to 'interfere' with the determination of a trial judge, the court had to 'come to the view that the trial judge was wrong'.[323]

Justices North and Mansfield referred to 'the advantage [normally] enjoyed by the trial judge in having seen and heard the witnesses directly', in contrast to the appeal court.[324] As they went on to remark, though, the 'unusual circumstances' in this case meant that 'the primary judge did not have a significant advantage over this Court in evaluating the evidence' as would usually be the case.[325] They recounted the circumstances that had led to this situation: the twenty-four days of evidence on country and expert evidence heard by Justice Beaumont; his illness; the transfer of the case to Justice French; and the parties' agreement about the primary judge making the determination principally on the basis of transcript. They noted that Justice French had heard three days of evidence in order 'to meet the developments in the law which had occurred between the end of the trial before Beaumont J and the hearing before the primary judge'.[326]

Previously I referred to what appeared to me to be a strategy on behalf of the respondent parties in relation to Jawi territory and the claim to sea. In the early days of the case, it had first been suggested that Jawi (as a Jawi community) were extinct, and later, as the issue of society in native title jurisprudence emerged, that they had ceased to exist as a society. The strategy included arguing that all of the islands were Jawi, that only Jawi had traditionally used mangrove log rafts, and that Bardi had acquired their knowledge of these rafts at Sunday Island mission, in a post-sovereignty context. The mangrove log rafts allowed people to use the currents to travel between islands, and became a vital component of arguments about whether native title existed offshore, beyond the resource-rich intertidal zone. Although there are records and stories of people swimming between the islands – William Dampier (1937 [1697], p. 315) recorded seeing groups of men swimming between the islands in 1688 – the use of mangrove log rafts clearly extends the offshore distance that people are able to travel. Peterson and Rigsby (1998, p. 7) estimate that the usual range of Aboriginal bark canoes or rafts was around 6.5 to 13 kilometres, although in the King Sound region, where people used their mangrove log rafts to travel with the force of the swiftly moving currents, these distances are likely to have been greater.[327] In the 2005 determination, Justice French took the view 'that the Jawi relied to a much greater extent than

Bardi on resources beyond the intertidal and reef zones and used rafts to a much greater extent for that purpose'.[328]

The reasons for the Full Court's decision run to 162 paragraphs. It canvasses the evidence the trial judge drew on to conclude that Bardi and Jawi had been two societies at sovereignty and discusses the trial judge's findings, along with the submissions the various parties made on the issues under appeal. In its determination on the issue, the Full Court shared the view the applicants had put forward in their submissions. It stated that 'central to the consideration of whether a group of people constitute a society in the sense used by the joint judgment in Yorta Yorta is whether the group acknowledged the same body of laws and customs relating to rights and interests in land and waters'.[329] Language, territory and self-identification were not seen as determinative of the society issue: rather, it was laws and customs that counted. The Full Court found that:

> The primary judge should have inferred from the evidence that the Bardi and Jawi people constituted a single society from sovereignty until the present. The primary judge should not have excluded the country of the Jawi people from the determination. The determination should, subject to resolution of the remaining arguments, include the territory of both the Bardi and Jawi people (Sampi FCAFC 26, at paragraph 79).

In including Jawi territory within the determination on appeal, the Full Court did not have anything further to say about the boundary between Bardi and Jawi or the identities of the contested islands. Further, the question of whether Bardi had acquired marine-craft technology from Jawi post-sovereignty became largely irrelevant. As the Full Court said:

> When the primary judge came to consider the sea claim he had determined that the Bardi society had had a continuous existence since sovereignty, but that the Jawi society had not.

Consequently, the question he asked in respect of the sea areas was whether the evidence established native title rights and interests in the Bardi people. As we have explained earlier in these reasons, the relevant society which held any rights or interests established by the evidence was the Bardi *and* Jawi society. Thus, the proper enquiry was whether the Bardi *and* Jawi people had established native title rights or interests in the sea claim area (Sampi FCAFC 26, at paragraph 102, my emphasis).

The Full Court's review of the evidence referred to the extraordinarily detailed knowledge of the tidal currents, and of *numurr*, the 'roads in the sea' that Bardi and Jawi used to travel between the islands by raft.[330] As well as citing Bagshaw's evidence at various points, the Full Court drew extensively on his anthropological reports in stating their findings, indicating the significance of this contribution to the case (Wilson 2016). The Full Court found that:

In our view the evidence as a whole...established that it is, and has been since sovereignty, customary for the Bardi and Jawi people to use the sea around the coast of the mainland of the Dampier Peninsula and among the islands for hunting, fishing and travelling. That evidence supports customary rights to access, move about in and on, and use and enjoy those areas, to hunt and gather including for dugong and turtle, and to access, use and take any of the resources of the sea for food and trapping fish. There was also evidence that resources from the ocean such as trochus shell were used for religious, spiritual, ceremonial and communal purposes.[331]

Given the reference to ritual and spiritual purposes, and Justice French's finding in Sampi No. 1 that Bardi and Jawi 'continue to enjoy their rights to the use of pearl shell for purely ceremonial purposes and the taking of oysters for subsistence in accordance with their traditional laws and customs' (*Sampi v State of Western Australia* FCA 777, at paragraph 9), my view is that what the appeal court meant to say here was, in fact, pearl shell.

The Croker Island case in 2002 had previously established that native title rights to sea could only be non-exclusive rights because of the public right to fish and the right to navigate. Bardi and Jawi native title rights recognised on appeal thus included 'possession, occupation, use and enjoyment as against the whole world' over land and over the islets and islands in the claim area; non-exclusive rights to 'the intertidal zone together with reefs within and adjacent to that zone and offshore reefs otherwise exposed'; and a 'right to access, use and take the resources of the sea' for 'religious, spiritual, ceremonial and communal purposes'.[332]

Male-only restricted evidence had been given about the cosmological significance of two sites offshore. In the initial determination, claimed rights in relation to these had not been successful. On appeal, in view of their particular significance to Bardi and Jawi people, the Full Court found a right to 'care for, maintain and protect' Alarm Shoals and a 'right to protect' Lalariny (an offshore feature).[333] The Full Court's determination was that native title should extend 3 nautical miles offshore from the eastern and western coastlines of the Dampier Peninsula, as the applicants had claimed in their amended application in the second trial.[334] In short, while still constrained by the limitations at law of the recognition of native title offshore, Bardi and Jawi had finally been successful in having native title rights recognised over sea.[335] A media report described the Full Court's appeal decision this way:

> The Bardi Jawi people of WA's remote Kimberley region have won a 15-year battle for native title rights over the sea off an area of WA's north coast.
>
> Yesterday's Federal Court ruling is the first time that traditional owners in the Kimberley have been recognised as having significant title over the sea, islands and reefs.[336]

Then deputy director of the Kimberley Land Council and Bardi man Nolan Hunter described the result as 'a major victory for our people'.[337]

Bardi Jawi

A year after the Bardi and Jawi native title claim was resolved through the Full Court decision, I returned to the peninsula. I wanted to catch up with people I had worked with now that the native title case was finally resolved, to visit the graves of people I had known who were no longer alive, and to pay my respects to their families. I also wanted to further consider whether to write this book, and to see what people thought about it. With the case over, and so many people who were involved in the case having passed away, perhaps it was time to simply move on. For most people I spoke with, the Bardi and Jawi native title claim was completed, and, in the words of one of the Bardi men who gave evidence in the trial, 'we just have to try and learn to live with it now'. As he put it, 'this native title is still a white-man kind of thing, and we have our own ways...I think I can see a way to work with it, but it's hard for these younger people to understand'.

While I was there, the Kimberley Land Council was holding Prescribed Body Corporate meetings, the purpose of which, people told me, was to talk about 'governance'. Successful applicant groups with a determination of native title must incorporate under the *Aboriginal Councils and Associations Act 1976* (Cth) legislation as prescribed bodies corporate (PBCs) or registered native title bodies corporate (RNTBCs). The Bardi Jawi Niimidiman Aboriginal Corporation is the registered native title body corporate for the Sampi claim ('niimidiman' is a term meaning 'shared', used to describe the shared country between estates and shared sea country). The corporation was registered in 2007, after the 2005 determination but prior to the appeal decision in 2010. Such bodies corporate are designed, in large part, to facilitate external dealings between governments (and other interests) and native title holding groups. Those whom I spoke with were attending the meetings with additional agendas: disputes about genealogical connections and rights in country, most particularly (but not solely) with respect to the neighbouring Mayala native title claim, from which some registered native title claimants had been receiving benefits in relation to a significant mining agreement. Indeed, during this visit, most of the discussions I had with people centred not on the final success of the Sampi claim, but on ways in which local people were connected to various parts of the Bardi and Jawi claim area, the Mayala claim area, and, in a couple of cases, their connections to Jabirr Jabirr country to the south, where controversy was then raging about the proposed gas hub at James Price Point (see Glaskin 2014).

In addition to tourism facilities at Kooljaman and Lombadina, tourism enterprises (camping grounds and cultural tours) had emerged at several outstations. Cygnet Bay Pearl Farm, which had been a respondent to the native title claim, had also set up tourist accommodation, pearl farm tours, boat tours and a cafe. With the road from Beagle Bay to Lombadina, Djarindjin and One Arm Point now bituminised, tourist facilities seemed to be proliferating. In a conversation with one of the workers from the Bardi-owned tourist enterprise Kooljaman at Cape Leveque, and one of the Bard tour guides, the Kooljaman worker referred to the successful native title claim, saying that 'things are different now. People have to understand that it's your country, and they can't just do anything they want to do, or go where they want to go'. At the time of my visit, the 'Bardi Jawi' rangers were active, working on dugong and turtle conservation, feral weed and animal control. One Arm Point School had published a book celebrating 'Bardi Jawi' culture (One Arm Point Remote Community School 2010). The Commonwealth Department of Environment's website noted that:

In 2011, parts of Bardi Jawi were registered on the national heritage list. The reasons behind the listing include the area's natural beauty, and the historic usage of *galwa* (double log raft) for transport and *guwarn* (pearl shell) for trading.[338]

The Commonwealth was, of course, one of the parties which strongly contested Bardi 'historic usage' of *galwa* in the court.

In 2013, a 95,000 hectare 'Bardi Jawi Indigenous Protected Area' – defined as a voluntary declaration 'by Indigenous people with no legal basis' – was declared.[339] The use of the term 'Bardi Jawi' in these different contexts and as evidenced in recent publications (for example, Travési 2015) suggests that, while Sampi claimants once regularly differentiated between their Bardi and Jawi identities, these identities – at least as articulated amongst younger generations and by the institutions with which Bardi and Jawi people must deal – are becoming significantly less differentiated.

Povinelli (2002, p. 6) has argued that Australian liberal multiculturalism requires 'authentic' Indigenous subjects with forms of 'tradition' that do not offend the moral sensibilities of the nation, referring to this as the 'cunning of recognition'. While I agree that one can see the 'tradition' requirement in native title as a form of 'cunning', the paradox of recognition is, as I see it, more complex. Not only are claims to native title mediated through the ontological lens of a Western property rights regime, and ultimately contingent on complex intersections between sets of relationships entangled in history, ethnography, legal process and individual actions, the very process of recognition is, itself, inherently transformative. Given the apparent issues having two named groups created in the context of native title's requirement for a 'society', the sedimenting of 'Bardi Jawi' as the public face of Bardi and Jawi may be recognition's paradox.

Moments in Time

Gave Baaji and Jinju copies of the transcriptions I'd done from the tape-recording at One Arm Point. Baaji scoured through his for mistakes in [the] Bardi words while Jinju was just really,

really pleased. As they were going through they were telling me stories too. Jinju said *we never told you about the Seven Sisters* and told me a sketchy, unfollowable version. Then he said, *we never told you about the dugong story*, either. So Baaji told me that…

I take Baaji down to the Aboriginal Legal Service to sort out his insurance claim. We return via the TAB (a betting agency), sit down, talk some more. Jinju has been going through the transcript…going through the things he said about Sunday Island mission and really likes it. *That's right, you got it here*, he says (extract from fieldnotes, 7 November 1997).

Part of the transcript that Jinju poured over that day was his detailed description of seeing the Japanese planes flying overhead on the way to bomb Broome. He talked about how Sunday Island mission had closed down because of the war and how the missionaries had left the Sunday Island residents on the mainland to 'just wander around', getting rations from the lighthouse keeper at Cape Leveque. He retold me the story of the public ancestral being, Galalung, and how he had forbidden people from eating one species of fish, the red emperor, analogising that this story had similarities to the biblical story of Adam and Eve:

> And that's just like the story about Adam and Eve, the way you see it you tell like a bible story too, you know, where God said to Adam eh, he said to him, there's one fruit tree there, tree of life, you can't touch it. But any other fruits what's in the field here, you can (extract from fieldnotes, 7 November 1997).

These extracts from my fieldnotes evoke a strong memory of these two brothers and the time I spent sitting down with them. They exemplify lives of 'mixtures, of translations and transculturations, of indistinguishably complex, experienced realities' (Dousset 2016, p. xiii) in which divisions between 'tradition' and its imaginary other can only be heuristic devices leant on to support native title claims required to be advanced in such terms.

Native title is neither the wholly beneficial legislation some imagined it might be before successive judicial decisions and legislative amendments transformed it into the more limited legal creature than the one that began its life as the 1993 Native Title Act. Nor is it simply the imposition of the state, divorced from the realities of indigenous relationships to country and the aspirations many Indigenous Australians hold to gain legal recognition of their rights. As legislation and as process, native title is necessarily ambiguous. Its social, cultural and legal effects and the relational processes in which these are embedded are complex and multidimensional, and this reflects on the law of native title and its application as part of a trajectory first set in train when British colonists arrived: a shifting and uneven structural relationship between people who were in Australia prior to colonisation and those who have made Australia their home since.

Jinju, and others like him, are part of the hidden history of the Sampi native title claim, those who did not give evidence in the case and yet remain an integral part of its story. The people who extended their hospitality to Geoffrey Bagshaw and myself, the people who painstakingly taught us things we sought to know, the people who initially saw in native title not the burden of legislative definition and exhaustive requirements about proof; but a promise.

Notes

1   For example, Beckett (1994, 1995), Sharp (1996) and Keon-Cohen
     (2000) discuss the Mabo case; Redmond (2011) and Strelein (2005) have
     discussed the Sampi case in terms of how the term 'society' was applied; for
     discussions concerning the Yulara case, see Burke (2007); Dousset & Glaskin
     (2007); Glaskin (2007a); Keen (2007); Morton (2007); Sackett (2007);
     Sansom (2007); Sutton (2006, 2007). Frances Morphy (2007) discusses
     issues of communication that occurred during the hearing for Blue Mud
     Bay. Burke (2011) provides in-depth discussion of Mabo No. 2, Rubibi
     No. 6, De Rose Hill and Yulara in terms of the ethnographic archive and
     the evidence of the anthropologists who acted as expert witnesses in these
     cases. To date, the publication of Cane's (2002) *Pila Nguru* (based on his
     report for the Spinifex native title claim), Bagshaw's (2003) anthropological
     monograph of the Karajarri native title claim, the historical report (South
     West Aboriginal Land and Sea Council & Host 2009) and Kingsley Palmer's
     (2016) publication of an edited version of his anthropological report in the
     same case, the Single Noongar Claim, are exceptional as being the only
     publications of expert reports provided to the courts in native title cases. As
     Palmer (2016, xv) points out, Cane's (2002) book is not really presented as
     an expert report.

2   *Mabo v Queensland (No. 2)* [1992] HCA 23, at paragraphs 96 and 97(2).

3   In the Mabo case, Justice Brennan had noted that the 'Court is not free to
     adopt rules that accord with contemporary notions of justice and human
     rights if their adoption would fracture the skeleton of principle which
     gives the body of our law its shape and internal consistency' (*Mabo v
     Queensland (No. 2)* [1992] HCA 23, at paragraph 29), and views that Mabo
     might 'fracture the skeleton' of the common law were derived from this
     metaphor.

4   *Mabo v Queensland (No. 2)* [1992] HCA 23, at paragraph 75.

5   See, for example, the Canadian judgment *Delgamuukw v British Columbia*
     [1997] 3 SCR 1010 and the Malaysian judgment *Sagong Bin Tasi & Ors v
     Kerajaan Negeri Selangor & Ors* (Dalam Mahkamah Tinggi Di Shah Alam,
     Guaman Sivil No: Mti-21-314-1996).

6   *Native Title Act 1993* (Cth) S223(1).

7   *Members of the Yorta Yorta Aboriginal Community v Victoria* [2002] HCA 58, at
     paragraph 47.

8   *Hamlet of Baker Lake v Minister of Indian Affairs and Northern Development* (1979) 107 DLR (3d) 513.

9   *Delgamuukw v British Columbia* (1997) 153 DLR (4th) 193 (Delgamuukw) and *Tsilhqot'in Nation v British Columbia* 2007 BCSC 1700; [2008] 1 CNLR 112 (Tsilhqot'in) respectively.

10   At the time of writing, extended anthropological analyses of particular native claims in Australia from their inception to their conclusion are difficult to find, though see Williams (1986) account of the Gove land rights case (*Milirrpum v Nabalco Pty Ltd* (1971) 17 FLR 141) and Sharp's (1996) account of the Mabo claim (which both preceded native title legislation). Both Macdonald (2004) and Weir (2009) have provided broad accounts of land rights struggles (for Wiradjuri and Gunditjmara respectively). Paul Burke's (2011) analysis of various native title cases provides a close analysis of the interaction between law, anthropology and applicant evidence in four litigated native title settings, and there is some parallel between this and aspects of this book in that regard. Burke's exposition, based primarily on published ethnography, transcripts and interviews with the anthropologists who worked on the cases concerned, necessarily has a different focus than the one I present here, even as it provides an important complement to it. As Burke (2011, p. 32) notes, 'detailed accounts of native title hearings by participant anthropologists are rare'.

11   Petri (1948, p. 238) reported that one of the beings in Bardi cosmology was a Rainbow Serpent, Alungun, who lives in a round cave of saltwater 'and here makes all the bright coloured shells of the sea, which she excretes out of her body'. According to Worms (1952, p. 545), Galalung has more than one name: 'his second name is *Lulul* or *Lulur*, "the Shark-Man"'. This latter observation appears to conflate Lululu the whale shark with Galalung the law-giver.

12   *Sampi v State of Western Australia* at paragraph 635.

13   For example, see 'Ornithologist seeks to prove theory NT desert hunting birds spread fire to flush out prey', http://www.abc.net.au/news/2016-03-03/smart-bushfire-birds/7216934, accessed 16 August 2016.

14   Petri (1938–40, p. 234) tells the story of Djungalbellen, 'a small brown bird' (Jungalbil), involving Kanbali and Kedo [giido], 'two red-bill gulls'. In these stories the events occur between Sandy Point and 'Olga Creek' (Urlg, or Chile Creek) at Lombadina. Nilili also told a story involving Jungalbil in which two birds were fighting over land, and fire was spread (Bagshaw 1995, p. 58). If there was once a narrative that connected his activities between the various locales with which he is associated, though, it is no longer apparent.

15   'Interested parties' to native title claims are covered by S84(3) of the Native Title Act. Becoming an interested party signals that the claim

is contested, and confers automatic rights on the parties to be involved
in mediation and negotiation with the claimant group, to be notified
concerning relevant claim developments, and to be a party to the Federal
Court hearing.

16   Nominated interests of the parties included government, fishing, pearling,
      mining, telecommunications, and 'indigenous', a group who also referred to
      themselves as the 'independent Bard claimants'.

17   Dampier infamously wrote that 'The Inhabitants of this Country are the
      miserablest People in the World' Dampier (1937 [1697], p. 312), although
      an earlier handwritten manuscript of the same book depicts the people
      whom Dampier encountered in New Holland in, as Marchant (1988, p. 121)
      states, a 'more scientific and less apparently subjective' manner than in his
      published account.

18   Various writers have advanced theories about the nature of maritime
      exploration of the Australian coast. Holthouse (1986, p. 2) speaks of Chinese
      records of a fleet of 62 junks 'scattered by a cyclone south of Sumatra',
      which reportedly sailed right around Australia; Bain (1982, p. 201) discusses
      indications that Japanese from the settlements of Guam, the Gilbert Islands
      and New Ireland, journeyed as far south as Tasmania during early trading
      expeditions; McCarthy (1993, p. 1) refers to American whalers off the
      coast of Western Australia in 1844; he says American whalers are 'believed
      to have preceded all but the first explorer' at Nickol Bay in the Pilbara.
      Von Brandenstein believed that the Portuguese established a colony around
      1520, extending from the Buccaneer Archipelago in the west to as far east as
      Fitzroy Crossing (Broome Advertiser 1993a, 1993b).

19   Mondial Films 1932. See Robinson (1976a, 1976b) and Smith (1996) for
      further discussion of this footage.

20   Bain (1982, pp. 79, 92, 109) reports that reports of 'remarkable finds' of
      mother-of-pearl shell at Cygnet Bay in the King Sound area had occurred
      by 1884, and that Cygnet Bay became known as 'the Graveyard' because so
      many divers died from the bends there. This is not to be confused with the
      Graveyard on the eastern side of the King Sound that received its name for
      the same reasons.

21   See Marchant (1988, pp. 103–07) for a discussion of the inconsistencies
      in Dampier's written accounts, and the difficulties engendered by this in
      relation to defining a precise location for the *Cygnet* to have landed.

22   In an effort to prevent the trade that occurred between Aborigines and
      others, early colonial legislation distinguished between Asians, Europeans
      and Aborigines, with the aim of restricting Aboriginal and 'Asian'
      interaction (Ganter 1994, p. 51).

23   Gibney (1886, point 5) recorded that 'the licence for pearl shell fishing is
      1 pound per annum and there is a duty of 4 pounds per ton for its export.
      Hitherto it has been sold for about 100 pounds per ton.'

24   For fuller discussion of the pearling industry and matters such as blackbirding in this region, see Anderson (1978); Bain (1982); Edwards (1983); Robinson (1973, pp. 135–37).

25   Rations included flour, tea, sugar, clothes, tobacco and blankets. In 1908, Hunter received rations to distribute to twenty-eight people, as follows: (all spellings except where indicated in parentheses as in original documents): Mudgee, Tinker [Dingga], Wallinburra, Wahbahlee [Wobali], Dungleia, Jeedoong [Jidung], Tadpole [Jadbu], Daylight [Dilai], Old Noddy, Meichehow, Old Bobby, Gipsy [Jibadji], Kudall [Gurdal], Laura, Coomungoo, Neeliwill [Niliwil], Dolly, Punch [Panj], Amy, Susan, Judy, Mindo [Mindau], Cuminoorha, Kingold [Ginggul], Lalenmara, Jimij, Dynamite Charlie [probably Charlie Bumba], and Old Peter. Battye Library, AN1/2; Acc 255; 19/1908. Notwithstanding issues of orthography, most of these people are readily identifiable as antecedents of contemporary Bardi people.

26   Exemptions were not easily gained and those who gained exemptions could have them revoked at any time (Haebich 1998 [1988], pp. 89, 126–27, 163).

27   For example, in 1923 a Broome police report discussed the perceived problems that cancellation of the Hunters' exemption certificates would create, saying that it would require 'very careful consideration owing to the conduct of the Hunter boys and the results that may follow once they are classified again as Aborigines if the certificates are cancelled. They would have free entry to the mission reserves and may and no doubt would cause considerable trouble amongst the inmates and to the management of these institutions…' (Broome Police Report 1923).

28   Blundell and Woolagoodja (2005, p. 39) refer to a Yawjibaya woman, Nellie Wurimbuloin, who lived on Sunday Island as an adult.

29   In 1901 the WA government subsidy to Sunday Island mission consisted of blankets for aged natives: in that year Hadley reported that sixteen 'aged natives' had been recipients of these blankets (Hadley 1901a).

30   Gibson (1951, p. 40) says that Hadley underwent different stages of initiation, which, if correct, indicates that this was something more than patronage. Robinson (1973, p. 161) suggests, however, that Hadley's involvement may have been limited to occasional ceremonial participation, advising that 'the Bardi themselves say that there was no serious attempt to incorporate him within the group although he displayed an appreciation of traditional culture'.

31   Walter (1982 [1928], p. 124).

32   The 'little time' Garndingunjun refers to here is the holiday time in which children were able to go out camping with their parents, at least in the 1930s when she was a child at Lombadina. She refers to 'One Arm Point people' because One Arm Point community was largely formed by people who were formerly associated with Sunday Island mission.

33   Also see Raible (1938, pp. 273–74) who states that:
      'The first difficulty which the missionary encounters is ultimately connected with the nomadic life of the primitive black...There is really no alternative in tackling this problem. There is only one way, that is: try and make the native settle on a certain place where he will be able to earn his living by doing a reasonable amount of work every day.'

34   The UAM was originally the Australian Aborigines Mission (AAM). The organisation divided in 1928 and the main body was re-named the United Aborigines Mission (Robinson 1973, p. 167).

35   In 1926 Jim Jago, a UAM missionary, reported that tooth evulsion (*rijil*) had ceased (in Gibson 1951, p. 70); however, when Elkin visited the island in 1928, he observed tooth evulsion while there (Elkin 1928b). Gibson (1951, p. 70) records that in 1929 tooth evulsion was again said to have ceased: 'Cocky [Gagi] (somewhat of a leader) informed the lady missionary while she was visiting his camp on the edge of the corroboree ground that the knocking out of teeth was finished'.

36   During the Sampi native title hearing, Dennis Davey described *raya* this way: '*Raya* is like fairy, you know, spirit kids? They choose their own person... They can save him from danger, protect him...[If] that bloke is a married guy and his *raya* want to come in the real world, conceive in – in his wife or in his sweetheart...he comes out in real life' (transcript *Sampi v State of Western Australia* T546, pp. 35–42).

37   As one man described this, 'I was *raya* before I was born. My father seen turtle passing by, speared a turtle' (Galiwar 15 May 2001).

38   See Elkin (1933, p. 444), too, who noted that 'any irregularity is caused by the father being on a visit to another "country" at the time her finds the child, who is thus associated with the *dzalnga* [jarlnga] of that "country"'.

39   In 1998 the latter had not yet commenced operation since it required repairs; the craft was subsequently stolen.

40   Examples of these include Ngililngburu, Miligunburu, Gambarnanburu, Ngamagunburu and Gurrbalgunburu. In the case of Ngamagunburu, the various outstations all belong to brothers who are the senior patrifiliates for the estate. They described their rationale for attempting to 'cover' their *buru* with outstations as a means to fulfil their religious obligations to protect significant sites within their country (in the absence of other satisfactory means to do so).

41   After addressing a number of requisite criteria, including that of incorporation, applications for land to form an outstation were submitted to the Aboriginal Affairs Planning Authority (AAPA) which administers the *Aboriginal Affairs Planning Authority Act 1972* (WA) that established the Aboriginal Lands Trust. One criterion was to demonstrate that the applicants had traditional attachment to the area in question, although the corroborating documentation required was not substantial. Such

documentation could include genealogies prepared by anthropologists,
by resource agency workers (who generally assisted with all facets of the
incorporation process), or by the applicants themselves.

42   Davis & Prescott (1984, p. 1); Green and Turner (1984). Aspects of Bardi
and Jawi relationships to sea are described in published material by Akerman
(n.d., 1975), Elkin (1933), Green (1988), Robinson (1979), Smith (1984–85,
1987, 1997), Tindale (1974), Wiggan (1990), Worms (1940a). Unpublished
material includes Robinson's (1973) Master's thesis, Green and Turner's
submission to the Seaman Inquiry (1984), Rouja's (1998) PhD thesis focusing
on Bardi fishing practices, and reports submitted to the Federal Court in the
Sampi case (Bagshaw 1999, 2001a, 2001b; Bagshaw and Glaskin 2000).

43   Recommendation 11.27, Seaman (1984, pp. 81–82).

44   At that time there were some smaller parcels of land with different legal
tenures over them, such as the lighthouse reserve at Cape Leveque, and the
land held by the Catholic Church at Lombadina.

45   Cygnet Bay's promotional material describes their pearling endeavour
as having begun in 1946, although it does not specify that until 1962
this activity occurred from Sunday Island mission (see: http://www.
cygnetbaypearls.com.au/about-us-2/, accessed 23 July 2016).

46   F. E. Gare, Commissioner of Native Welfare to Under Secretary for Lands,
3 November 1969 stated that 'it is contrary to the policy of this Department
to excise areas from reserves set apart for the use of Aborigines'.

47   Bagayi, plenary meeting with the Native Title Tribunal at One Arm Point,
6 March 1997, (my notes).

48   See Volumes 2, 3 and 4 of 1559/62; 3229/84 (Volume 3); 467/985 and
3266/69 of the Lands and Surveys Department.

49   *Ejai v Commonwealth* (unreported, Supreme Court of Western Australia,
No. 1744 of 1993, 18 March 1994).

50   While the two land councils would ultimately work cooperatively on the
successful Neowarra claim, *Neowarra v State of Western Australia* [2004] FCA
1092, in these early days of native title the relationship was so fractious that
the Kamali Land Council contested the Kimberley Land Council's right to
be registered as a Native Title Representative Body under the Native Title
Act (Edmunds 1995, p. 3).

51   Justice French, President of the National Native Title Tribunal to Bardi and
Jawi claimants, 6 March 1997, at One Arm Point, (my notes).

52   Interestingly, the Mabo decision was the outcome of a similar predicament,
but in this case the claimants did separate their claim to sea from their
claim to land. Their claim to sea was finally determined (in 2010) in what
was known as the Torres Strait Island sea claim, *Akiba v State of Queensland*
(No. 2) [2010] FCA 643 (*The Torres Strait sea claim*).

53   Justice Sackville said in that case that: 'It is evident from the Yulara
Anthropology Report that each author spent considerable time interviewing

the applicants and other indigenous people who have given evidence in the proceedings. This appears to be the bulk of the "fieldwork" undertaken by them. There is an obvious risk that much of this effort duplicated the work undertaken (so I infer from what I have been told) by lawyers in preparing written statements from Aboriginal witnesses to be tendered at the hearing... it is by no means clear to me why it was apparently thought necessary for the anthropologists to carry out such extensive interviews of witnesses and potential witnesses for the purpose of preparing their Report' (*Jango v Northern Territory of Australia (No. 2)* [2004] FCA 1004, at paragraph 15).

54   *Yorta Yorta Aboriginal Community v Victoria* (Federal Court of Australia, Olney J, 18 December 1998, unreported) [1998] FCA 1606 at paragraph 129.

55   Barrister Raelene Webb acting for the State of Western Australia, during oral submissions in the Full Court appeal, WAD188/2006 27 February 2007, T114, pp. 30–4.

56   ibid., T114, pp. 34–5.

57   Bagshaw (1999) is the main anthropological report, with Bagshaw (2001a & 2001b) being supplementary reports. Bagshaw & Glaskin (2000) specifically dealt with marine tenure and resource use. Glaskin & Bagshaw (1999) is the genealogies that were submitted to the court in the case.

58   According to his CV, Greenfeld's primary training is in archaeology but he also has a qualification (a Postgraduate Diploma) in Anthropology (http://bradgoode.com.au/wp-content/uploads/2014/06/paul-greenfield-cv.pdf).

59   Sansom's (2000:15) observation that 'the Bardi raft was nicknamed the "marine velocipede" by King and was present in the King Sound in 1837 and so was an aspect of Bardi tenure by that time' did not become part of the respondents' case. In fact, the place where King recorded seeing these craft was considerably to the south of Bardi country, off Lewis Island in the Pilbara region, several hundred kilometres away. This mistake is probably a result of confusion between the Dampier Archipelago (off the Burrup Peninsula in the Pilbara) and the Buccaneer Archipelago (in the King Sound in the Kimberley).

60   E.g., Petri 1938–40; Nevermann, Worms & Petri 1968; Worms 1940a, 1942, 1950b, 1955, 1957b, 1959.

61   Copies of these workbooks are located in *Records of Daisy M. Bates* [MS 365] in the manuscript section of the National Library of Australia, Canberra. Bates evidently used these books during a certain period of her ethnographic investigations, although she is not the only one to have done so.

62   These are located in *Records of Daisy M. Bates,* MS 365, Box 27, Item Numbers 53/110, 53/111, and 53/116, National Library of Australia, Canberra.

63   See Worms (1940a, 1942, 1944, 1949, 1950a, 1950b, 1952, 1957a, 1957b, 1957c, 1959), Nekes and Worms (1953) and Nevermann, Worms & Petri (1968).

64 Helon (1998, p. 14) identifies the following alternatives to Jawi: Buccaneer Islanders, Chowie, Djaoi, Djau, Djawi, Ewanji, Ewenu, Eweny-oon, I:wanja, Jawi, Sunday Islanders, Tohau-I, Tohaui, Tohawi, Towahi, 'Djaui.

65 The name Jayirri refers both to Jackson Island and to Tyra Island. Tyra Island (Munburran) is a small island immediately south of Jackson and joined to it by reef. Because it is joined to Jackson Island, it is considered part of the island, which bears the overall name Jayirri.

66 Robinson (1973, p. 103) also wrote that while Long Island (Unggaliyun) 'is regarded today as Djawi territory, older informants maintain that it was more properly part of the territory of the Ugarung people of the Yampi Peninsula, and that Djawi only settled there after European contact.' Ugarung is alternatively pronounced Uggarang, Ungarang, Uggarangu, Ungarangu.

67 For example, see evidence given by Paul Sampi: Federal Court of Australia 2001 Transcript WAG 49/98, T1094.00–1095.10.

68 E.g. Elkin (1933) depicted the boundary at Pender Bay; Tindale (1974) located the boundary north of Pender Bay; Robinson (1979) showed the boundary at Pender Bay.

69 See *Sampi v Western Australia* [2005] FCA 777, at paragraph 1094.

70 This was Bagshaw's (1999, p. 12) estimate of the population, and was arrived at by a process of examining the genealogies prepared for the native title case. It represents Jawi patrifiliates, those people with Jawi fathers.

71 To be fair, this is really Campbell's observation. Bird is listed as a co-author because he contributed a vocabulary to the article. Elsewhere Bird writes about the 'Chowie language of the Buccaneer Islanders' (see Bird 1910, 1915).

72 As part of my fieldwork I had spoken with a senior Bardi woman whose adoptive father was Jawi in an explicit attempt to see whether she could remember, from her father, differences in Jawi kinship terminology as compared to Bardi. She could not.

73 In the Sampi case, we examined Elkin's 1927–28 fieldnotes, correspondence and genealogies (Elkin 1928a, 1928b, 1927–8a, 1927–8b), the relevant portions of Tindale's (1953a, 1953b) fieldnotes and genealogies and Tindale and Birdsell's unpublished field maps (1954).

74 *Sampi v State of Western Australia* [2005] FCA 777, at paragraph 789.

75 *Sampi v State of Western Australia* [2005] FCA 777, at paragraph 789.

76 From 24 April 2001 to 17 May 2001, when the request for their return was formally made in the court; these were returned a few days afterwards. Federal Court of Australia 2001 Transcript WAG 49/98, T695:19–698:47.

77 Federal Court of Australia 2001 Transcript WAG 49/98, T697.40–47.

78 Federal Court of Australia 2001 Transcript WAG 49/98, T556.33–557.05.

79 Federal Court of Australia 2001 Transcript WAG 49/98, T557.07–10.

80 Geoffrey Bagshaw, personal communication, 14 August 2015.

81 E.g., Western Australian Fishing Industry Council 2001, at point 5.10.9.

82 Federal Court of Australia Transcript 2001, WAG49/98, T2102.44–T2013.17.

83 For example, see Eades (1993, 1995); Koch (1991); Liberman (1978, pp. 94–6, 1981, pp. 247–55), and Williams (1986, pp. 166, 170). Based on his examination of the transcript in the Rubibi No. 1 case, Burke (2011, p. 141) refers to some of the applicant evidence as 'highly contradictory', and identifies 'language difficulties' as constituting a significant problem for several of the witnesses concerned.

84 In land claims under the ALRA, formal rules of evidence did not apply.

85 Federal Court of Australia Transcript 2002, WAG6016/96, T6361, pp. 25–45.

86 While the term 'on country' evidence is usually taken to refer to evidence heard on the country that the applicants are claiming, the term has also sometimes been used to refer to any evidence obtained distantly from the Federal Court registry, in contexts which require the Federal Court to 'set up' a hearing in a place other than a court normally designated for this purpose. The Chief Justice of the High Court, Robert French, described this and associated innovations in the hearing of Aboriginal evidence as follows:
'Customary law interacts directly with the national legal system in Australia in the hearing and determination of claims for the recognition of customary native title. In such cases, the Federal Court of Australia has frequently taken evidence on the country the subject of the claim. It has rules of court providing for the reception of evidence, not only in the form of oral testimony, but also in the form of art, dance and song. Some witnesses may give testimony with a group of their community and be permitted to consult with members of the group before answering questions. Some evidence relates to restricted traditional knowledge. In such cases the Federal Court has heard evidence in the presence only of male legal practitioners and expert witnesses and has restricted distribution of the transcript' (French 2011).

87 Federal Court of Australia Transcript 2001, WAG49/98, T93:13.

88 Federal Court of Australia Transcript 2001, WAG49/98, T93:13–16.

89 The evidence that corroborated the annotations on the map included information about the currents Milimil (the current between Jalan and Jayirri Islands), Gardadin (the current between Jalan and Bulnginy and Ralral Islands), Lirruljin (the current that runs between Bulngniny and Ralral), Iwanyunu (the current near Sunday Island that runs through Meda Passage), the whirlpool Jindirrabalgun (in Sunday Strait, which has mythological significance), Ardiolan (the current near One Arm Point), and Wanan (described as the second big *lu*, or current, after Jindirrablagun). Claimants identified Ilarr, Jingaljirri and Jirrawanj (the three currents between Sunday Island and East and West Roe Islands just to its north);

Ambulanj (a current not far from One Arm Point); Biyananj (a current between Biyana – Waterlow Island – and Jackson Island), Gurir (which was described as a 'big *lu* [current] for married turtle' between Sunday Island and East Roe Island), Jurundanggun (a current close to Sunday Island), Jawul (a current near East Roe Island), and Unburrgunbard (a passage, also the name of Mid Rock, lying between East and West Roe Islands), representing fifteen named currents as well as the whirlpool, Jindirrabalgun, overall. The claimants provided evidence about most of the islands in the claim area, including Iwanyi (Sunday Island), Ralral (Salural Island), Bulnginy (Poolngin Island), Niwardinggun (Rees Island), Ungalgun (Leonie Island), Ngolorron (Allora Island), Belayn (West Roe Island), Garndalayn (East Roe Island), Unburrgunbard (Mid Rock), Kumuriyngan (Pinnicombe Shoal), Ngulminjin (Apex Island), Julum (Middle Island), Jayirri (Jackson Island), Munu (Holtham Island, the east side of Jayirri), Munburran (Tyra Island), Biyana (Waterlow Islands), Irrabardayn (Talboys Island), Jalan (Tallon Island), Kalmbarr (Dingo Rock), Juwarnan and Murrudulun (Twin Islands), Maybinjun (the eastern end of Anchor Shoal) and Juljinabur (Brue Reef), as well as about numerous islands in the Mayala claim area.

90   Federal Court of Australia Transcript 2001, WAG49/98, T149:30–31. This became Exhibit #C.

91   Federal Court of Australia Transcript 2001, WAG49/98, T162:20–23.

92   This became Exhibit #E.

93   Federal Court of Australia Transcript 2001, WAG49/98, T201.30.

94   Federal Court of Australia Transcript 2001, WAG49/98, T207.32. This became Exhibit #F.

95   Jackson's footage has largely been lost or destroyed: the only known reel of the 'legendary lost Jackson footage', is *Chez Les Sauvages Australiens* (Mondial Films 1932, 7 minutes). See Robinson (1976a, 1976b); Smith (1996).

96   Ken Pettit, Federal Court of Australia Transcript 2001, WAG49/98, T217.25–34.

97   Greg McIntyre, Federal Court of Australia Transcript 2001, WAG49/98, T217.43–4.

98   Extract from journal entry, Friday 11 May 2001.

99   *Western Australia v Ward* [2002] HCA 28, paragraph 64.

100   Federal Court of Australia Transcript 2000, WAG6017/1996, T5539:05.

101   Federal Court of Australia Transcript 2001, WAG49/98, T139:14–16.

102   One of the Bardi men recounted to me how he and two other teenagers once swam from One Arm Point to Sunday Island, swimming from One Arm Point to Jackson Island on the full tide, walking across the island, then swimming over to Tallon Island, walking along the reef and then swimming over to Poolngin Island, and then over to a point at Allora Island and from there to Sunday Island (Baaji, personal communication 30 September 1997).

103   The term *barrawarr* was said to be the term that was used on the eastern side of the King Sound, while *inbargun* was the term Bardi and Jawi used (Jinju, personal communication 30 September 1997).

104   This became Exhibit G: Video and transcript of evidence given by Khaki Stumpagee on Sunday Island.

105   Federal Court Transcript WAG49/98, T1609.

106   In relation to the gathering of affidavits, a senior Bardi woman told me she had admonished one of the legal personnel for 'barging in and demanding to know everything about our culture and [to] put it down in black and white right now, one time' (Marnung, personal communication, 8 March 2003).

107   For example, in the exchange between Counsel for the Applicants and one of the Bardi witnesses, Counsel for the Applicants asked the witness about an area for which he did not have the right to speak.

      Witness: ...Well, I'm not from there, I said a couple of them. I only talked about my area, Ardiolon...They've got their own names, there, I don't know half of them.
      Counsel (Apps): Okay. It's not right for you to call those ones?
      Witness: Yes, you ask - - -
      Counsel (Apps): Ask them....Baniol people...
      Counsel (Apps): Okay, I will.
      Witness: You're getting me confused. You're asking me of a place that's not mine. (Federal Court of Australia Transcript 2001, WAG49/98, T2574.00–45).

108   He sought to cross-examine a middle-aged Jawi woman on the basis of something that senior Jawi man Khaki Stumpagee had said to the anthropologists as recorded in the fieldnotes.

109   The relevant passages are at Federal Court of Australia Transcript 2001, WAG49/98, T323.4–18. Eades (1993, 1995), Koch (1991) and Liberman (1978, 1981) have all discussed the communicative burden to which I refer.

110   Federal Court of Australia Transcript 2001, WAG49/98, 17 May 2001, T646.04–646.05.

111   Federal Court of Australia Transcript 2001, WAG49/98, 17 May 2001, T651.43.

112   De-restricted passages were Federal Court of Australia Transcript 2003, WAG49/98, T2887:17–22, and T2901:25–35, being from restricted evidence given in 2003.

113   Federal Court of Australia Transcript 2001, WAG49/98,T596.44–597.22.

114   Elkin (1928a) wrote that 'Kalalong first time sat down Djalam [Julum] (island west of Djairi [Jayirri] from Irwan [Iwanyi, Sunday Island]), then over to Irwan and just to east of Cocky's camp a big rock – he climbed up and went on top' (Field notebook 2, p. 214).

115   Federal Court of Australia Transcript 2001, WAG49/98, T605.13–606.02.

116 Bell had not previously worked with Bardi and Jawi people. Irving had some familiarity with the case through his role as Principal Legal Officer with the Kimberley Land Council.

117 *Sampi v State of Western Australia (No. 1)* [2005] FCA 777, at paragraph 49.

118 *Sampi v State of Western Australia (No. 1)* [2005] FCA 777, at paragraph 54.

119 *Sampi v State of Western Australia (No. 1)* [2005] FCA 777, at paragraph 54.

120 Federal Court transcript *Sampi v State of Western Australia*, T92:35–9.

121 *Western Australia v Ward* [2000] FCA 611.

122 *Daniel v State of Western Australia* [2003] FCA 666.

123 Letter, Geoffrey Bagshaw and Katie Glaskin to Wayne Bergmann, Executive Director of the Kimberley Land Council, 12 June 2003.

124 ibid., at paragraph 49, p. 20.

125 ibid., at paragraph 55, p. 22.

126 Federal Court of Australia 2004. Transcript WAG 49/98, 2 March 2004, T2937:22–4.

127 Federal Court of Australia 2004. Transcript WAG 49/98, 2 March 2004, T2937:26–30.

128 Federal Court of Australia 2004. Transcript WAG 49/98, 2 March 2004, T2937:33.

129 Federal Court of Australia 2004. Transcript WAG 49/98, 2 March 2004, T2938:23–5.

130 Federal Court of Australia 2004. Transcript WAG 49/98, 2 March 2004, T2939:04.

131 Federal Court of Australia 2004. Transcript WAG 49/98, 2 March 2004, T2948:24–5.

132 Federal Court of Australia 2004. Transcript WAG 49/98, 2 March 2004, T2948:39–T2949:39-04.

133 Federal Court of Australia 2004. Transcript WAG 49/98, 2 March 2004, T2949:13, 23–5.

134 Federal Court of Australia 2004. Transcript WAG 49/98, 2 March 2004, T2949:13, 39–45.

135 Federal Court of Australia 2004. Transcript WAG 49/98, 2 March 2004, T2950:37–45.

136 Federal Court of Australia 2004. Transcript WAG 49/98, 2 March 2004, T2950:47–T2951:02.

137 Federal Court of Australia 2004. Transcript WAG 49/98, 2 March 2004, T2951:05–7.

138 Federal Court of Australia 2004. Transcript WAG 49/98, 2 March 2004, T2951:09–10.

139 Federal Court of Australia 2004. Transcript WAG 49/98, 2 March 2004, T2951:17–20, my emphasis.

140 Federal Court of Australia 2004. Transcript WAG 49/98, 2 March 2004, T2955:45–6.

141 Federal Court of Australia 2004. Transcript WAG 49/98, 2 March 2004, T2956:06–13, 24–5.

142 Federal Court of Australia 2004. Transcript WAG 49/98, 2 March 2004, T2958:11–22.

143 Federal Court of Australia 2004. Transcript WAG 49/98, 2 March 2004, T2956:23–30.

144 Federal Court of Australia 2004. Transcript WAG 49/98, 2 March 2004, T2960:10–13; 27–8.

145 Federal Court of Australia 2004. Transcript WAG 49/98, 2 March 2004, T2961:30–2.

146 Federal Court of Australia 2004. Transcript WAG 49/98, 2 March 2004, T2961:34–41.

147 Federal Court of Australia 2004. Transcript WAG 49/98, 2 March 2004, T2965:12–17.

148 Federal Court of Australia 2004. Transcript WAG 49/98, 2 March 2004, T2965:24–6.

149 Federal Court of Australia 2004. Transcript WAG 49/98, 2 March 2004, T2962:4–5.

150 Federal Court of Australia 2004. Transcript WAG 49/98, 2 March 2004, T2967:6.

151 Federal Court of Australia 2004. Transcript WAG 49/98, 2 March 2004, T2966:2–5 (my emphasis).

152 Federal Court of Australia 2004. Transcript WAG 49/98, 2 March 2004, T2966:5–6.

153 Federal Court of Australia 2004. Transcript WAG 49/98, 2 March 2004, T2976:19–25.

154 Federal Court of Australia 2004. Transcript WAG 49/98, 2 March 2004, T2976:41–2; WAG49/98 2 March 2004, T2977:14-17.

155 Federal Court of Australia 2004. Transcript WAG 49/98, 2 March 2004, T2977:24–6.

156 Federal Court of Australia 2004. Transcript WAG 49/98, 2 March 2004, T2978:36–9.

157 Federal Court of Australia 2004. Transcript WAG 49/98, 2 March 2004, T2979:10–12.

158 Federal Court of Australia 2004. Transcript WAG 49/98, 3 March 2004, T2990:5–11.

159 Federal Court of Australia 2004. Transcript WAG 49/98, 3 March 2004, T2990:13–14.

160 Federal Court of Australia 2004. Transcript WAG 49/98, 3 March 2004, T2990:14–15.

161 Federal Court of Australia 2004. Transcript WAG 49/98, 3 March 2004, T2990:20–5.

162   Federal Court of Australia 2004. Transcript WAG 49/98, 3 March 2004, T2991:4–6.

163   Federal Court of Australia 2004. Transcript WAG 49/98, 3 March 2004, T2991:10–13.

164   Federal Court of Australia 2004. Transcript WAG 49/98, 3 March 2004, T2993:29–33.

165   Federal Court of Australia 2004. Transcript WAG 49/98, 3 March 2004, T2993:37–9.

166   Federal Court of Australia 2004. Transcript WAG 49/98, 3 March 2004, T2993:43–5; T2994:4–7.

167   Federal Court of Australia 2004. Transcript WAG 49/98, 3 March 2004, T2994:9–12.

168   Federal Court of Australia 2004. Transcript WAG 49/98, 3 March 2004, T2994:27–30.

169   Federal Court of Australia 2004. Transcript WAG 49/98, 3 March 2004, T2994:36–42.

170   Federal Court of Australia 2004. Transcript WAG 49/98, 3 March 2004, T2994:44–T2995:2.

171   Federal Court of Australia 2004. Transcript WAG 49/98, 3 March 2004, T2995:10–13.

172   *Northern Territory v Alyawarr* (2005) 145 FCR 442, quoted in *Griffiths v Northern Territory of Australia* [2006] FCA 903, paragraph 513l; and see Hiley (2008, p. 1).

173   Federal Court of Australia 2004. Transcript WAG 49/98, 3 March 2004, T2995:27–31.

174   Federal Court of Australia 2004. Transcript WAG 49/98, 3 March 2004, T2996:4–7.

175   Federal Court of Australia 2004. Transcript WAG 49/98, 3 March 2004, T2996:14–16.

176   Federal Court of Australia 2004. Transcript WAG 49/98, 3 March 2004, T2996:28–9.

177   Federal Court of Australia 2004. Transcript WAG 49/98, 3 March 2004, T2996:34–5.

178   Federal Court of Australia 2004. Transcript WAG 49/98, 3 March 2004, T2996:8.

179   Federal Court of Australia 2004. Transcript WAG 49/98, 3 March 2004, T2996:44–6.

180   Federal Court of Australia 2004. Transcript WAG 49/98, 3 March 2004, T2997:1–2.

181   Federal Court of Australia 2004. Transcript WAG 49/98, 3 March 2004, T2999:7–10.

182   Federal Court of Australia 2004. Transcript WAG 49/98, 3 March 2004, T2999:24–6.

183   Federal Court of Australia 2004. Transcript WAG 49/98, 3 March 2004, T2999:39–40.

184   Federal Court of Australia 2004. Transcript WAG 49/98, 3 March 2004, T3000:26–30.

185   Federal Court of Australia 2004. Transcript WAG 49/98, 3 March 2004, T3000:45–7.

186   Federal Court of Australia 2004. Transcript WAG 49/98, 3 March 2004, T3002:4–9.

187   Federal Court of Australia 2004. Transcript WAG 49/98, 3 March 2004, T3002:28–9.

188   Federal Court of Australia 2004. Transcript WAG 49/98, 3 March 2004, T3002:33–7.

189   Federal Court of Australia 2004. Transcript WAG 49/98, 3 March 2004, T3002:45–6.

190   Federal Court of Australia 2004. Transcript WAG 49/98, 3 March 2004, T3003:5–6.

191   Federal Court of Australia 2004. Transcript WAG 49/98, 3 March 2004, T3003:10–16.

192   Federal Court of Australia 2004. Transcript WAG 49/98, 3 March 2004, T3004:7–9.

193   http://www.nativetitle.dpc.wa.gov.au/index.cfm?fuseaction=claims_kimberley.bardi_jawi

194   Kimberley native title decision due. Available from http://www.abc.net.au/news/newsitems/200506/s1389122.htm, accessed 10 June 2005.

195   *Sampi v State of Western Australia (No. 1)* [2005] FCA 777, at paragraph 870.

196   *Sampi v State of Western Australia (No. 1)* [2005] FCA 777, at paragraphs 1094 and 1098.

197   E.g., see *Gumana v Northern Territory of Australia* [2005] FCA 50 at paragraph 3.

198   Figures for tidal variation in the Kimberley vary around the coastline and also vary within the claim area. 5.5 metres is the mean neap water tide and 8 metres the mean spring-water tide. 8.8 metres is the highest astronomical tide. These figures are derived from readings at Karrakatta Bay in the northwest of the claim area, taken from AusTides data (available from: http://www.hydro.gov.au/prodserv/publications/ausTides/tides.htm, accessed 9 January 2013. I am grateful to Paul Davill, Data Manager at the National Tidal Centre, for his assistance in this regard.

199   *Sampi v State of Western Australia (No. 2)* [2005] FCA 1567, at paragraph 17.

200   *Sampi v State of Western Australia (No. 2)* [2005] FCA 1567, at paragraphs 7–27.

201   Robert Blowes, acting for the applicants, Federal Court of Australia 2007. Transcript WAD 188/266, 26 February 2007, T26:7–8.

202   Robert Blowes, acting for the applicants, Federal Court of Australia 2007. Transcript WAD 188/266, 26 February 2007, T26:10.

203   Robert Blowes, acting for the applicants, Federal Court of Australia 2007. Transcript WAD 188/266, 26 February 2007, T26:13–14.

204   More precisely, this meant exclusive possession over those areas of land where native title had not been extinguished. 'Exclusive possession' is 'the right of possession and occupation…as against the whole world', and it included the following rights:
'(a) the right to live on the land;
(b) the right to access, move about on and use the land and waters;
(c) the right to hunt and gather on the land and waters;
(d) the right to engage in spiritual and cultural activities on the land and waters;
(e) the right to access, use and take any of the resources of the land and waters (including ochre) for food, shelter, medicine, fishing and trapping fish, weapons for hunting, cultural, religious, spiritual, ceremonial, artistic and communal purposes;
(f) the right to refuse, regulate and control the use and enjoyment by others of the land and its resources;
(g) the right to have access to and use the water of the land for personal, domestic, social, cultural, religious, spiritual, ceremonial and communal purposes' (Sampi No. 3 at paragraph 4).

205   These non-exclusive rights were:
'(a) the right to access, move about in and on and use and enjoy those areas;
(b) the right to hunt and gather including for dugong and turtle;
(c) the right to access, use and take any of the resources thereof (including water and ochre) for food, trapping fish, religious, spiritual, ceremonial and communal purposes.
Provided that, in respect of areas within that defined in Schedule 4 which are seaward of the mean low water mark, the preceding native title rights and interests are limited to reefs and islets within that area when they are exposed or covered by not more than 2 metres of water' (Sampi No. 3 at paragraph 5).

206   Sampi No. 3 at paragraph 51, citing the Australian Hydrographic Services Tidal Glossary.

207   The variation between the highest astronomical tide at 8.8 metres and the mean high water spring tide at 8 metres is 0.8 metres – a difference that is not insignificant. If this difference was to be calculated as lying between the mean high water spring tide and the mean high water neap tide levels (the latter being 5.5m), then the difference would be much greater – 1.75 metres. This figure is arrived at by taking the mid-point between the mean high water springs (at 8m) and the mean high water neap (at 5.5m), i.e., 6.75m, and then calculating the difference between this and the highest astronomical tide (which is 8.8m), these figures being derived from readings at Karrakatta Bay, taken from AusTides data (available

from: http://www.hydro.gov.au/prodserv/publications/ausTides/tides.htm, accessed 9 January 2013. I am grateful to Paul Davill, Data Manager at the National Tidal Centre, for his assistance in this regard.

208   Robert Blowes, barrister for the applicants, Federal Court of Australia 2007. Transcript WAD 188/266, 26 February 2007, T22:27–8.

209   I refer here to the High Court's decision in *Northern Territory of Australia v Arnhem Land Aboriginal Land Trust* [2008] HCA 29 (Blue Mud Bay), which recognised Aboriginal landowners in the Northern Territory as having exclusive possession of the intertidal zone – that is, the right to exclude persons from tidal waters adjoining land by Aboriginal landowners under the *Aboriginal Land Rights (Northern Territory) Act 1976* (the 'ALRA'). The majority of the court found that the Northern Territory Fisheries Act had statutorily abrogated the public right to fish (paragraph 27), and that the sea boundaries of the land grants in question under the ALRA, having been defined in 'metes and bounds' (paragraph 55), extended to the low water mark (paragraph 46) and hence included the intertidal zone. This case is a product of the intersection of two sets of legislation, the ALRA and the Native Title Act – and hence as a precedent does not extend to native title cases Australia-wide. In effect, it confirmed key aspects of the ALRA in the intertidal zone.

210   Kevin Bell, who represented the applicants during the 'second trial' in 2003, had been appointed a Justice to the Supreme Court of Victoria in February 2005. This meant that, had there been an intention to brief him to run the appeal, he would have been unavailable.

211   This can occur for the provision of confidential legal advice though. For example, Bagshaw reviewed key aspects of the anthropology for the Central Land Council representing the applicants on appeal in the Yulara case.

212   For example, in the Ngarluma/Yindjibarndi case (*Daniel v State of Western Australia* [2003] FCA 666 3 July 2003), Nicholson J discussed factors affecting the weight that should be given to one of the expert reports, discussing 'methodological defects' that included such things as 'proceeding on an implicit assumption' and then proceeding to ask 'leading questions' on that basis (see paragraphs 1530–31).

213   Federal Court of Australia Transcript 2001, WAG49/98, T593.01; T593.02.

214   For example, after Transcript Australia audio-checked the recording it was agreed that Djarindjin (which is the name of the community) should be changed to Jarrinyan (the name of a *buru*) in relation to at least eight references in the applicant evidence (T844.22; T844 24; T844.26; T844.28; T244.30; T858.11; T858.13; T858.15).

215   Commonwealth of Australia (2003) at 76(i).

216   For example, at paragraph 411, the witness's evidence (from T551.20–35) was summarised as referring to Jalan (Tallon Island), when the reference should have been to Yalun (Cone Bay); a transcript error that had been previously

identified and agreed. There are references in the judgment to 'Chaffered Island', which should have been Cafarelli Island (see paragraph 148). There is no 'Chaffered Island' in this region. At paragraph 406, the judgment refers to the witness's wife as being from Bulnginy (Poolngin Island), a transcript error that had been previously identified (at T540.25), which should have been Bulgin. Paragraph 139 of the judgment also retains a previously identified transcript error, this time referring to Bulnginy (Poolngin Island) rather than to Bulgun (a named place on Sunday Island; the transcript reference is to T593.25–30).

217　There is a reference to these transcript errors towards the conclusion of the 2001 expert evidence in the case:

> *Counsel (Cth):* Yes. One other minor matter, your Honour. The applicants in this matter have prepared a document of 11 pages long identifying errors in the transcript.
>
> *His Honour:* Yes.
>
> *Counsel (Cth):* I have that document. There are some which are not agreed, but I've spoken to Mr Donges [of Transcript Australia]. If, at the end of the day, the respondents and the applicants do not agree on this list of changes, Mr Donges will review the matter and if that doesn't resolve it, we'll have recourse to your Honour.
>
> *His Honour:* I'll have to – I'll have to rule on it, at some stage.
>
> *Counsel (Cth):* Yes.
>
> *His Honour:* Perhaps in final addresses - - -
>
> *Counsel (Cth):* Yes, your Honour. There's no urgency. I don't think any of these matters is – is crucial...(Federal Court of Australia 2001. Transcript WAG 49/98, T2062.27–45).

218　E.g., evidence given by three separate witnesses, at Federal Court of Australia 2001. Transcript WAG 49/98, T512.00–15 (Aubrey Tigan); T2547.15–20 (Joe Davey); T598.10–15 (Jimmy Ejai).

219　Federal Court of Australia 2001. Transcript WAG 49/98, T1500:31–33.

220　Federal Court of Australia 2001. Transcript WAG 49/98, T1371.35–1372.20; T1373.00.

221　E.g., Federal Court of Australia 2001. Transcript WAG 49/98, evidence at T512.15–20 (Aubrey Tigan); T2547.25 (Joe Davey); T611.30–35 (Jimmy Ejai).

222　Justice French, summarising WAFIC's submissions, pointed out that they noted that Khaki Stumpagee had not been called at the second trial (paragraph 990).

223　E.g., Khaki Stumpagee's evidence, Federal Court of Australia 2001. Transcript WAG 49/98, at T1515.35–45; Aubrey Tigan's evidence at T192.20–25; Dennis Davey's evidence at T540.30–43. Albert Lennard, recognised as the senior traditional owner for Tyra Island (Munburran, adjacent to Jayirri) was also widely recognised as Bardi.

224 As described in Federal Court of Australia 2001. Transcript WAG 49/98,
Aubrey Tigan's evidence at T191.30–T192.47.

225 Federal Court of Australia 2001. Transcript WAG 49/98, T1515.35.

226 Federal Court of Australia 2001. Transcript WAG 49/98, T1515.35–45.

227 Federal Court of Australia 2001. Transcript WAG 49/98, T2612.10–20.

228 Federal Court of Australia 2001. Transcript WAG 49/98, T1501.00–22.

229 Federal Court of Australia 2001. Transcript WAG 49/98, T1506.03–07.

230 Federal Court of Australia 2001. Transcript WAG 49/98, T2003.10–30.

231 Federal Court of Australia 2001. Transcript WAG 49/98, T477.45–478.05.

232 Federal Court of Australia 2001. Transcript WAG 49/98, T478.15–20.

233 Federal Court of Australia 2001. Transcript WAG 49/98, Khaki Stumpagee's
evidence at T1514.00–35.

234 Federal Court of Australia 2001. Transcript WAG 49/98, T1515.25–37.

235 Federal Court of Australia 2001. Transcript WAG 49/98, T611.00–10.

236 Federal Court of Australia 2001. Transcript WAG 49/98, T611.05–20.

237 Federal Court of Australia 2001. Transcript WAG 49/98, T1503.00–10.

238 See *Sampi v State of Western Australia* FCA777, paragraph 190.

239 This was rendered as Bulgin (on the mainland, at Hunter's Creek, Federal
Court of Australia 2001. Transcript WAG 49/98, at T1503.23 in the
transcript; although correctly rendered as Bulnginy soon afterwards at
T1503.31).

240 Federal Court of Australia 2001. Transcript WAG 49/98, T1503.15–30.

241 Federal Court of Australia 2001. Transcript WAG 49/98, T1339.43–44.

242 *Jul* (the name of the being) *jina* (belonging to, from) *bur* (a polysemic term,
meaning country, estate, camp, ground, place: Bowern (2009, p. 330)
suggests that it also refers to 'time, tide', but this is not a usage I have
encountered. Dennis Davey gave evidence at the reef that '*Juljinabur* is what
we call fish, but at that time this was old man and – and we believed that
Jul[u] was a human being' (T1325.17–18).

243 Federal Court of Australia 2001. Transcript WAG 49/98, T1325.17–18, and
Sampi v State of Western Australia FCA 777 at paragraph 424.

244 Sampi No. 1, at paragraph 1116.

245 This expression 'of some antiquity' is derived from J. Von Doussa in
Chapman & Ors v Luminis & Ors. Action No. SG 33 of 1997, FCA 21 at
paragraph 399.

246 Metcalfe (2000, p. 15) refers to the difficulty Bardi had in translating some
ceremonial songs word-for-word, since the words did not have meanings
in everyday speech; he argues that this is evidence of the antiquity of
these ritual songs. Clendon (2001, p. 7) suggests that another possibility is
that the songs were not translatable in this manner because 'secret/sacred
material may be disguised, so that occult meanings are rendered inaccessible
to uninitiated audiences'. In the case of the *ilma* I am referring to here,
Metcalfe's view would seem more applicable, since *ilma* as a genre are

widely accessible to Bardi audiences, and the *Juljinabur* narrative is an 'open' (unrestricted) myth.

247   Federal Court of Australia 2001. Transcript WAG 49/98, T511.30.

248   Federal Court of Australia 2001. Transcript WAG 49/98, T542.25–30; T2565.40–2566.05.

249   Federal Court of Australia 2001. Transcript WAG 49/98, T2522.25.

250   Federal Court of Australia 2001. Transcript WAG 49/98, T1515.35–45; T1504.00–15; T1504.25–30; T1505.40–45.

251   Federal Court of Australia 2001. Transcript WAG 49/98, T478.05–15; T464.45–465.00.

252   Federal Court of Australia 2001. Transcript WAG 49/98, T1007.15–1008.35. Importantly, he also included Albert Lennard whose country was Munburran (Tyra Island), right next door to Jayirri.

253   Federal Court of Australia 2001. Transcript WAG 49/98, T1005.25–1006.05.

254   Federal Court of Australia 2001. Transcript WAG 49/98, T318.40–T319.00; T921.35–45.

255   Federal Court of Australia 2001. Transcript WAG 49/98, T922.15.

256   Bernadette Angus's deferral to Khaki Stumpagee's knowledge is in Federal Court of Australia 2001. Transcript WAG 49/98, at T321.26–28. Khaki Stumpagee referred to the island as 'Inalabul'; he said 'they was talking Bardi language, that one, all them mob' (T1504.26–28).

257   Federal Court of Australia 2001. Transcript WAG 49/98, T482.10–40; T494.25–40; T494.45–495.15.

258   Federal Court of Australia 2001. Transcript WAG 49/98, T483.00–10; T483.25–35.

259   Federal Court of Australia 2001. Transcript WAG 49/98, T591.15–25, T592.35–45; T593.10–15; T593.35–45.

260   Federal Court of Australia 2001. Transcript WAG 49/98, T592.40–45.

261   Federal Court of Australia 2001. Transcript WAG 49/98, T593.00–10. Paragraph 139 of *Sampi v State of Western Australia* FCA 777 records these places as Bulnginy, a previously identified transcript error, and Gawinungunu, which is neither true to the transcript nor a corrected transcript error.

262   Federal Court of Australia 2001. Transcript WAG 49/98, T596.45–597.15.

263   Federal Court of Australia 2001. Transcript WAG 49/98, T597.15–25.

264   Federal Court of Australia 2001. Transcript WAG 49/98, T598.40–45.

265   Federal Court of Australia 2001. Transcript WAG 49/98, T593.35–45.

266   Bowern (2012, pp. 715–34) reproduces an extended narrative version (in Bardi, with English and interlinear translation) of Galalung's travel on the mainland and the islands that linguist Gedda Aklif recorded from David Wiggan in 1990. This narrative refers to Galalung travelling from the mainland over to various islands including Julum (Middle Island), Jayirri (Jackson Island), Jalan (Tallon Island), Ralral (Salural Island), Boolnginy

(Poolngin Island), and Iwany (Sunday Island), creating specific places as he went.

267 Federal Court of Australia 2001. Transcript WAG 49/98, T594.00–10.

268 See *Sampi v State of Western Australia* FCA 777 at paragraph 139. This part of Ejai's evidence is not included.

269 Such as Gurrngygalal, see Federal Court of Australia 2001. Transcript WAG 49/98, T801.29–31. See Semeniuk (1983) and Mathews, Semeniuk & Semeniuk (2011) who have described the ecology underpinning these subsurface rivulets of freshwater that emerge offshore.

270 See *Sampi v State of Western Australia* FCA 777 at paragraph 9, in which Justice French says that the claimants 'continue to enjoy their rights to the use of pearl shell for purely ceremonial purposes and the taking of oysters for subsistence in accordance with their traditional laws and customs'.

271 See *Sampi v State of Western Australia* FCA 777 at paragraph 80.

272 Federal Court of Australia 2001. Transcript WAG 49/98, T426.05–15.

273 Federal Court of Australia 2001. Transcript WAG 49/98, T464.45–465.00.

274 Federal Court of Australia 2001. Transcript WAG 49/98, T321.29–30. The witness is likely to have meant 'spring chicken'.

275 *Sampi v State of Western Australia* FCA 777, at paragraph 1103.

276 Federal Court of Australia 2001. Transcript WAG 49/98, T2036.30–31.

277 Federal Court of Australia 2001. Transcript WAG 49/98, T1656.35-1657.32.

278 Federal Court of Australia 2001. Transcript WAG 49/98, T1703.17–32.

279 Federal Court of Australia Transcript 2001, WAG 49/98, T1648.26–27; T1662.11–14; T1692.29–32.

280 Federal Court of Australia 2007. Transcript WAD188/2006 26 February 2007, T28:6–10.

281 Federal Court of Australia 2007. Transcript WAD188/2006 26 February 2007, T25:34–41. Robert Blowes and Tom Keely were the two barristers acting in the appeal.

282 Ken Pettit, representing the Commonwealth of Australia. In Federal Court of Australia 2007. Transcript WAD188/2006 28 February 2007, T156:19–22.

283 Ken Pettit, representing the Commonwealth of Australia. In Federal Court of Australia 2007. Transcript WAD188/2006 28 February 2007, T156:10–13. WAFIC's and the Commonwealth's submissions that the determination should specify that the recognised native title rights to fish were non-commercial rights only – an argument made on the basis that this would afford greater 'clarity'– was not successful on appeal. See Sampi FCAFC 26, at paragraphs 154–60.

284 http://www.familycourt.gov.au/wps/wcm/connect/FCOA/home/ judgments/about_judgments/, accessed 7 January 2014.

285 http://www.fedcourt.gov.au/case-management-services/appeals/from-courts/ appellate-jurisdiction, accessed 7 January 2014.

286 Federal Court of Australia 2007. Transcript WAD188/2006 26 February 2007, T3:31–32.

287 Federal Court of Australia 2007. Transcript WAD188/2006 26 February 2007, T3:32–36.

288 http://www.fedcourt.gov.au/case-management-services/appeals/from-courts/appellate-jurisdiction, accessed 7/1/2014. Given the logistical difficulties of an on-country trial and the expenses involved, the idea of re-hearing a case is unlikely to be one that those who have already been through one would immediately and optimistically embrace.

289 Federal Court of Australia 2007. Transcript WAD188/2006 26 February 2007, T2:37.

290 Federal Court of Australia 2007. Transcript WAD 188/2006, Paul Sampi and Others and the State of Western Australia and Others. Prepared by Auscript Australasia. This transcript contains even more transcript errors than that of the original case.

291 Federal Court of Australia 2007. Transcript WAD188/2006 26 February 2007, T43:42–T44:03. 'In rem' (from Latin, 'against a thing') in this instance refers to the court's power to make a decision that there was no native title over the islands.

292 Sampi v State of Western Australia [2010] FCAFC 26, at paragraph 33. See also Sampi (No. 1) at paragraphs 1043–46.

293 Sampi v State of Western Australia [2010] FCAFC 26, at paragraph 41.

294 Federal Court of Australia 2007. Transcript WAD188/2006 27 February 2007, T102:22.

295 Federal Court of Australia 2007. Transcript WAD188/2006 27 February 2007, T102: 23–30, my emphasis.

296 Robert Blowes, representing the Applicants, in Federal Court of Australia 2007. Transcript WAD188/2006 26 February 2007, T26:30–34.

297 Geoffrey Bagshaw, personal communication, March 2016.

298 Raelene Webb, representing the State of Western Australia, in Federal Court of Australia 2007. Transcript WAD188/2006 27 February 2007, T102:36.

299 Raelene Webb, representing the State of Western Australia, in Federal Court of Australia 2007. Transcript WAD188/2006 26 February 2007, T6:21–43, my emphases.

300 Federal Court of Australia 2007. Transcript WAD188/2006 27 February 2007, T102:6–7.

301 Federal Court of Australia 2007. Transcript WAD188/2006 27 February 2007, T208:17–19.

302 Federal Court of Australia 2007. Transcript WAD188/2006 26 February 2007, T42:19–23.

303 Federal Court of Australia 2007. Transcript WAD188/2006 26 February 2007, T42:28–29.

304 Federal Court of Australia 2007. Transcript WAD188/2006 26 February 2007, T28:29–34, my emphasis.

305 Federal Court of Australia 2007. Transcript WAD188/2006 26 February 2007, T28:36–40.

306 Federal Court of Australia 2007. Transcript WAD188/2006 26 February 2007, T46:34–38.

307 Federal Court of Australia 2007. Transcript WAD188/2006 26 February 2007, T29:3–4.

308 Federal Court of Australia 2007. Transcript WAD 188/266, 26 February 2007, T30:42.

309 The claim over Worrorra country is called Dambimangarri, the claim over Ngarinyin country is called Neowarra after the first named applicant, and the Wunambal claim is called Uunguu.

310 Federal Court of Australia 2007. Transcript WAD188/2006 26 February 2007, T29:11–17.

311 Federal Court of Australia 2007. Transcript WAD188/2006 26 February 2007, T29:21–27.

312 *Jango v Northern Territory of Australia* [2006] FCA 318 at paragraph 397. Yulara was appealed to the Full Federal Court of Australia: see *Jango v Northern Territory of Australia* [2007] FCAFC 101.

313 Federal Court of Australia 2007. Transcript WAD188/2006 26 February 2007, T29:34–26.

314 Federal Court of Australia 2007. Transcript WAD188/2006 26 February 2007, T29:38–39.

315 Federal Court of Australia 2007. Transcript WAD188/2006 26 February 2007, T30:20.

316 Federal Court of Australia 2007. Transcript WAD188/206 26 February 2007, T30:22–25.

317 Federal Court of Australia 2007. Transcript WAD188/206 26 February 2007, T51:47–T52:02.

318 *Sampi v State of Western Australia* [2010] FCAFC 26, at paragraph 37.

319 *Sampi v State of Western Australia* [2010] FCAFC 26, at paragraph 38.

320 Letter, State Solicitor's Office to Kimberley Land Council, 24 August 2007.

321 *Sampi v State of Western Australia* [2010] FCAFC 26, at paragraph 5.

322 *Sampi v State of Western Australia* [2010] FCAFC 26, at paragraph 7.

323 *Sampi v State of Western Australia* [2010] FCAFC 26, at paragraph 7.

324 *Sampi v State of Western Australia* [2010] FCAFC 26, at paragraph 8.

325 *Sampi v State of Western Australia* [2010] FCAFC 26, at paragraph 9.

326 *Sampi v State of Western Australia* [2010] FCAFC 26, at paragraph 9.

327 I heard stories about people swimming, in their younger days, from One Arm Point to Sunday Island in the 1950s. This is a distance of about 10 kilometres, albeit a distance that could be broken up by stopping at different islands along the way.

328   Sampi (No.1) at paragraph 1043, also cited in *Sampi v State of Western Australia* [2010] FCAFC 26, at paragraph 29, my emphasis.

329   *Sampi v State of Western Australia* [2010] FCAFC 26, at paragraph 51.

330   *Sampi v State of Western Australia* [2010] FCAFC 26, at paragraph 107.

331   *Sampi v State of Western Australia* [2010] FCAFC 26, at paragraph 111.

332   *Sampi v State of Western Australia* [2010] FCAFC 26, at paragraphs 85, 111, 146, 147, 153.

333   *Sampi v State of Western Australia* [2010] FCAFC 26, at paragraphs 133, 140.

334   This 3 nautical mile limit was a retraction of the 12 nautical miles of the original application, and represents the limit of the State of Western Australia's territorial waters (Sampi FCAFC 26, paragraph 111).

335   Detailed maps of the determination area can be accessed at: http://www.nntt.gov.au/searchRegApps/NativeTitleRegisters/NNTR%20 Extracts/WCD2005_003/WCD2005_003%201.%20The%20Maps.pdf, accessed 2 September 2015.

336   Source: http://www.watoday.com.au/wa-news/kimberley-aborigines-win-rights-over-sea-20100319-qlk1.html, accessed 2 September 2015.

337   Source: http://www.watoday.com.au/wa-news/kimberley-aborigines-win-rights-over-sea-20100319-qlk1.html, accessed 2 September 2015.

338   http://www.environment.gov.au/indigenous/ipa/declared/bardijawi.html, accessed 20 August 2015.

339   See: http://www.environment.gov.au/indigenous/ipa/sea.html; http://www. environment.gov.au/indigenous/ipa/declared/bardijawi.html, accessed 20 August 2015.

References

Akerman, Kim n.d., 'People of the ocean: Tide riders of the Dampier Peninsula', Booklet produced and funded as a project of National Significance by the Commonwealth Schools Commission, pp. 1–17. WA Social Science Education Consortium of the WA Institute of Technology, Perth.

Akerman, Kim 1975, 'The double raft or kalwa of the West Kimberley', *Mankind,* vol. 10, no. 1, pp. 20–3.

Akerman, Kim with John Stanton 1994, *Riji and jakoli: Kimberley pearlshell in Aboriginal Australia*, Northern Territory Museum of Arts and Sciences Monograph Series 4, Northern Territory Museum of Arts and Sciences, Darwin.

Aklif, Gedda 1999, *Ardiyooloon Bardi ngaanka: One Arm Point Bardi dictionary*, Kimberley Language Resource Centre, Halls Creek.

Alroe, M. J. 1988, 'A Pygmalion complex among missionaries', in T. Swain & D. B. Rose, (eds), *Aboriginal Australians and Christian Missions: Ethnographic and historical studies*, pp. 30–44, Australian Association for the Study of Religions, Adelaide.

Anderson, Lois 1978, 'The role of Aboriginal and Asian labour in the origin and development of the pearling industry, Broome, Western Australia, 1862–1940', Honours thesis, Murdoch University, Perth.

Appadurai, Arjun (ed.) 1986, *The social life of things*, Cambridge University Press, Cambridge.

Applicant's Supplementary Substances of Evidence (Filed Pursuant to Order 17 of Lee J of 17 December 1999), in The Federal Court of Australia, Western Australia District Registry, WAG 49 of 1998, between Paul Sampi & Ors and The Premier & State of Western Australia and the Commonwealth of Australia.

Austin-Broos, Diane 2009, *Arrernte present, Arrernte past: Invasion, violence, and imagination in Indigenous central Australia*, The University of Chicago Press, Chicago & London.

Bagshaw, Geoffrey C. 1995, 'Bardi/Jawi native title claim', Anthropologist's report, Prepared for the Kimberley Land Council.

Bagshaw, Geoffrey C. 1999, 'Native Title Claim WAG 49/98 (Bardi and Jawi)', Anthropologist's Report, Prepared for the Kimberley Land Council on behalf of the native title claimants, February 1999.

Bagshaw, Geoffrey C. 2001a, 'Bardi and Jawi supplementary anthropology report parts 1, 2 & 3', Filed in the Federal Court of Australia, Western Australia District Registry, General Division, in *Paul Sampi & Ors v The Premier and State of Western Australia & The Commonwealth of Australia*, 27 August 2001.

Bagshaw, Geoffrey C. 2001b, 'Applicants' additional anthropological report concerning distribution and spatial extent of local estates (bur[u]) within the Bardi and Jawi native title claim area', Filed in the Federal Court of Australia, Western Australia District Registry, General Division, in *Paul Sampi & Ors v The Premier and State of Western Australia & The Commonwealth of Australia*, 8 February 2001.

Bagshaw, Geoffrey C. 2003, *The Karajarri claim: A case-study in native title anthropology*, Oceania Monograph 53, Oceania Publications, Sydney.

Bagshaw, Geoffrey C. & Katie Glaskin 2000, 'Anthropologists' supplementary report: Aspects of Bardi and Jawi marine tenure and resource usage', Filed in the Federal Court of Australia, Western Australia District Registry, General Division, in *Paul Sampi & Ors v The Premier and State of Western Australia & The Commonwealth of Australia*, 30 October 2000.

Bain, Mary Albertus 1982, *Full fathom five*, Artlook Books, Perth.

Bardi Aborigines Association 1983, Letter to Paul Seaman QC, 12 August 1983.

Barker, Wayne 1998, *The stolen series* (video), Gunada Productions, Broome.

Bateman, F. E. A. 1948, *Report on survey of Native Affairs*, Wyatt, Government Printer, Perth.

Bates, Daisy Mary n.d., *Records of Daisy M. Bates*, Box 50, Items 97/439–458. Manuscript Section, National Library of Australia.

Bates, Daisy Mary 1966 [1938], *The passing of the Aborigines*, William Heinemann, Melbourne.

Beckett, Jeremy 1987, *Torres Strait Islanders: Custom and colonialism*, Cambridge University Press, Cambridge.

Beckett, Jeremy 1994, 'The Murray Island land case and the problem of cultural continuity', in W. Sanders (ed.), *Mabo and native title: Origins and institutional implications*, pp. 7–24, CAEPR Research Monograph No.7. Centre for Aboriginal Economic Policy and Research, Canberra.

Beckett, Jeremy R. 1995, 'The Murray Island land case', *The Australian Journal of Anthropology*, vol. 6, pp. 15–31.

Bird, W. H. n.d., 'Notes on Habits and Customs of Sunday Island Natives', in *Records of Daisy M. Bates*, MS 365, Box 8, Folio 16/36–108, Item 16/114, Manuscript Section, National Library of Australia.

Bird, W. H. 1910, 'Some remarks on the grammatical construction of the Chowie-Language, as spoken by the Buccaneer Islanders, North-Western Australia', *Anthropos*, Bd. 5, H. 2, pp. 454–56.

Bird, W. H. 1911, 'Ethnographical notes about the Buccaneer Islanders, North Western Australia', *Anthropos*, Bd. 6, H. 1, pp. 174–78.

Bird, W. H. 1915, 'A short vocabulary of the Chowie-language of the Buccaneer Islanders (Sunday Islanders), North Western Australia' *Anthropos*, Bd. 10/11, H. 1/2, pp. 180–86.

Bischofs, P. Jos 1908, 'Die Niol-Niol, ein Eingenborenenstamm in Nordwest-Australien', *Anthropos* Bd. 3, H. 1, pp. 32–40. German text trans. C. Fennell for the Kimberley Land Council.

Blundell, Valda & Donny Woolagoodja 2005, *Keeping the Wanjinas fresh: Sam Woolagoodja and the enduring power of Lalai*, Fremantle Arts Press, Fremantle.

Bottrill, Angus M. n.d., 'Mission Lands Review', Unpublished report commissioned by the Western Australian government.

Bourdieu, Pierre 1977, *Outline of a theory of practice*, Cambridge University Press, Cambridge.

Bourdieu, Pierre 1987, 'The force of law: Towards a sociology of the juridical field', *Hastings Law Journal*, vol. 38, pp. 814–54.

Bowern, Claire 2009, 'Naming Bardi places', in Harold Koch & Luise Hercus (eds), *Aboriginal Placenames: Naming and re-naming the Australian landscape*, pp. 615–49, Aboriginal History Monograph 19, ANU E-Press and Aboriginal History Inc., Canberra.

Bowern, Claire 2012, *A grammar of Bardi*, Walter de Gruyter, Boston and Berlin.

Brennan, Sean 2007, 'Recent developments in native title case law', Paper presented at the Human Rights Law Bulletin Seminar, HREOC, Sydney, 4 June 2007.

Broome Advertiser 1993a, 'Portugal colonised Kimberley: Professor', Thursday 29 May 1993, p. 3.

Broome Advertiser 1993b, 'Professor claims Portuguese first whites to colonise the state', Thursday 3 June 1993, p. 7.

Broome Police Report 1923, 'H.C. Hunter family of Boolgin [sic] Creek', AN 1/4; Acc 653; 851/1923, Battye Library, Western Australia State Archives, Perth.

Brown, Lyndon (Cygnet Bay Pearls) 1975, Letter to Alan Ridge, Minister for Lands, 29 October 1975, From vol. 2, 3 and 4 of 1559/62; 3229/84 (vol. 3); 467/985 and 3266/69 of the Lands and Surveys Department, in: Bottrill, Angus M. n.d., Brown – Cygnet Bay, Typescript.

Brown, Bruce (Cygnet Bay Pearls) 1984, Letter to Mr Peter Dowding, MLC, Member for North Province 12 December 1984, From Volume 2, 3 and 4 of 1559/62; 3229/84 (vol. 3); 467/985 and 3266/69 of the Lands and Surveys Department, in Bottrill, Angus M. n.d., Brown – Cygnet Bay, Typescript.

Burke, Paul 2007, 'The problem when flexibility *is* the system', *Anthropological Forum*, vol. 17, no. 2, pp. 162–65.

Burke, Paul 2010, 'Overlapping jural publics: A model for dealing with the "society" question in native title', in T. Bauman (ed.), *Dilemmas in Applied Native Title Anthropology in Australia*, pp. 55–71, Native Title Research Unit, Australian Institute of Aboriginal and Torres Strait Islander Studies, Canberra.

Burke, Paul 2011, *Law's anthropology: From ethnography to expert testimony in native title*, ANU E-Press, Canberra.

Burns, Marcelle 2011, 'Challenging the assumptions of positivism: An analysis of the concept of society in *Sampi on behalf of the Bardi and Jawi People v Western Australia* [2010] and *Bodney v Bennell* [2008]', *Land, Rights, Laws: Issues of Native Title*, vol. 4, Issues Paper no. 7, Native Title Research Unit, Australian Institute of Aboriginal and Torres Strait Islander Studies, Canberra.

Campbell, W. D. & W. H. Bird 1915, 'An account of the Aboriginals of Sunday Island, King Sound, Kimberley, Western Australia', *Journal and Proceedings of the Royal Society of Western Australia* vol. 1, p. 55–82.

Cane, Scott 2002, *Pila Nguru: The Spinifex People*, Fremantle Arts Centre Press, Fremantle.

Chanock, Martin 1985, *Law, Custom and Social Order: The Colonial Experience in Malawi and Zambia*, Cambridge University Press, Cambridge.

Chez Les Sauvages Australiens (film) 1932, Mondial Films, France.

Chi, Jimmy & Kuckles 1991, *Bran Nue Dae: A musical journey*, Magabala Books, Broome.

Choo, Christine 2001, *Mission Girls: Aboriginal women on Catholic missions in the Kimberley, Western Australia, 1900–1950*, University of Western Australia Press, Crawley.

Clendon, Mark 2001, 'Response to Dr C. D. Metcalfe's Bardi and Jawi linguistics expert report', First Respondents' Preliminary Linguist's Report, prepared for the Western Australian Crown Solicitor's Office, January 2001, Filed in the Federal Court of Australia, Western Australia District Registry, General Division, in *Paul Sampi & Ors v The Premier and State of Western Australia & The Commonwealth of Australia*, 10 January 2001.

Commonwealth of Australia 2003, Submissions of the Commonwealth of Australia (Facts), in The Federal Court of Australia, Western Australia District Registry, WAG 49 of 1998, between Paul Sampi & Ors and The Premier & State of Western Australia and the Commonwealth of Australia.

Connolly, Anthony J. 2006, 'Judicial conceptions of tradition in Canadian Aboriginal Rights Law', in James F. Weiner and Katie Glaskin (eds), 'Custom: Indigenous tradition and law in the twenty-first century', *The Asia-Pacific Journal of Anthropology,* Special Issue, vol. 7, no. 1, pp. 27–44.

Connolly, Anthony J. 2010, *Cultural Difference on Trial: The Nature and limits of judicial understanding,* Ashgate, Farnham.

Coombs, H. C. 1974, 'Decentralisation trends among Aboriginal communities', Presidential Address to the Anthropology Section, 45th ANZAAS Congress, Perth, 14 August 1973, reprinted in Department of Aboriginal Affairs WA, Newsletter, vol. 1, no. 8, Sep. 1974, pp. 4–25.

Coombs, H. C., McCann, H., Ross, H. and Williams, N. (eds.) 1989, *Land of Promises: Aborigines and development in the East Kimberley,* Centre for Resource and Environmental Studies, Australian National University and Aboriginal Studies Press, Australian Institute of Aboriginal Studies, Canberra.

Crawford, Ian 2001, *We won the victory: Aborigines and outsiders on the north-west coast of the Kimberley,* Fremantle Arts Centre Press, Fremantle.

Culhane, Dara 1998, *The pleasure of the Crown: Anthropology, law, and first nations,* Talon Books, Vancouver.

Dampier, William 1937 [1697], *A New Voyage Round the World,* Adams and Charles Black, London.

Davidson, Daniel S. 1935a, 'The chronology of Australian watercraft (continued)', *The Journal of the Polynesian Society,* vol. 44, no. 2, pp. 69–84.

Davidson, Daniel S. 1935b, 'The chronology of Australian watercraft (continued)', *The Journal of the Polynesian Society,* vol. 44, no. 3, pp. 137–53.

Davis, Stephen L. & J. R. V. ('Victor') Prescott 1984, *Maritime claims by Aboriginal Communities in Northwest Australia: A submission to the Aboriginal Land Inquiry,* June 1984, presented on behalf of the Dampierland Peninsular [sic] Aboriginal Communities, Bardi Aboriginal Association Inc., One Arm Point; Beagle Bay Aboriginal Council Inc. and Lombardina [sic] Community Inc.

Dirlik, Arif 2001, Comment on 'Lost Worlds: environmental disaster, "culture loss" and the law', by Stuart Kirsch, *Current Anthropology*, vol. 42, no. 2, pp. 181–82.

Donges, Graham 1999, 'Sitting on the transcript', *Butterworths Native Title News*, vol. 4, no. 1, pp. 16–17.

Donovan, James M. 2008, *Legal anthropology: An introduction*, AltaMira Press, Lanham.

Douglas, Malcom 1991, *Follow the sun*, Malcolm Douglas Films, Cable Beach.

Douglas, Wilf 1992, *Bardi language word-book: A revision of 'Word gems from Iwanya – Sunday Island'*, Typescript.

Dousset, Laurent & Katie Glaskin 2007, 'Western Desert and native title: how models become myths', *Anthropological Forum*, vol. 17, no. 2, pp. 127–48.

Dousset, Laurent 2016, 'Introduction', in Lizzie Marrkilyi Ellis, *Pictures from my memory*, pp. xi–xv, Aboriginal Studies Press, Canberra.

Drysdale, Ingrid and Mary Durack 1974, *The end of the Dreaming*, Rigby, Adelaide.

Durack, Mary 1997 [1969], *The rock and the sand*, Corgi, Great Britain.

Eades, Diana 1993, 'Language and the law: White Australia v Nancy', in M. Walsh & C. Yallop (eds), *Language and Culture in Aboriginal Australia*, pp. 181–90, Aboriginal Studies Press, Canberra.

Eades, Diana (ed.) 1995, *Language in evidence: Issues confronting Aboriginal and multicultural Australia*, University of New South Wales Press, Sydney.

Edmunds, Mary 1995, 'Conflict in native title claims', Land, Rights, Laws: Issues of Native Title Issues Paper No. 7, Native Title Research Unit, Australian Institute of Aboriginal and Torres Strait Islander Studies, Canberra.

Edwards, Hugh 1983, *Port of pearls*, Rigby, Adelaide.

Elkin, A. P. 1928a, Field notebook IV, Box 2, Item 1/1/11, Elkin Archives, Fisher Library, University of Sydney.

Elkin, A. P. 1928b, Letter home to Sally, 18 March 1928, in: Letters home to Sally from A. P. Elkin – on field trip to Kimberley Division 1927–28, Box 1, Item 1 (1/1/1), Elkin Archives, Fisher Library, University of Sydney.

Elkin, A. P. 1927–8a, Genealogy Notebooks 1927–8, Book 2, 'Bād Tribe', Item 1/1/19, Elkin Archives, Fisher Library, University of Sydney.

Elkin, A. P. 1927-8b, Genealogy Notebooks 1927–8, Book 3, 'Djau Tribe', Item 1/1/20, Elkin Archives, Fisher Library, University of Sydney.

Elkin, A. P. 1932, 'Social organization in the Kimberley division, North-Western Australia', *Oceania*, vol. 2, no. 3, pp. 296–333.

Elkin, A. P. 1933, 'Totemism in north-Western Australia (the Kimberley Division), Part II', *Oceania*, vol. 3, no. 4, pp. 435–81.

Emo, Father Nicholas Maria 1907, Protector of Natives at Cygnet Bay, letter to Chief Protector of Aborigines, 10 September 2007, AN 1/3; Acc 652; 803/1909, Folios 1-8, 'J. Isdell, Native crews on boats – re-regulations governing employment of natives', Battye Library, Western Australia State Archives, Perth.

Ejai, Tudor 1986, 'The killing of the 'Bilikin' brothers', transcribed by C. D. Metcalfe, in L. Hercus & P. Sutton (eds), *This Is What Happened: Historical narratives by Aborigines*, pp.140–50, Australian Institute of Aboriginal Studies, Canberra.

Farrell, P. G. 1887, Journal of P. Farrell, West Kimberley District, Derby Station. AN5; Acc 430; 600/1887, Battye Library, Western Australia State Archives, Perth.

Federal Court of Australia 2000, Transcript WAG6017/1996 *Daniel v State of Western Australia & Ors*, Transcript produced by Transcript Australia.

Federal Court of Australia 2001, Transcript WAG 49/98 *Paul Sampi & Ors v State of Western Australia & Ors*, Transcript produced by Transcript Australia.

Federal Court of Australia 2002, Transcript WAG 6016/96 *Neowarra v State of Western Australia & Ors*, Transcript produced by Transcript Australia.

Federal Court of Australia 2003, Transcript WAG 49/98 *Paul Sampi & Ors v State of Western Australia & Ors*, Transcript produced by Transcript Australia.

Federal Court of Australia 2004, Transcript WAG 49/98, *Paul Sampi & Ors v State of Western Australia & Ors*, Final Submissions, Transcript produced by Transcript Australia.

Federal Court of Australia 2007, Transcript WAD 188/266, *Paul Sampi & Ors v State of Western Australia & Ors*, Transcript produced by Auscript.

French, Robert 2011, 'Home grown laws in a global neighbourhood – Australia, the United States and the Rest', Albritton Lecture, given at the University of Alabama School of Law, 18 January 2011, Alabama.

Fuller, Chris 1994, Legal anthropology, legal pluralism and legal thought. *Anthropology Today*, vol. 10, no. 3, pp. 9–12.

Ganter, Regina 1994, 'Australia's Asian connection', *Eureka Street*, vol. 4, no. 9, pp. 51–2.

Gare, F. E. 1969, Letter, Commissioner of Native Welfare to Under Secretary for Lands, 3 November 1969, Kimberley Land Council Library, Derby.

Gibney, Matthew 1886, Memo on the prospects for a mission to the Aboriginals of WA, Unpublished memo, Perth 6 January 1886.

Gibson, Edward Gordon 1951, 'Culture contact on Sunday Island', Unpublished MA thesis, University of Sydney, Sydney.

Glaskin, Katie 2000, 'Limitations to the recognition and protection of native title offshore: The current "accident of history"', *Land, Rights, Law, Issues of Native Title*, Issues Paper no. 5, June 2000, Native Title Research Unit, Australian Institute of Aboriginal and Torres Strait Islander Studies, Canberra.

Glaskin, Katie 2002, 'Claiming Country: A case study of historical legacy and transition in the native title context', a thesis submitted for the degree Doctor of Philosophy, Australian National University, Canberra, January 2002.

Glaskin, Katie 2003, 'Native title and the "bundle of rights" model: Implications for the recognition of Aboriginal relations to country', *Anthropological Forum*, vol. 13, no. 1, pp. 67–88.

Glaskin, Katie 2005, 'Innovation and ancestral revelation: the case of dreams', *Journal of the Royal Anthropological Institute* (N.S.), vol. 11, no. 2, pp. 297–314.

Glaskin, Katie 2006a, 'Death and the person: reflections on mortuary rituals, transformation and ontology in an Aboriginal society', *Paideuma*, vol. 52, pp. 107–26.

Glaskin, Katie 2006b, Summaries of witnesses' evidence, Prepared for the Kimberley Land Council for the Full Federal Court Appeal in *Sampi v State of Western Australia,* Tabulated summary, 284 pp.

Glaskin, Katie 2006c, Summary of evidence about places (sites, islands, sea country), Prepared for the Kimberley Land Council for the Full Federal Court Appeal in *Sampi v State of Western Australia*, Tabulated summary, 82 pp.

Glaskin, Katie 2006d, Summary of evidence about laws, customs and society, Prepared for the Kimberley Land Council for the Full Federal Court Appeal in *Sampi v State of Western Australia*, Tabulated summary, 48 pp.

Glaskin, Katie 2006e, Comparative analysis of witness evidence (all witnesses) and witness summaries in judgment, Prepared for the Kimberley Land Council for the Full Federal Court Appeal in *Sampi v State of Western Australia*, Tabulated summary, 33 pp.

Glaskin, Katie 2007a, 'Manifesting the latent in native title litigation', *Anthropological Forum*, vol. 17, no. 2, pp. 165–68.

Glaskin, Katie 2007b, 'Outstation incorporation as precursor to a prescribed body corporate', in J. F. Weiner & K. Glaskin (eds),

Customary Land Tenure and Registration in Australia and Papua New Guinea: Anthropological Perspectives, pp. 199–221, Asia-Pacific Environment Monograph 3, ANU E-Press, Canberra.

Glaskin, Katie 2007c, Obituary Khaki Stumpagee *circa* 1924–2007, *TAJA (The Australian Journal of Anthropology)*, vol. 18, no. 2, pp. 223–26.

Glaskin, Katie 2007d, 'Claim, culture and effect: property relations and the native title process', in B. Smith & F. Morphy (eds), *The social effects of native title: recognition, translation, co-existence*, pp. 59–77, Centre for Aboriginal Economic Policy and Research, Research Monograph no. 27, ANU E-Press, Canberra.

Glaskin, Katie 2014, 'Territoriality, traditionality and transformation in the context of an Australian native title claim', in Allan C. Dawson, Laura Zanotti and Ismael Vaccaro (eds), *Negotiating Territoriality: Spatial Dialogues between State and Tradition*, pp. 129–41, Routledge.

Glaskin, Katie 2015, '"They used to frighten us…" Other-than-humans and the re-making of the social', Unpublished paper, winner of the 2015 Royal Anthropological Institute of Great Britain and Ireland's Curl Essay prize.

Glaskin, Katie & Geoffrey C. Bagshaw 1999, Bardi and Jawi genealogies, Prepared for the Kimberley Land Council on behalf of the claimants.

Glaskin, Katie & Laurent Dousset 2011, 'Asymmetry of recognition: Law, society, and customary land tenure in Australia', *Pacific Studies*, vol. 34, no. 2/3, pp. 142–56.

Glaskin, Katie, Myrna Tonkinson, Yasmine Musharbash & Victoria Burbank (eds) 2008, *Mortality, mourning and mortuary practices in Indigenous Australia*, Farham, Ashgate.

Gluckman, Max 1955, *The judicial process among the Barotse of Northern Rhodesia*, University Press, Manchester.

Good, Anthony 2008, 'Cultural evidence in courts of law', *The Objects of Evidence: Anthropological Approaches to the Production of Knowledge, Special Issue of the Journal of the Royal Anthropological Institute*, vol. 14, pp. S47–S60.

Green, Neville 2000, First respondents' preliminary history report (filed pursuant to the order of Lee J of 17 December 1999, as amended), in The Federal Court of Australia, Western Australia District Registry General Division, between Paul Sampi & Ors on behalf of the Bardi and Jawi People, and the State of Western Australia & Ors, WAG 49/1998.

Green, Nicholas 1988, 'Aboriginal affiliations with the sea in Western Australia', in F. Gray, & L. Zann (eds), *Traditional knowledge of the marine environment in northern Australia*, pp. 19–29, Workshop Series 8, Great Barrier Reef Marine Park Authority, Townsville.

Green, Nicholas & Jan Turner 1984, *Aboriginal rights to the sea in the Dampierland Peninsula – King Sound – Buccaneer Archipelago area of Western Australia,* A joint submission for sea closure to the Aboriginal Land Inquiry, Bardi Aborigines Association, Lombadina Community Inc., Beagle Bay Aboriginal Council Inc.

Grey, Sir George 1841, *Journals of two expeditions of discovery in north-west and Western Australia*, Boone, London.

Hadley, Sydney 1901a, Letter to Protector of Aborigines, 6 May 1901, in 'FS Hadley, Sunday Island Mission', AN 1/2; Acc 255; 10/1901, Battye Library, Western Australia State Archives, Perth.

Hadley, Sydney 1901b, Letter to Chief Protector, October 17/10/1901, in 'FS Hadley, Sunday Island Mission', AN 1/2; Acc 255; 10/1901, Battye Library, Western Australia State Archives, Perth.

Haebich, Anna 1998 [1988], *For their own good: Aborigines and government in the south-west of Western Australia 1900–1940*, University of Western Australia Press, Nedlands.

Harwood-Brown, G. 1901, Resident magistrate of Derby, letter to the Chief Protector of Aborigines 16/10/1901, AN 1/2; Acc 255; 10/1901, 'FS Hadley, Sunday Island Mission', located in Battye Library, Western Australia State Archives, Perth.

Helon, George William 1998, *Aboriginal Australia: Register of tribe, clan, horde, linguistic group, language names, and AIATSIS Language Codes*, Centre for Historical, Aboriginal and International Research, Bundaberg.

Hercus, Louise and Peter Sutton (eds) 1986, *This is what happened: Historical narratives by Aborigines*, Australian Institute of Aboriginal Studies, Canberra.

Hiatt, Lester R. 1996, *Arguments about Aborigines: Australia and the evolution of social anthropology*, Cambridge University Press, Cambridge.

Hiley, Graham 2008, 'What is the relevant "society" for the purposes of native title? Will any society do?' Unpublished paper distributed at the Office of Native Title Connection Workshop, Perth, November 12–13, 2008, dated 4 July 2008.

Holthouse, Hector 1986, *Ships in the coral: Explorers, wrecks and traders of the northern Australian coast*, Angus & Robertson, North Ryde.

Hosokawa, Komei 1994, 'Retribalization and language mixing: Aspects of identity strategies among the Broome Aborigines, Western Australia', *Bulletin of the National Museum of Ethnology*, vol. 19, no. 3, pp. 491–534.

Hunter, Henry 1908, List of people at Boolgin receiving rations 1908, AN 1/2; Acc 255; 19/1908, 'Boolgin Native Affairs', Battye Library, Western Australia State Archives, Perth.

Johnson, Darlene (dir.) 2002, *Gulpilil: One red blood*, Ronin Films, Australia.

Keen, Ian 1999, 'Cultural continuity and native title claims', *Land, Rights, Laws: Issues of Native Title*, Issues Paper No. 28, Native Titles Research Unit, Australian Institute of Aboriginal and Torres Strait Islander Studies, Canberra.

Keen, Ian 2007, 'Sansom's misreading of "The Western Desert vs. the Rest"', *Anthropological Forum*, vol. 17, no. 2, pp. 168–70.

Keneally, Kevin F., Daphne Choules Edinger & Tim Willing 1996, *Broome and beyond: Plants and people of the Dampier Peninsula, Kimberley, Western Australia*, Department of Conservation and Land Management, Como.

Keon-Cohen, Bryan A. 2000, 'The Mabo litigation: A personal and procedural account', *Melbourne University Law Review*, vol. 24, pp. 893–951.

Khaki Stumpagee Video Transcript 2001, interview with Geoffrey Bagshaw at Nillargoon outstation, Iwanyi, Sunday Island 16 July 1997, transcribed by Katie Glaskin & Geoffrey Bagshaw. Tendered in the Federal Court of Australia, Western Australia District Registry General Division, between Paul Sampi & Ors on behalf of the Bardi and Jawi People, and the State of Western Australia & Ors, WAG 49/1998.

Kimberley Land Council 2002, Closing submissions on behalf of the Applicants (filed pursuant to the directions of Beaumont J dated 28 August 2002). Filed in the Federal Court of Australia, Western Australia District Registry, in the matter No. WAG 49 of 1998, *Paul Sampi and Others on behalf of the Bardi and Jawi peoples v State of Western Australia and Others*.

Kimberley Land Council 2003, Further closing submissions on behalf of the Applicants (filed pursuant to the directions of French J. dated September 2003), filed in the Federal Court of Australia, Western Australia District Registry, in the matter No. WAG 49 of 1998, *Paul Sampi and Others on behalf of the Bardi and Jawi peoples v State of Western Australia and Others*.

King, Phillip Parker 1827, *Narrative of a survey of the inter-tropical and western coasts of Australia: Performed between the years 1818 and 1822, Volume 2*, John Murray, London.

Koch, Harold 1991, 'Language and communication in Aboriginal land claim hearings', in S. Romaine (ed), *Language in Australia*, pp. 94–103, Cambridge University Press, Melbourne.

Latour, Bruno 2010 [2002], *The making of law: An ethnography of the Conseil D'État*, Marina Brilman and Alain Pottage (trans.), Polity Press, Cambridge.

Latour, Bruno, & Steve Woolgar 1979, *Laboratory life: The construction of scientific facts*, Princeton University Press, Princeton.

Lewis, Stephen E., Craig R. Sloss, Colin V. Murray-Wallace, Colin D. Woodroffe & Scott G. Smithers 2013, 'Post-glacial sea-level changes around the Australian margin: a review', *Quaternary Science Reviews*, vol. 74, pp. 115–38.

Liberman, Kenneth 1978, 'Problems of communication in Western Desert courtrooms', *Legal Service Bulletin*, vol. 3, pp. 94–6.

Liberman, Kenneth 1981, 'Understanding Aborigines in Australian courts of law', *Human Organization*, vol. 40, no. 3, pp. 247–55.

Liberman, Kenneth 1985, *Understanding interaction in Central Australia: An ethnomethodological study of Australian Aboriginal people*, Routledge and Kegan Paul, Boston.

Love, J. R. B. 1939, 'The double raft of north-western Australia', *Man,* vol. 39, pp. 158–60.

Lurie, Nancy Oestrich 1988, 'The contemporary American Indian scene', in E. B. Leacock & N. O. Lurie (eds), *North American Indians in historical perspective*, pp. 418–80, Waveland Press, Illinois.

Macdonald, Gaynor 2001, 'Does "culture" have "history"? Thinking about continuity and change in central NSW', *Aboriginal History*, vol. 25, pp. 176–99.

Macdonald, Gaynor 2004, *Two steps forward, three steps back. A Wiradjuri land rights journey*, LhR Press, Canada Bay, NSW.

MacLean, James 2012, *Rethinking law as process: Creativity, novelty, change*, Routledge, New York.

Macknight, Charles C. 1976, *The voyage to Marege': Macassan trepangers in northern Australia*, Melbourne University Press, Melbourne.

Marchant, Leslie 1988, *An island unto itself: William Dampier and New Holland*, Hesperian Press, Perth.

Marks, S. R. 1960, 'Mission policy in Western Australia 1846–1959', *University Studies in Western Australian History*, vol. 3, no. 4, pp. 60–106.

Mathews, D., V. Semeniuk & C. A. Semeniuk 2011, 'Freshwater seepage along the coast of the Western Dampier Peninsula, Kimberley region, Western Australia', *Journal of the Royal Society of Western Australia*, vol. 94, pp. 207–12.

McCarthy, Mike 1993, 'Before Broome', paper presented at the New Directions in Maritime History conference, Fremantle, 6–10 December 1993.

McClay, Constable 1921, Police report, AN 1/4; Acc 653; 1094/1922, 'De Antione [sic] brothers, Tommy and Ginger – Cohabiting with native women', Battye Library, Western Australia State Archives, Perth.

Merlan, Francesca 2006, 'Beyond tradition', in James F. Weiner & Katie Glaskin (eds), *Custom: Indigenous tradition and law in the twenty-first century. The Asia Pacific Journal of Anthropology Special Issue*, vol. 7, no. 1, pp. 85–104.

Metcalfe, Christopher D. 1970–71, Bardi public corroborees, culture heroes, and narratives, Field Tape No. 5, In the Metcalfe collection, Archive Nos. 02134, located in the AIATSIS sound collection, Canberra.

Metcalfe, Christopher D. 1975, *Bardi verb morphology*, Pacific Linguistics, Canberra.

Metcalfe, Christopher D. 1979, 'Some aspects of the Bardi language: a non-technical description', in R. M. Berndt & C. H. Berndt (eds), *Aborigines of the West: their past and present*, pp. 197–213, University of Western Australia Press, Nedlands.

Metcalfe, Christopher D. 2000, Bardi/Jawi Land Claim – Linguistic Report, Bardi and Jawi Expert report: Linguist, prepared for the Kimberley Land Council. Filed in the Federal Court of Australia, Western Australia District Registry, General Division, in *Paul Sampi & Ors v The Premier and State of Western Australia & The Commonwealth of Australia*, 13 November 2000.

Mitchell, Scott 2001, First respondents' preliminary archaeologist's report, (Filed pursuant to the order of Lee J of 17 December 1999, as amended). In The Federal Court of Australia, Western Australia District Registry General Division, between Paul Sampi & Ors on behalf of the Bardi and Jawi People, and the State of Western Australia & Ors, WAG 49/1998.

Moore, Sally F. 1986, *Social facts and fabrications: "Customary" Law on Kilimanjaro, 1880–1980*, Cambridge University Press, Cambridge.

Morphy, Frances 2007, 'Performing law: The Yolngu of Blue Mud Bay meet the native title process', in B. Smith & F. Morphy (eds), *The social effects of native title: Recognition, translation, co-existence*, pp. 31–57, Centre for Aboriginal Economic Policy and Research, Research Monograph No. 27, ANU E-Press, Canberra.

Morphy, Howard 2006, 'The practice of an expert: anthropology in native title', *Anthropological Forum*, vol. 16, no. 2, pp. 135–51.

Morton, John 1997, 'Why can't they be nice to one another? Anthropology and the generation and resolution of land claim disputes', in D. E. Smith & J. Finlayson (eds), *Fighting over country: anthropological perspectives*, pp. 83–92, CAEPR Research Monograph No. 12, Centre for Aboriginal Economic Policy Research, The Australian National University, Canberra.

Morton, John 2007, 'Sansom, Sutton and Sackville: Three expert anthropologists?', *Anthropological Forum*, vol. 17, no. 2, pp. 170–3.

Munn, Nancy 1973, *Walbiri iconography: Graphic representation and cultural symbolism in a central Australian society*, Cornell University Press, Ithaca.

Myers, Fred 1986, *Pintupi country, Pintupi self: Sentiment, place, and politics among Western Desert Aborigines*, Smithsonian, Washington.

Nadasdy, Paul 2002, '"Property" and Aboriginal land claims in the Canadian subarctic: Some theoretical considerations', *American Anthropologist*, vol. 104, no. 1, pp. 247–261.

Napier, Constable 1903, 'Report 15th July 1903 relative to the Sunday Island Mission Station and the Condition of Abo [sic] Natives on the Island', AN 1/2; Acc 255; 28/1903, Battye Library, Western Australia State Archives, Perth.

Nekes, Hermann & Ernest Ailred Worms 1953, 'Australian Languages', *Bibliotheca Anthropos*, vol. 10.

Nettheim, Garth 1994, 'Mabo and Aboriginal political rights: The potential for inherent rights and Aboriginal self-government', in W. Sanders (ed), *Mabo and Native Title: Origins and Institutional Implications*, pp. 46–60, Research Monograph No. 7, Centre for Aboriginal Economic Policy Research, ANU, Canberra.

Nevermann, Hans, Ernest Ailred Worms & Helmut Petri 1968, *Die Religionen der Südsee und Australiens,* W. Kolhammer Verlag, Stuttgart.

Nunn, Patrick 2014, 'Geohazards and myths: ancient memories of rapid coastal change in the Asia-Pacific region and their value to future adaptation', *Geoscience Letters*, vol. 1, no. 3, pp. 1–11.

Nunn, Patrick & Nicholas J. Reid 2015, 'Aboriginal memories of inundation of the Australian coast dating from more than 7000 years ago', *Australian Geographer*, DOI: 10.1080/00049182.2015.1077539.

O'Barr, William & John Conley 1988, 'Ideological dissonance in the American legal system', *Anthropological Linguistics*, vol. 30, no. 3/4, pp. 345–68.

O'Connor, Sue 1990, '30,000 years in the Kimberley: A Prehistory of the Islands of the Buccaneer Archipelago and Adjacent Mainland, West Kimberley, Western Australia', PhD Thesis, University of Western Australia, Perth.

O'Connor, Sue 2000, Bardi and Jawi expert report: archaeologist. Expert report submitted to the Federal Court of Australia in *Sampi & Ors v the Premier and State of WA & Ors*, No. WAG 49 of 1998, 13 November 2000.

Omerod, 1901, Letter to Hadley, 17 October 1901, in: 'FS Hadley, Sunday Island Mission', AN 1/2; Acc 255; 10/1901, Battye Library, Western Australia State Archives, Perth.

One Arm Point Remote Community School 2010, *Our world: Bardi Jaawi: Life at Ardyaloon*, Magabala Books, Broome.

Ottenberg, Simon 1990, 'Thirty years of fieldnotes: Changing relationships to the text', in Roger Sanjek (ed.), *Fieldnotes: The makings of anthropology*, pp. 139–60, Cornell University Press, Ithaca, N.Y.

Palmer, Kingsley 2010, 'Understanding another ethnography: The use of early texts in native title inquiries', in Toni Baumann (ed), *Dilemmas in applied native title anthropology in Australia*, pp. 72–96, Australian Institute of Aboriginal and Torres Strait Islander Studies, Canberra.

Palmer, Kingsley 2016, *Noongar people, Noongar land: The resilience of Aboriginal culture in the south west of Western Australia*, Aboriginal Studies Press, Canberra.

Peterson, Nicolas & Bruce Rigsby 1998, *Customary Marine Tenure in Australia*, Oceania Monograph 48, University of Sydney, Sydney.

Petri, Helmut 1938–40, 'Mythical heroes and dreamtime legends in Northern Dampierland, Northwest Australia', *Paiduema*, vol. 1, pp. 217–40, [Translated into English by Christiane Fennell].

Petri, Helmut 1948, 'Ideas of the soul and totemism in northern Dampierland, North Western Australia', *Studium Generale*, vol. 1, no. 4, pp. 237–48, [Translated into English by Shirley Deutscher, AIATSIS manuscript P16271].

Porteus, Stanley D. 1931, *The psychology of a primitive people: A study of the Australian Aborigine*, Edward Arnold & Co, London.

Povinelli, Elizabeth A. 2002, *The cunning of recognition: Indigenous alterities and the making of Australian multiculturalism*, Duke University Press, Durham.

Raible, Otto [Most Reverend Otto Raible, P. S. M., Vicar Apostolic of Kimberley] 1938, 'The Aborigines', in Edward M. Dasey (ed), *The Story of the Regional Missionary and Eucharistic Congress, Newcastle NSW Australia, 16th–20th February 1938*, pp. 272–77, Specialty Publications & Sales Promotion Co. Ltd, Newcastle, NSW.

Ray, Arthur J. 2011, *Telling it to the judge: Taking native history to court*, McGill-Queens University Press, Montreal & Kingston.

Redmond, Anthony 2011, 'Identifying the relevant level of society in native title claims', *Anthropological Forum*, vol. 21, no. 3, pp. 287–305.

Ripper, Benjamin H. 2014, 'Depoliticising native title: Mediation, uncertainty and the extension of state government power in Western Australian native title determinations', MA thesis, University of Western Australia, Perth.

Robinson, Michael V. 1973, 'Change and adjustment among the Bardi of Sunday Island, North-Western Australia', MA thesis, University of Western Australia, Perth.

Robinson, Michael V. 1976a, 'The Jackson film of 1917', Australian Institute of Aboriginal Studies Newsletter, June, pp. 17–20.

Robinson, Michael V. 1976b, 'The film that vanished…the Jackson film of 1917, *WA Department of Aboriginal Affairs Newsletter*, vol. 2, no. 6, pp. 10–19.

Robinson, Michael V. 1979, 'Local organization and kinship in northern Dampier Land', in R. Berndt & C. H. Berndt (eds), *Aborigines of the West: Their Past and Present*, pp. 186–96, University of Western Australia Press, Nedlands.

Rosen, Lawrence 2008, *Law as culture: An invitation*, Princeton University Press, Princeton.

Rouja, Philippe Max 1998, *Fishing for culture: Toward an Aboriginal theory of marine resource use among the Bardi Aborigines of One Arm Point, Western Australia*, PhD thesis, Department of Anthropology, University of Durham, Durham.

Sackett, Lee 2007, 'A potential pathway', *Anthropological Forum*, vol. 17, no. 2, pp. 173–75.

Sansom, Basil 2000, First Respondents preliminary anthropological report (Filed pursuant to the order of Lee J of 17 December 1999, as amended). In The Federal Court of Australia, Western Australia District Registry General Division, between Paul Sampi & Ors on behalf of the Bardi and Jawi People, and the State of Western Australia & Ors, WAG 49/ 1998.

Sansom, Basil 2001, First Respondents second preliminary anthropological report (Filed pursuant to the order of Lee J of 17 December 1999, as amended). In The Federal Court of Australia, Western Australia District Registry General Division, between Paul Sampi & Ors on behalf of the Bardi and Jawi People, and the State of Western Australia & Ors, WAG 49/ 1998.

Sansom, Basil 2007, '*Yulara* and future expert reports in native title cases', *Anthropological Forum*, vol. 17, no. 1, pp. 71–92.

Seaman, Paul Laurence 1984, *The Aboriginal land inquiry*, Report by Paul Seaman, Q.C, to the West Australian Government, September 1984, Government Printer, Perth.

Semeniuk, V. 1983, 'Mangrove distribution in northwestern Australia in relationship to regional and local freshwater seepage', *Vegetatio*, vol. 53, issue 1, pp. 11–31.

Sharp, Nonie 1996, *No ordinary judgment*, Aboriginal Studies Press, Canberra.

Shigaro, Y. 1901, Letter 22 August 1901, apparently to the Resident Magistrate in Derby, in 'FS Hadley, Sunday Island Mission', AN 1/2; Acc 255; 10/1901, Battye Library, Western Australia State Archives, Perth.

Skyring, Fiona 2000, Bardi and Jawi expert report: historian. Expert report submitted to the Federal Court of Australia in Sampi & Ors v the Premier and State of WA & Ors, No. WAG 49 of 1998, 30 October 2000.

Skyring, Fiona 2001, Bardi and Jawi: supplementary history report. Expert report submitted to the Federal Court of Australia in *Sampi & Ors v the Premier and State of WA & Ors*, No. WAG 49 of 1998, 27 August 2001.

Smith, Moya 1983, 'Joules from pools: social and techno-economic aspects of Bardi stone fish traps', in M. Smith (ed.), *Archaeology at ANZAAS 1983*, pp. 29–45, Western Australian Museum, Perth.

Smith, Moya 1984–85, 'Bardi relationships with sea', *Anthropological Forum*, vol. 5, no. 3, pp. 443–47.

Smith, Moya 1987, 'Dots on the map: sites and seasonality, the Bardi example', *Australian Archaeology*, vol. 25, pp. 4–52.

Smith, Moya 1996, Jackson's film of the North West Scientific Expedition, 1917. *COMA: Bulletin of the Conference of Museum Anthropologists* no. 29, October 1996, pp. 30–3.

Smith, Moya 1997, *Fish-Capture Sites and the Maritime Economies of Some Kimberley Coastal Aboriginal Communities*, West Australian Museum, Perth.

Smith, Moya 2000, Report on the archaeological and ethnoarchaeological evidence for occupation of the area included in the Bardi and Jawi claim Expert report submitted to the Federal Court of Australia in *Sampi & Ors v the Premier and State of WA & Ors*, No. WAG 49 of 1998, 30 October 2000.

Smith, Ben & Frances Morphy (eds) 2007, *The social effects of native title: Recognition, translation, co-existence*, Centre for Aboriginal Economic Policy and Research, Research Monograph No. 27, ANU E-Press, Canberra.

Solms, Mark & Oliver Turnbull 2002, *The brain and the inner world: An introduction to the neuroscience of subjective experience*, Other Press, New York.

South West Aboriginal Land and Sea Council & John Host 2009, *It's still in my heart, this is my country: The single Noongar claim history*, UWA Publishing, Crawley.

Stokes, John Lort 1846, *Discoveries in Australia: With an account of the coasts and rivers explored and surveyed during the voyage of H.M.S.* Beagle *in the years 1837–38–39–40–41–42–43, Volume 1*, T. and W. Boone, London. Digitised version, available at: http://www.gutenberg.org/files/12115/12115-h/12115-h.htm (Accessed 4 August 2015).

Stow, Randolph 1982[1958], *To the islands*, Secker & Warburg, London.

Strelein, Lisa 2005, 'Native title-holding groups and native title societies: *Sampi v State of Western Australia* [2005]', *Land, Rights, Laws: Issues of Native Title*, Vol. 3, Issues Paper No. 4, Native Title Research Unit, Australian Institute of Aboriginal and Torres Strait Islander Studies, Canberra.

Strelein, Lisa 2006, *Compromised jurisprudence: Native title cases since Mabo*, Aboriginal Studies Press, Canberra.

Stuart, E. J. 1923, *A land of opportunities*, John Lane the Bodley Head, London.

Sutton, Peter 1996, 'The robustness of Aboriginal land tenure systems: Underlying and proximate customary titles', *Oceania*, vol. 67, no. 1, pp. 7–29.

Sutton, Peter 2001, 'Aboriginal country groups and the "community of native title holders"', National Native Title Tribunal Occasional Papers Series, No. 1/2001, National Native Title Tribunal, Perth.

Sutton, Peter 2003, *Native title in Australia: An ethnographic perspective*, Cambridge University Press, Cambridge.

Sutton, Peter 2006, 'Norman Tindale and native title: His appearance in the Yulara case', The 2006 Norman B. Tindale Memorial Lecture, presented at the South Australian Museum, Adelaide, 2 December.

Sutton, Peter 2007, 'Norms, statistics and the *Jango* case at Yulara', *Anthropological Forum*, vol. 17, no. 2, pp. 175–92.

Sutton, Peter & Peter Veth 2008, Introduction and themes, in P. Sutton, P. Veth & M. Neale (eds), *Strangers on the shore: Early coastal contact in Australia*, pp. 1–5, National Museum of Australia Press, Canberra.

Sutton, Peter & Petronella Vaarzon-Morel 2003, Yulara anthropology report, Central Land Council, Alice Springs.

Thieberger, Nicholas 1993, *Handbook of Western Australian Aboriginal languages south of the Kimberley region*, Pacific Linguistic Series C-124,

Pacific Linguistics, Research School of Pacific Studies, Australian National University, Canberra.

Tindale, Norman B. 1940, Map showing the distribution of the Aboriginal tribes of Australia, Located in AIATSIS map collection, Canberra.

Tindale, Norman B. 1953a, Anthropological Field Notes on the UCLA-UA Anthropological Expedition, North-west Australia, Tindale Collection housed in the South Australian Museum, Adelaide.

Tindale, Norman B. 1953b, 'Genealogical Data on the Aborigines of Australia gathered during the University of California at Los Angeles and University of Adelaide Anthropological Expedition 1952–1954 by Norman B. Tindale', Vol. III, Tindale Collection housed in the South Australian Museum, Adelaide.

Tindale, Norman B. 1974, *Aboriginal tribes of Australia: Their terrain, environmental controls, distribution, limits and proper names*, University of California Press, Berkeley, Los Angeles & London.

Tindale, Norman B. & J. B. Birdsell 1954, Unpublished field maps, Tindale Collection housed in the South Australian Museum, Adelaide.

Travési, Céline 2015, 'Au-delà des revendications foncières aborigènes: le tourisme, nouvelle voie de reconnaissance ou cul-de-sac?', in C. Travési & M. Ponsonnet (eds), *Les conceptions de la propriété foncière à l'épreuve des revendications autochtones: Possession, propriété et leurs avatars*, pp.275–97, Cahiers du Credo, Marseille.

Tsang, Steve 2015, 'China dredges up a frontline', *The Guardian Weekly*, 5–11 June 2015, p. 1.

Ubink, Janine M. 2008, *In the land of the chiefs: Customary law, conflicts and the role of the state in semi-urban Ghana*, Leiden University Press, Leiden.

Walter, Georg 1982 [1928], Inge Danaher [trans.], *Australia: Land, people, mission*, Bishop of Broome, Broome.

Weiner, James F. & Katie Glaskin (eds) 2006, *Custom: Indigenous tradition and law in the twenty-first century*, Special issue of *The Asia-Pacific Journal of Anthropology*, vol. 7, no. 1.

Weiner, J. F. & K. Glaskin (eds) 2007, *Customary Land Tenure and Registration in Indigenous Australia and Papua New Guinea: Anthropological Perspectives*, Asia-Pacific Environment Monograph 3, Australian National University E-press, Canberra.

Weir, Jessica 2009, *The Gunditjmara land justice story*, Native Title Research Monograph 1/2009, Australian Institute of Aboriginal and Torres Strait Islander Studies, Canberra.

Western Australian Fishing Industry Council 2001, Submissions of the Western Australian Fishing Industry Council (Inc) in Relation to Factual Issues (pursuant to to the orders of Justice Beaumont made on

18 September 2001), in the case *Sampi v State of Western Australia* No. WAG 49 of 1998.

Wiggan, David 1990, *Loolooloo and Marrgaliyn*, One Arm Point School, One Arm Point.

Williams, Nancy M. 1986, *The Yolngu and their land: A system of land tenure and the fight for its recognition*, Stanford University Press, Stanford.

Wilson, Richard Ashby, 2016, *Expert evidence on trial: Social researchers in the international criminal courtroom,* forthcoming in *American Ethnologist* vol. 43, no. 4, November 2016.

Wise, Tigger 1985, *The self-made anthropologist: A life of A. P. Elkin*, Allen & Unwin, Sydney.

Worms, Ernest A. 1940a, 'Religiöse Vorstellungen und Kultur einiger Nord-Westaustralischer Stämme in fünfzig Legenden', *Annal Lateranensi*, vol. 4, pp. 230–82.

Worms, Ernest A. 1940b, Letter to A. P. Elkin 23/2/40, in Elkin Archives, University of Sydney, Box 6, Item 1/1/64.

Worms, Ernest A. 1942, 'Die Gonara-Feier Im Australischen Kimberley', *Annali Lateranensi*, vol. 6, pp. 207–35.

Worms, Ernest A. 1944, 'Aboriginal place names in the Kimberley, Western Australia: an etymological and mythological study', *Oceania*, vol. 14, no. 4, p. 284–310.

Worms, Ernest A. 1949, 'An Australian Migratory Myth', *Primitive Man*, vol. 22, no. 1–2, pp. 33–8.

Worms, Ernest A. 1950a, '[restricted name of mythical being], the Creator: a myth of the Bad (West Kimberley)', *Anthropos*, Bd. 45, H. 4/6, pp. 641–58.

Worms, Ernest A. 1950b, 'Feuer und Feuerzeuge in Sage und Brach der Nordwest-Australier', *Anthropos*, Bd. 45, H. 1/3, pp. 145–64.

Worms, Ernest A. 1952, '[restricted name of mythical being] and his relation to other Culture Heroes', *Anthropos*, Bd. 47, H. 3/4, pp. 539–60.

Worms, Ernest A. 1955, 'Bei den Australiern (Among the Australian Aborigines)', *Die Kath Missionen*, Bd. 5, pp. 145–47.

Worms, Ernest A. 1957a, 'Australian mythological terms, their etymology and dispersion', *Anthropos*, Bd. 52, H. 5/6, pp. 732–68.

Worms, Ernest A. 1957b, 'Mythologische Sebstbiographie eines Australischen Ureinwohners (Mythological autobiography of an Australian aborigine)', *Wiener Völkerkundliche Mitteilungen*, Bd. 5, H. 1, pp. 40–8.

Worms, Ernest A. 1957c, 'The poetry of the Yaoro and Bād, North-Western Australia', *Annali Lateranensi* , vol. 21, pp. 213–19.

Worms, Ernest A. 1959, 'Verbannungslied eines australischen Wildbeuters: ein Beitrag zur Lyrik der Bād', *Anthropos*, Bd. 54, H. 1/2, pp. 154–68.

Worms, Ernest A. & Petri, Helmut 1998, *Australian Aboriginal Religions,* Nelen Yubu Missiological Series No. 5, Nelen Yubu Missiological Unit, Kensington.

Young, Simon 2009, 'Native title in Canada and Australia post Tsilhqot'in: Shared thinking or ships in the night?', *Land, Rights, Laws: Issues of Native Title*, vol. 4, Issue Paper no. 2, Native Title Research Unit, Australian Institute of Aboriginal and Torres Strait Islander Studies, Canberra.

Legal Cases

Australian Cases

Akiba v State of Queensland (No. 2) [2010] FCA 643 ('the Torres Strait sea claim')

Barunga v State of Western Australia [2011] FCA 518 ('Dambimangarri')

Bennell v State of Western Australia [2006] FCA 1243 ('the Single Noongar claim')

Chapman & Ors v Luminis & Ors. Action No. SG 33 of 1997, FCA Judgment 21

Daniel v State of Western Australia [2003] FCA 666 ('Ngarluma/ Yindjibarndi')

Ejai v Commonwealth, Unreported, Supreme Court of Western Australia, No. 1744 of 1993, 18 March 1994

Griffiths v Northern Territory of Australia [2006] FCA 903

Gumana v Northern Territory of Australia [2005] FCA 50 ('Blue Mud Bay')

Harrington-Smith v State of Western Australia (No. 9) [2007] FCA 31 ('Wongatha')

Jango v Northern Territory of Australia (No. 2) [2004] FCA 1004 ('Yulara')

Jango v Northern Territory of Australia [2006] FCA 318

Jango v Northern Territory of Australia [2007] FCAFC 101

Lardil Peoples v Queensland [2004] FCA 298 ('Wellesley Islands')

Lorrie Utemorrah and others v Commonwealth and others (F.C. S.92/004 (1992) 108 ALR 225

Mabo v Queensland (No. 2) [1992] HCA 23 ('Mabo')

Milirrpum v Nabalco Pty Ltd (1971) 17 FLR 141 ('the Gove land rights case')

Nangkiriny v State of Western Australia [2002] FCA 660 ('Karajarri')

Neowarra v State of Western Australia [2003] FCA 1402 ('Neowarra')

Neowarra v State of Western Australia [2004] FCA 1092

Northern Territory of Australia v Arnhem Land Aboriginal Land Trust [2008] HCA 29 ('Blue Mud Bay')

Northern Territory v Alyawarr (2005) 145 FCR 442

Sampi v State of Western Australia [2005] FCA 777 ('Sampi' or 'Sampi No 1')

Sampi v State of Western Australia (No. 2) [2005] FCA 1567 ('Sampi No 2')

Sampi v State of Western Australia (No. 3) [2005] FCA 1716 ('Sampi No 3')

Sampi v State of Western Australia [2010] FCAFC 26

Western Australia v Ward [2002] HCA 28 ('Ward')

Wik Peoples v Queensland [1996] 187 CLR 1 ('Wik')

Yarmirr v Northern Territory [2001] HCA 56 ('Croker Island')

Yorta Yorta Aboriginal Community v Victoria [1998] FCA 1606

Yorta Yorta v State of Victoria [2002] HCA 58 ('Yorta Yorta')

International Cases

Delgamuukw v British Columbia [1997] 3 SCR 1010 (Canada)

Delgamuukw v British Columbia (1997) 153 DLR (4th) 193 (Delgamuukw) (Canada)

Hamlet of Baker Lake v Minister of Indian Affairs and Northern Development (1979) 107 DLR (3d) 513 (Canada)

Sagong Bin Tasi & Ors v Kerajaan Negeri Selangor & Ors (Dalam Mahkamah Tinggi Di Shah Alam, Guaman Sivil No: Mti-21-314-1996). (Malaysia)

Tsilhqot'in Nation v British Columbia 2007 BCSC 1700; [2008] 1 CNLR 112 (Tsilhqot'in.) (Canada)

Legislation

Commonwealth of Australia

Aboriginal Councils and Associations Act 1976 (Cth)

Native Title Act 1993 (Cth) ('NTA')

New South Wales

Aboriginal Land Rights Act 1983 (NSW)

Northern Territory

Aboriginal Land Act 1978 (Northern Territory)

Aboriginal Land Rights (Northern Territory) Act 1976 (Cth)

Queensland

Land Act (Aboriginal and Islander Land Grants) Amendment Act 1982 (Qld)

Local Government (Aboriginal Lands) Act 1978 (Qld)

Aboriginal Land Act 1991 (Qld)
Torres Strait Islander Land Act 1991 (Qld)
Aboriginal and Torres Strait Islander Land Amendment Act 2008 (Qld)

South Australia
Aboriginal Land Trust Act 1966 (SA)
Pitjantjatjara Land Rights Act 1981 (SA)
Maralinga Tjarutja Land Rights Act 1984 (SA)

Tasmania
Aboriginal Land Act 1995 (Tas)

Western Australia
Aboriginal Protection Act 1886 (WA)
Aborigines Act 1889 (WA)
Aborigines Act 1905 (WA)
Aboriginal Affairs Planning Authority Act 1972 (WA)

Victoria
Aboriginal Land Acts 1970 (Vic)
Aboriginal Land (Lake Condah and Framlingham Forest) Act 1987 (Vic)
Aboriginal Land (Aboriginal Advancement League) (Wall St, Northcote) Act 1982 (Vic)
Aboriginal Land (Northcote Land) Act 1989 (Vic)
Aboriginal Land Act 1991 (Vic)
Aboriginal Land (Manatunga Land) Act 1992 (Vic)

Papua New Guinea
Land Groups Incorporation Act (1972) (Papua New Guinea)

Index

www.ingramcontent.com/pod-product-compliance
Lightning Source LLC
Chambersburg PA
CBHW031206240326
R18026200001B/R180262PG41599CBX00002B/3